JUDAISM AND THE VATICAN

© VICOMTE LÉON DE PONCINS 1967

Reprinted 1985
Reprinted 1999

JUDAISM
and the
VATICAN
AN ATTEMPT AT SPIRITUAL SUBVERSION

Translated from the French of
VICOMTE LÉON DE PONCINS
by
Timothy Tindal-Robertson

Christian Book Club of America
Post Office Box 900566
Palmdale, California 93590-0566

"It is a vital principle never to deform the truth. Truth is always fundamental for all responsible men. It should always prevail."
Pope John XXIII

"It is a veritable competition as to who can make the Jews appear most hateful. Richly chequered and pathetic as is the narrator of the fourth Gospel (St. John), the palm goes to Matthew; his unerring hand unleashed the poisoned arrow that can never be withdrawn."
Jules Isaac: Jésus et Israel, p. 483

"Professor Isaac, a distinguished French-Jewish historian . . . devoted the last years of his life to a study of the religious roots of anti-Semitism. He had audiences with the late Popes Pius XII and John XXIII, the latter being of considerable importance and leading to subsequent emendation of certain passages offensive to Jews in the Roman liturgy."
Jewish Chronicle 29th October 1965, p. 14

". . . the permanent and latent source of anti-Semitism is none other than Christian religious teaching of every description, and the traditional, tendentious interpretations of the Scriptures."
Jules Isaac: Jésus et Israel, p. 572

CONTENTS

PART I

THE "TEACHING OF CONTEMPT"

Chapter		page
1	The Jewish Question and the Council	9
2	Jules Isaac and the Evangelists	14
3	Jules Isaac and the Church Fathers	20

PART II

THE PROBLEM OF THE AGES

4	The Complexity of the Jewish Problem	45
5	Mosaic Law and the Talmud	53
6	The Marranos	60
7	Assimilation	64
8	A State within a State	73
9	Anti-Semitism	82
10	World Revolution	96
11	Eternal Antagonism	111
12	"Portrait of a Jew"	123

PART III

THE COUNCIL'S SOLUTION

13	The Vatican Vote	133
14	Tracts against the Council	159
15	How the Jews changed Catholic Thinking	167
Appendix I	Appeal to Heads of State	175
Appendix II	Six Million Innocent Victims	178
Bibliography		191
Index		193

DEDICATED

To the Memory of the Church Fathers who constructed Christian civilisation.

PART I

THE "TEACHING OF CONTEMPT"

" 'The Ecumenical Council's Declaration on the Church and non-Christians lifting the charge of collective guilt from the Jewish people was impudent, cheap politics, and an insult to God,' said Dr. Eliezer Berkovitz, Professor of Jewish Philosophy at the Jewish University of America, in Toronto last week.

"He said that Christianity was spread throughout Europe not by the Gospel but by the sword, and the spirit of ecumenism and interfaith understanding now put forward was little more than a public relations stunt."

Jewish Chronicle, 28th January, 1966, p. 17

"The Gospel version of the Jesus trial, as presented to us by the scribes of the Bishop of Rome as the great judicial event of the first century, is terrifying in its cunning malevolence."

D. G. Runes: *The Jew and the Cross*, 1965, p .26

"The difficult and slow process of building a happier relationship between Christian and Jew can only proceed if stereotypes and prejudices are cast aside and replaced by rational and intelligent reappraisal. It is essential that we understand more about each other. We must talk, but conversation does not mean conversion."

Jewish Chronicle editorial, 27th January, 1967

I

THE JEWISH QUESTION AND THE COUNCIL

ON the 19th November 1964, the bishops and cardinals of the Catholic Church gathered in Council at Rome passed by an overwhelming majority the Schema dealing with the attitude of the Church towards Judaism.

Le Monde of the 27th November referred to the violent reactions provoked by this vote among the Eastern Rite Catholic churches and among the Arab states.

The article concluded with a post-script from the paper's Rome correspondent, H. Fesquet, who was considered the spokesman for Father Congar, the leader of the Catholic progressive wing. Fesquet began by recalling that conciliar votes are secret, and then went on to add:

"Ninety-nine Fathers voted 'No'. One thousand six hundred and fifty-one voted 'Yes' and two hundred and forty-two voted 'Yes' with reservations. Moreover, this was only a provisional vote, and the final ballot will take place at the end of the fourth session of the Council in 1965.

"In the general assembly the Eastern bishops intervened as a body, saying that they were opposed in principle to a declaration on the Jews by the Council. We can therefore conjecture that the ninety-nine Fathers who had voted in the negative were in the main the Eastern ones."

The following is a passage taken from the text of the declaration on the Jews voted by the Council Fathers on the 20th November 1964:

". . . Since such is the inheritance accepted by Christians from the Jews, this holy Council resolves expressly to further and to recommend reciprocal understanding and appreciation, to be obtained by theological study and fraternal discussion and, beyond that, inasmuch as it severely disapproves of any wrong inflicted upon men wheresoever, it equally deplores and condemns hatred and maltreatment (vexationem) of Jews. . . .

"Everyone should be careful, therefore, not to expose the Jewish people as a rejected nation, be it in catechetical tuition, in preaching of God's Word or in worldly conversation, nor should anything be said or done which may alienate the minds of men from the Jews. Equally, all should be on their guard not to impute to the Jews of our time that which was perpetrated in the Passion of Christ."

(*The Tablet*, 26th September 1964, p. 1094—the revised text on the agenda for the third session)

At first sight, this motion seems to conform to the unchanging doctrine of the Church which, while striving to protect the Christian community against Jewish influences, has always condemned persecution, a fact which has indeed been candidly acknowledged by a Jewish writer, Max I. Dimont:

"Popes and princes of the Middle Ages could have wiped out the Jews completely had they wanted to, but they did not want to. . . . When, because of social, economic, or even religious pressures, the presence of the Jews became unwanted, they were banished, not killed. The Church endowed all human beings with a soul, and it took a man's life only to save his soul. It was only when religion lost its deterrent hold on man that Western society could entertain the idea of coolly murdering millions because it felt there was no room for them."

(M. I. Dimont: *Jews, God and History*, p. 286)

In fact, however, the motion voted on in Rome implies that the majority of the Council Fathers are under a serious misapprehension as to what constitutes the very essence of Judaism. It would seem that they have only applied themselves to the humanitarian aspect of the problem skilfully submitted by the spokesmen of World Jewry and by a Press largely favourable to Jewish interests.

The truth, it is suggested, is that a number of Jewish organisations and personalities are behind the reforms which were proposed at the Council with a view to modifying the Church's attitude and time-honoured teaching about Judaism: Jules Isaac, Label Katz, President of the B'nai B'rith, Nahum Goldman, President of the World Jewish Congress, etc.

These reforms are very important because they suggest that for two thousand years the Church had been mistaken and that she must make amends and completely reconsider her attitude to the Jews.

Among the Catholic laity, a similar campaign is being carried on by progressive prelates who, taking their stand on the historical fact that Christianity is in direct line of descent from Judaism, claim a toleration for Jews, which the latter as we shall see, are far from professing with regard to Christians. In actual fact, for both parties, it is a weapon designed to overthrow traditional Catholicism, which they consider the chief enemy.

Of the Jewish personalities mentioned above, there was one who played a vital role: the writer, Jules Isaac, of Aix-en-Provence, who died recently. He was at one time Inspector-General of Public Education in France and the author of academic books on history.

Isaac turned the Council to advantage, having found there considerable support among progressive bishops. In fact he became the principal theorist and promoter of the campaign being waged against the traditional teaching of the Church.

This is the gist of his thesis:

We must have done with anti-Semitism, the logical outcome of which was the liquidation of European Jews at Auschwitz and other death camps during the Second World War.

According to him, the most dangerous form of anti-Semitism is Christian anti-Semitism, which is fundamentally theological. Indeed, the Christian attitude to Judaism has always been based on the account of the Passion as described by the four Evangelists and as commented on by the Fathers of the Church such as St. John Chrysostom, St. Ambrose, St. Augustine, Pope Gregory the Great, St. Agobard, Primate of the Gauls, and many others.

Thus it is this theological foundation that Jules Isaac sought to undermine in disputing the historical value of the Gospel accounts and in discrediting the arguments advanced by the Fathers of the Church to protect Christians from being influenced by the Jews who were charged with everlasting plotting against the Christian order.

Now let us consider in detail what steps Jules Isaac took, both in the Vatican and in the heart of the Council, to get his views accepted.

After the disappearance of his wife and daughter, who died during deportation, he dedicated the last twenty years of his life to a critical study of relations between Judaism and Christianity, and to this end he wrote two important books, *Jésus et Israel*, first published in 1946 and republished in 1959, and *Genèse de l'Antisémitisme*, first published in 1948 and republished in 1956.

In these books Jules Isaac fiercely censures Christian teaching, which he says has been the source of modern anti-Semitism, and preaches, though it would be more correct to say he demands, the "purification" and "amendment" of doctrines two thousand years old. Further on we shall briefly examine these two books; for the moment let us continue our review of the part played by Jules Isaac in bringing the Jewish question to the attention of the Council.

As early as the end of the war he began organising both national and international gatherings attended by sympathetic Catholics who were favourably disposed towards his arguments.

In 1947,[1] following Judaeo-Catholic dialogues of this kind, which were attended, among the Jews, by Edmond Fleg and Samy Lattés, and among the Catholics, by Henri Marrou, Father Daniélou, and the Abbé Vieillard of the Episcopal Secretariat, he drew up an 18 point memorandum on "The rectification of Christian teaching concerning Israel".

The same year he was invited to the international conference in Seelisberg in Switzerland attended by seventy members from nineteen countries, among whom were Father Callixte Lopinot, Father Demann, Pastor Freudenberg and the Grand Rabbi Kaplan. In general session the conference adopted the "Ten Points of Seelisberg", which suggested to the Christian Churches measures to be adopted to purify religious teaching concerning the Jews.

Then Jules Isaac established the first Judaeo-Christian friendship society with the help of the Grand Rabbi of France and his assistant, Jacob Kaplan, and the Jews Edmond Fleg and Leon Algazi, Catholic friends such as Henri Marrou, Jacques Madaule, Jacques Nantet, and Protestant friends such as Professor Lovsky and Jacques Martin. The society's regulations debarred members from trying to convert one another, and its establishment was soon followed by others in Aix, Marseilles, Nîmes, Montpellier, Lyons and lastly in Lille, where Jules Isaac secured the help of a nun of Dom Bosco's order and the support of Cardinal Liénart. Later on he founded another in North Africa.

In 1949 he made contacts with the clergy in Rome, and through them he was able to obtain a private audience with Pius XII, to whom he pleaded on behalf of Judaism, asking him to have the "Ten Points of Seelisberg" examined.

In 1959 he held a conference at the Sorbonne on the need for revising Christian teaching on the Jews and he closed with an appeal to Pope John's sense of justice and love of truth.

Shortly afterwards he met several prelates of the Roman Curia, in particular Cardinals Tisserand, Jullie, Ottaviani, and Cardinal Bea; and on the 13th June 1960 he was granted an audience by the Pope, whom he asked to condemn the "teaching of contempt", suggesting

---

[1] All the following information is taken from statements made by Jules Isaac himself.

that a sub-commission should be set up specifically to study the problem.

Some time afterwards Jules Isaac "learned with joy that his suggestions had been considered by the Pope and handed on to Cardinal Bea for examination". The latter set up a special working party to study relations between the Church and Israel, which finally resulted in the Council vote on the 20th November 1964.

2

JULES ISAAC AND THE EVANGELISTS

LET us now examine the objections to the Gospel writers raised by Jules Isaac, in particular with reference to their account of the Passion, and his objection to the Church Fathers whom he holds responsible for what he calls the "teaching of contempt" with which apparently the whole Christian mentality has been completely impregnated.

Jules Isaac frigidly denies that the account given by the Evangelists has any historical value:

> "The historian has the right and the duty, an absolute duty, to regard the Gospel accounts as witnesses for the prosecution (against the Jews), with the aggravating drawback that they are the sole witnesses and that all four of them write from the same angle: we have no Jewish or pagan evidence for comparison or with which to weigh one against the other. Now this bias of the Gospel writers is nowhere more evident or more marked, this absence of non-Christian documentation is nowhere more deplorable, than in the story of the Passion. . . . But it is quite striking how all four writers are preoccupied with reducing Roman responsibility to the minimum in order correspondingly to increase that of the Jews. Moreover, they are not equally biased: in this respect Matthew is far and away the worst, not only worse than Mark or Luke but perhaps even worse than John. Is this so surprising? There are no more bitter opponents than brothers in enmity: now Matthew was a Jew, fundamentally a Jew, the most Jewish of the Evangelists, and according to an apparently well-founded tradition he wrote 'in Palestine and for the Palestinians' to prove from the Old Testament that Jesus was indeed the Messiah prophesied by the Scriptures. . . . But does the cause of historical truth derive any value from this? We are at liberty to doubt it. It is not at all surprising that of the three Synoptic writers Matthew is the most biased, his account of the Passion

being the most tendentious, while the most impartial in the circumstances—or the least biased—is Luke, the only non-Jewish Gospel writer, the only one of Gentile origin.

(Jules Isaac: *Jésus et Israel*, pp. 428-9)

"But let us not forget . . . that they are all in agreement in asserting that there, in Pilate's presence, at a unique moment in time, at an hour which struck once for all mankind and which means more to humanity than any other moment in the whole world, the whole Jewish people expressly and explicitly took on itself the responsibility of the innocent Blood, the total responsibility, the national responsibility. It remains to be shown to what degree the texts and the reality of which they give an indication warrant the appalling gravity of such an assertion.

(Jules Isaac, ibid., p. 478)

"The Christian charge brought against Israel, that of deicide, an accusation of murder which is in itself murderous, is the most serious, the most injurious possible; it is also the most iniquitous.
"Jesus had been condemned to the agony of the Cross, a Roman punishment, by Pontius Pilate, the Roman Procurator.
"But the four evangelists, for once in agreement, state that Jesus was given up to the Romans by the Jews, and that, owing to irresistible pressure by the Jews, Pilate, although he wished to declare Jesus innocent, nevertheless had him put to death. Therefore, it is upon the Jews, not upon the Romans who were mere instruments, that responsibility for the Crime devolves, and it weighs them down with supernatural force and crushes them.

(Jules Isaac, ibid., p. 567)

"At first sight we are impressed by the unanimity—at least on the surface—of the four evangelists on the point at issue, namely Jewish responsibility.
"That the Roman pronounced the death sentence under pressure from the Jews all four Gospel writers to be sure earnestly bear witness with one voice. But as their testimony is an indictment which is prejudiced and impassioned, circumstantial and belated, frankly speaking, we find it impossible to accept it without reservation.

(Jules Isaac, ibid., p. 478)

"Matthew is the only one who recognised (xxvii. 24-25) that the Procurator Pilate ceremoniously washed his hands according to Jewish custom to rid himself of the guilt of innocent blood

which he was compelled to shed. He is the only one to observe that 'all the people' cried out, 'His blood be upon us and upon our children'. Mark, Luke and John know nothing and say nothing, either about the famous ablution or about the terrifying exclamation.
(Jules Isaac, ibid., p. 481)

"The suggestive gradation observed in the first phase of the trial is repeated again here, and it is highly perceptible from Mark to Matthew, according to whom (xxvii. 24-25), Pilate deliberately absolves himself from responsibility (through washing his hands), which 'the Jewish people', by contrast, takes almost joyfully on itself. In Luke's account Pilate three times declares Jesus innocent and obviously wishes to set him free (xxii. 14, 15, 16, 20, 22). John goes even further: he does not hesitate to prolong the extraordinary comings and goings of the Procurator in and out of the praetorium; after the interlude of the scourging comes the pitiable exhibition: 'Behold the man!'; then more conversation between Pilate and 'the Jews'; the agitation of Pilate when he learns that Jesus has claimed to be the 'Son of God'; then Pilate and Jesus exchange words; a further effort by Pilate to release Jesus; then blackmail by the Jews 'if you set him free, you are no friend of Caesar's' (John xix. 12), to which the vacillating Procurator at length gives way: 'then he delivered him up to them to be crucified'.
(John xix. 16)

"A veritable competition as to who can makes the Jews more hateful.

"What could not be said, what has not been said on the grounds of historical probability. But it is dangerous ground, as I well know: truth 'can sometimes appear improbable'. It makes me all the more inclined to remark that, conspicuously in Matthew and John, the figure of Pontius Pilate exceeds the bounds of improbability....

"It is hard to believe that the all-powerful Procurator in bewilderment had to consult the Jews, his subjects, and the high priests, his instruments, as to what he should do with the prisoner, Jesus.
(Mark xv. 12; Matthew xxvii. 22)

"It is hard to believe that the butcher of Jews and Samaritans, suddenly overcome by scruples about a Galilean Jew accused of messianic agitation, stooped to solicit the pity of the Jews for him: 'What evil has he done?'
(Mark xv. 14; Matthew xxvii. 23)

"It is hard to believe that a Roman official had to have recourse to the Jewish symbolic ritual of washing hands to rid himself of his responsibility—in the eyes of the God of Israel no doubt.
(Matthew xxvii. 24)

"It is hard to believe that the cunning politician in him took it into his head that day to take the side of the luckless prophet against the native oligarchy upon whom it was customary for the Roman rulers to rely and upon whom he himself depended, for Pilate held Judea through Hanan and Caiaphas.

"It is hard to believe that the representative of Rome, whose supreme duty and care was to ensure respect for Roman grandeur, went to and fro in honour of a few devout Jews from the judge's seat to the street outside where they were gathered.

"It is hard to believe that a strong ruler, though ready to shed blood to prevent any rising or threat of a rising, nevertheless to please the Jewish crowd agreed to release a 'well-known' rioter imprisoned on a charge of sedition and murder (and why did the crucifixion of Jesus have to follow the release of Barabbas?).

"It is hard to believe that the judge, the law-maker of the province, though apparently oblivious of the fact, said to the high priests his interlocutors: 'Take him yourselves and crucify him.'
(John xix. 6)

sceptic was impressed by the
—according to John xix. 7-8
be the Son of God' (in the
hensible at first sight either

lawyer, so precise in mind,
itional methods of procedure

, a thousand times more so,
le' of the Jews, patriotic and
gainst Jesus to the point of
nd demanding that the pro-
after the day before, a man
le, should be crucified in the

[ules Isaac, ibid., pp. 483-4)

which emphasised the con-
ishing his hands and the cry
'His blood be upon us and

"We have already referred to it, but not nearly enough when one considers all the evils to which it has given rise.

(Jules Isaac, ibid., p. 489)

"I still maintain that Pilate's gesture was 'completely at variance with the procedure of Roman trials'; that is sufficient. I have the right to draw the conclusion that in all probability the gesture never was in fact made. The whole performance is of doubtful authenticity and we find that it is in fact pushed to absurd lengths.

"The reply of the Jews 'His blood be upon us and upon our children' undoubtedly becomes less paradoxical when it is linked with ancient Hebraic traditions and expressions. But, as we have said, it is quite as incredible by reason of its heinous character and of the rage to which it claims to give utterance. . . .

(Jules Isaac, ibid., pp. 491-2)

"*Never has a narrative appeared so obviously tendentious, or anxiety to 'impress' been so marked, culminating in verses 24 and 25, which compel conviction in all open minds.*

"No, Pilate did not wash his hands according to the Jewish custom.

"No, Pilate did not protest his innocence.

"No, the Jewish crowd did not cry out: 'His blood be upon us and upon our children. . . .'

"But what is the good of stressing all this any more? The case is up for hearing in the eyes of all men of good faith. And I venture to say, in the eyes of God too.

(Jules Isaac, ibid., p. 493)

"Therefore the total responsibility of the Jewish people, of the Jewish nation and of Israel for condemning Jesus to death is a matter of legendary belief and not based on solid historical foundations. . . .

(Jules Isaac, ibid., pp. 514-15)

"To maintain the opposite viewpoint, one would have to be intractably and fanatically prejudiced, or have a blind belief in a tradition which, as we know, is not 'normal', and thus ought not to be laid down as a rule of thought for even the most docile sons of the Church—a tradition which, moreover, is infinitely noxious and murderous, and which, as I have said and shall repeat, leads to Auschwitz—Auschwitz and other places. Some six million Jews were liquidated solely because they were Jews and this brought shame not only upon the German people but upon the whole of Christianity, because without centuries of Christian teaching, preaching and vituperation, Hitler's teaching, propaganda and vituperation would have been impossible."

(Jules Isaac, ibid., p. 508)

In short, in their account of the Passion, now revised and corrected by Jules Isaac, the writers of the Gospels appear as arrant liars of whom Matthew is unquestionably the most venomous.

"He bears the palm. His unerring hand unleashed the poisoned arrow that can never be withdrawn."

(Jules Isaac, ibid., p. 483)

3

JULES ISAAC AND THE CHURCH FATHERS

As we have seen, the Evangelists have been disposed of, and Jules Isaac now proceeds to attack the Church Fathers, who for 1,500 years have codified Christian doctrine on Judaism.

"It is only too true that there was a strong current of anti-Semitism in the pagan world, long prior to Christian anti-Semitism.

"It is only too true that this anti-Semitism sometimes produced bloody conflicts and pogroms.

"It is only too true that its principal cause was the exclusiveness and separatism of Israel, which was essentially religious, dictated by Yahve and the Scriptures, and without which Christianity evidently could not have been conceived, since it is due to this Jewish separatism that faith in Yahve and the knowledge and cult of the one God was preserved intact from all defilement and transmitted from generation to generation until the coming of the Christ.

"But what do these facts justify?

"Just because there was a pagan anti-Semitism, which indeed took its origin from the divine commandment, what ground is this for Christianity in copying it (having fallen victim to it itself for a time), and further, for having developed it to a paroxysm of virulence, evil-mindedness, and slanderous and murderous hatred?

(Jules Isaac: *Jésus et Israel*, p. 353)

"Thus there began to develop in the Christian conscience (if I may venture to say so), the theme of the Crime, of the Unworthiness, of the Curse, of the Chastisement of Israel, a chastisement which was, like the Crime itself, collective, without appeal, embodying for ever 'carnal Israel', Israel fallen, outcast, Israel-Judas, Israel-Cain. This theme is closely interwoven but not to be confused with another, which became a doctrinal thesis, that of the Witness-People—chosen by God, the Jew Saint Paul had said, for the fullness of final conversion, unhappy witness 'to its own iniquities and to our truth', said St. Augustine 350 years later, bearing from God, as did Cain, a sign which is at once its protection and draws on it the execration of the Christian world."

(Jules Isaac, ibid., p. 359)

"No weapon has proved more successful against Judaism and her faithful than the teaching of contempt, forged principally by the Church Fathers in the fourth century, and within it, no thesis has been more harmful than that of the 'deicide people'. Christian mentality has become impregnated with these ideas to the very roots of its subconscience. Failure to recognise this fact is to ignore or disguise the major source of Christian anti-Semitism, and the spring which has nourished popular opinion. But the latter did not produce it, for the teaching of contempt is a theological creation."

(Jules Isaac: *Genèse de l'Antisémitisme*, p. 327)

" 'Deicide.' When did the defamatory epithet appear, later to be turned, oh happy discovery, to murderous use, to become an indelible brand, goading to fury and crime (homicide, genocide)? It is impossible to name an exact date. But one can discern among the confused flood of Judaeo-Christian polemics the main current from which it stemmed.

(Jules Isaac: *Jésus et Israel*, p. 360)

"In the fourth century a step forward was taken. The destinies of the Church and the Empire having united, all caution was put aside, and the tone of anti-Jewish controversy could be increased, as indeed it was. It became openly abusive. . . .

"The Christian anti-Semitism which then began to develop was essentially theological, but it could also be called 'ecclesiastical' or 'clerical'. Its foundation was the accusation of deicide.

(Jules Isaac, ibid., p. 361)

"Murderer of Jesus, the Christ-Messiah, murderer of the Man-God,
deicide !—
"Such is the accusation cast against the whole Jewish people . . . a capital accusation linked to the theme of capital chastisement . . . in such a way that by an ingenious alternating mechanism of doctrinal sentences and popular outbursts there is ascribed to God what, seen from the earthly sphere, is assuredly the work

of incurable human vileness, this perversity, variously and cleverly exploited from century to century, from generation to generation, to culminate in Auschwitz, and the gas chambers and crematorium ovens of Nazi Germany."

(Jules Isaac, ibid., pp. 351-2)

"One must recognise the sad fact that nearly all the Church Fathers have contributed their stone in this work of moral lapidation (not without material repercussions): St. Hilary of Poitiers, St. Jerome, St. Ephrem, St. Gregory of Nyssa, St. Ambrose and St. Epiphany—who was born a Jew—St. Cyril of Jerusalem, and many others. But two of this illustrious cohort, venerable in so many other respects, deserve a special mention: the great Greek orator, St. John Chrysostom (i.e. St. John of the Golden Mouth), who is distinguished by his abundant and truculent invective, and his excessive insults; and the great doctor of Christian latinity, St. Augustine, for the wonderful (and dangerous) ingenuity he displayed in elaborating a coherent doctrine."

(Jules Isaac: *Genèse de l'Antisémitisme*, p. 161)

We will now pass from this general review of the Church Fathers to examine particular instances, quoting passages from the study Jules Isaac has devoted to the great Doctors of the Church.

In 386 St. John Chrysostom began to preach at Antioch, where there was an important Jewish community. He began with eight homilies against the Jews in a tone which "is often of unparalleled violence".

"All the grievances and insults are to be found in Chrysostom. He displays better than any other, and often with unequalled violence and even coarseness, on occasions, the fusion of elements taken from popular anti-Semitism and from specifically theological grounds for complaint, and the use of biblical texts, which are the hall-mark of the Christian anti-Semite.

(Jules Isaac, ibid., p. 256)

"Let it be plainly said: whatever his intention, this inordinate piece of outrage and calumny is a revolting thing on the part of a sacred orator.

"Seeds of scorn and hatred such as these inevitably produce their harvest. You reap as you sow. Silhouetted down the ages to come beyond the holy declaimers of the fourth century, devoutly dragging their adversaries in the mud, I see the countless legion of theologians, Christian preachers, teachers and writers, eager to enlarge on striking themes of the carnal Jew, the lustful Jew, the covetous Jew, the Jew possessed of the devil, the accursed Jew, the Jew as a murderer of the prophets, and of Christ, the Jew guilty of deicide—all conscientiously endeavouring in all good faith to propagate these false, pernicious and deadly ideas; all equally ready, it follows logically, to admit with Chrysostom that if the hateful Jew received as his share exile, dispersion, servitude, misery and shame it was only justice (God's justice): he had to pay his forfeit. But these are only figures of speech you will say today—1,600 years later—to reassure your conscience; that may be so but 'one must understand' to what end figures of speech uttered by a 'golden mouth' may lead, taken up in chorus across the centuries by myriads of disciples; the figures of speech took vital and virulent root, they are encrusted in millions of souls. Who then would dare to believe that the Christian soul is free from them today? Who can tell if it will ever be freed? Look at the hideous lampoonists, the Streicher Nazis, who followed after the Christian preachers."

(Jules Isaac, ibid., pp. 162, 164-6)

Less violent than the Greek orator, according to Jules Isaac, St. Augustine:

". . . is equally hostile towards Judaism and the Jews, and equally determined to fight their persistent influence, to protect the faithful from it, and to provide them with a stock of valid arguments to use in controversy with these obstinate reprobates. He uses the same method, and their point of view and interpretation of the Scriptures is similar: long before the coming of the Saviour, Judaism had progressively become corrupt, faded and withered; after the revelation of Christ, it fell completely under Satan's inspiration; formerly the chosen children of God, they became the sons of the devil.

(Jules Isaac, ibid., p. 166)

"In all this passionate teaching which has survived the centuries and which still in our day dares to lift its voice, there is no more respect for Biblical truth than for historical truth. Both the deplorable Crucifixion and the Dispersion are fearlessly used as weapons cruelly sharpened in order the better to do to death old Israel. . . .

(Jules Isaac, ibid., p. 167)

"But most important of all is St. Augustine's own particular doctrinal contribution, the elaboration, in his sharp mind, of an ingenious, opportune thesis destined to the greatest (theological) success: the doctrine of the Witness-People. . . .

"If the Jews who refused to believe in Christ nevertheless continue to exist, it is because they must do so, because God in his supernatural wisdom has so ordained it; they continue to exist in order to bear witness to Christian truth, and they bear witness to it both by their sacred books and by their Dispersion.
(Jules Isaac, ibid., p. 168)

"Oh marvellous discovery of a subtle, creative genius: the astonishing survival of the Jewish people can only be ascribed to one object and one reason, to testify to the antiquity of biblical tradition and the authenticity of the sacred texts on which the Christian faith is founded; the blind (and 'carnal') Jews themselves do not understand the real meaning of their holy Scriptures, but they preserve them piously and reverently for the use of the Church, to whom, in other words, they are nothing more than enslaved 'book-rests' walking behind their master. Similarly, the Dispersion of the Jewish people, while not losing its significance as the chastisement brought down by God in punishment for the Cross of Christ, itself bears witness and corresponds to the designs of providence since it proves everywhere that the Jews continue to exist 'for the salvation of the nations and not for the salvation of their own', and thus serves to spread the same Christian faith which the Jews persist in denying.
"Such, in broad outline, is St. Augustine's theme.
(Jules Isaac, ibid, pp. 168-9)

"There is a corollary to these augustinian propositions, a corollary which is rendered formidable by its practical implications. The witness which the Jews bear (in favour of Christian truth) by their survival and by their dispersion, they should also bear by their visible downfall. The efficacy of their witness will be measured in terms of the harshness of the lot which has been reserved for them. . . .
"The teaching of contempt", adds Jules Isaac, "leads to the system of vilification which is its necessary justification.
"Henceforward we perceive the radical difference which separates the Christian system of vilification from its modern Nazi imitator—blind and ignorant are they who ignore their thousand profound connections: the latter was only a stage, a brief stage preceding the massive extermination; the former on the contrary involved survival, but a shameful survival in contempt and disgrace; thus it was created to endure and to injure and slowly torture millions of innocent victims. . . ."
(Jules Isaac: ibid., pp. 166-8, 171-2)

One is tempted to say that all exaggerations are valueless after reading such shameless slanders against the teaching of the Church. Our reply is given a few pages later. Meanwhile, says Jules Isaac:

"Let us first of all examine the doctrinal teaching of the Church in this period of the early Middle Ages. No more perfect expression of it is to be found than in the masterpiece of St. Gregory the Great, who comes half-way between St. Augustine and St. Agobard, at the end of the sixth century. After the Church Fathers, no work commanded more attention in Christendom, especially in Western Catholicism. No example could be more conclusive since . . . this great Pope, far from being a fanatic, is renowned for his remarkable qualities of generosity, moral elevation, equity and humanity.

"Gregory the Great never systematically defined his doctrinal position with regard to Judaism . . . but a Catholic theologian, V. Tollier, who has made a special, conscientious study of his work, came to this conclusion, which reference to the texts themselves would qualify as acceptable: 'He envisaged the history of this people as an enormous error, prepared at great length, committed in cold blood, rigorously punished, to be effaced one day by divine mercy.' For having treated God 'with the blackest ingratitude', 'the chosen people became accursed . . .; it will only arouse itself from its fatal slumbers at the last days of the world.'

"Gregory the Great could only follow existing tradition, firmly established by the Fathers of the fourth century. But let it be said to his credit that he never lost sight of the Jewish origins of the early Church, or of the Pauline vision of the final reconciliation—deferred by him (not by St. Paul) to the last days of the world; that he was not a party to the unjust and deadly accusation of 'deicide'; that while underlining the guilt of the majority of the Jews for the Passion, he never completely omitted the share in it borne by the procurator Pilate and the Romans; that it was he indeed who formulated the pre-eminently Christian idea—which was to dominate the spirit and the heart of all believers in Christ and which is taught in the catechism of the Council of Trent—of the universal responsibility of sinful humanity; and that finally, anti-Jewish controversy in his writings nowhere degenerates into the outrageous and scurrilous outbursts after the example of St. John Chrysostom.

"One is therefore all the more struck by the strict severity with which this great Pope, this noble person, speaks of Judaism and the Jewish people, and re-iterates themes that are mainly traditional without verifying their foundations. . . .

" 'Drunk with pride (writes the great Pope) the Jews have bent all their energy on closing their minds to God's representatives. . . . They lost humility and with it the understanding of the truth.'

"Like the fourth Evangelist, Gregory incessantly abuses the term the Jews to draw attention to the clique of Jesus' enemies, which amounts to condemning the whole of the Jewish people to the contempt and hatred of the faithful: 'The Jews handed over the Lord and accused him. . . .' (Jules Isaac, ibid., pp. 289-90)

" 'The finest examples failed to move this vulgar nation to serve God with love, not fear . . . Israel's faith consisted only in obeying the divine precepts to the letter . . . they became not a means for sanctification but a source of pride. . . . To rise up to God, Israel had the wings of the Law, but her heart, crawling in the lowest depths on earth, held her down. . . . The infidel people only understood the incarnation of God in the flesh, and would not accept him as more than a man . . . thus the spouse, given up to carnal judgment, failed to recognise the mystery of the Incarnation.' "

(St. Gregory the Great, quoted by Jules Isaac, ibid, pp. 289-90)

Jules Isaac continues:

"This theme of the 'carnal people' is infinitely dangerous since it leads inevitably to that of the people of 'the Beast', of 'the antichrist' and of 'the devil' actuated by perverse, diabolical hatred against God and his supporters. (ibid., p. 290)

" 'Because the hearts of the Jews are without faith,' said St. Gregory, 'they have submitted to the devil . . . the Synagogue is not only unwilling to accept the faith, but has fought it with the sword and has raised up against it the horrors of a merciless persecution . . . is it not true to say that the Beast has made his den in the hearts of Jewish persecutors? . . . the more the Holy Spirit filled the world the more perverse hatred enchained the souls of the Jews; their blindness has made them cruel and their cruelty has driven them to implacable persecution'.

(St. Gregory the Great, quoted by Jules Isaac, ibid., p. 290)

"Such is the teaching of the great Pope, in his opinion conciliatory and of a purely doctrinal nature, consistent with one's duty to humanity, Christian charity and respect for the law. It is his opinion, perforce not others'. For it was to leave in mediocre hearts and minds, everywhere and always in the majority, a stigma branded on the forehead of the Jewish people of its crimes, its curse, its satanic perverseness. It is all that is required today, or at any time, to unleash the savagery of 'the Beast'."

(Jules Isaac, ibid., p. 291)

Jules Isaac now turns to St. Agobard.

"The first point to note about Agobard is that his anti-Judaism is essentially ecclesiastical and theological, like the Church Fathers'; it doesn't spring from what Mr. Simon calls the vein of popular anti-Semitism. . . . (Jules Isaac, ibid., p. 274)

"In conflict with the Jews, Agobard appealed directly to the emperor in two letters; *de insolentia Judaeorum* (On the Insolence of the Jews), and *de judaicis superstitionibus* (On Jewish Superstitions).

"In the former, Agobard sets out a justification of his attitude and of the anti-Jewish measures which he has taken. It was easy for him to show that in denouncing the perfidia Judaeorum he was only obeying the precepts taught by the Fathers and the rules established by the Church. These precepts and rules, he assures the emperor, accord with reason and charity: 'Since the Jews live among us, and since we must not treat them spitefully nor do injury to their life, their health and their fortune, let us observe the moderation prescribed by the Church, which is to behave with prudence and humanity towards them. . . .'

(Jules Isaac, ibid., p. 278)

"The whole of his work, which is based on the Church Fathers —principally St. Ambrose—on the decisions of the Councils and on the Scriptures, tends to demonstrate that the Jews ought to be kept strictly apart, as a people whose society was the worst defilement a Christian could endure. Antichrists, sons of the devil, 'the impious Jews, enemies of the Son of God, themselves cut themselves off from the true house of David, the Church; all the divine threats and maledictions have been fulfilled with regard to the Synagogue of Satan'. There is nothing new in this; Agobard is merely repeating the habitual formulas, or rituals, as one might call them, of the teaching of contempt: banning the Jews from Christian society is one of the masterpieces of the system of vilification.

"To superstition, according to Agobard, the Jews add blasphemy and slander, and he gives examples of outrageous accounts of the life of Jesus spread abroad by Jews. It is indeed known that a detestable Jewish tradition to this effect sprang up in the second century, later to be recorded in the books of the Sepher Toledot Jeschu—the version Agobard quoted is akin to them, if not absolutely identical. These contemptuous, libellous stories are as indefensible as the manifold insults of certain Christian orators directed against the synagogue and the Jewish faith. Agobard himself does not deny it." (Jules Isaac, ibid., p. 280)

Jules Isaac concludes in these words:

"Agobard's attitude cannot be justified by putting forward the evils which the Jews or certain Jews may have committed, nor is it in accordance with 'reason' or 'wisdom' or 'Christian charity' to treat them all as Pariahs, to denounce them in public as the enemies of God, to call their sanctuaries synagogues of Satan and themselves a people cursed to their very bowels, with whom all contact ought to be avoided as the worst pollution. . . .

"For, and I will repeat it again and again, such teaching, hurled from the roof-tops to flocks of ignorant and credulous faithful leads not only to 'violent injustice', but to even more odious consequences, to criminal acts of homicide and genocide, to massive assassinations and monstrous 'pogroms'. It is too simple to believe or to let people believe that the most violent vocal outbursts are harmless, as if there was no risk that violent words would lead men to violent acts. Which is more to blame, the tongue's insults or the arm's blows? In spite of his apologists, 'St. Agobard' must bear his part of the responsibility." (Jules Isaac, ibid., pp. 284-5)

In other words, according to Jules Isaac, the Evangelists were liars, St. John Chrysostom is a delirious theologian and a scurrilous pamphleteer, St. Augustine uses his sharp, subtle mind to falsify the facts, Pope St. Gregory the Great invented the "formidable theme of the 'carnal people', which has unleashed the savagery of the Beast against the Jews throughout history", and St. Agobard, the celebrated Primate of Gaul, hurled "from the roof-tops to flocks of the faithful a teaching which leads to the most odious consequences, to crimes of genocide, to massive assassinations and to monstrous progroms."

All persecutors, filled with anti-Jewish hatred, the veritable forerunners of Streicher and others, morally responsible for "Auschwitz" and "six million innocent Jewish victims".

Thus, Jules Isaac denounces this, asserts that, and then condemns the great doctors without attempting to analyse any of the reasons which led them all, each of different character and origin—Jewish,

Greek and Latin—and each raised by the Church to the altar, to make such stern and weighty accusations against the Jews.

He asked, or rather insisted that the Council:

Condemn and suppress all racial, religious or national discrimination with regard to the Jews;

Modify or suppress liturgical prayers concerning the Jews, especially those on Good Friday;

Declare that the Jews are in no way responsible for the death of Christ, for which the whole of humanity is to blame;

Quash the passages, in the Evangelists, and principally the one in St. Matthew, whom Jules Isaac coldly describes as a liar and perverter of the truth, in which they relate the crucial story of the Passion;

Declare that the Church has always been to blame for this state of latent war which has persisted for two thousand years between the Jews, the Christians and the rest of the world;

Promise that the Church will definitely modify her attitude to a spirit of humility, contrition and forgiveness with regard to the Jews, and that she will make every effort to repair the wrongs that she has done them by rectifying and purifying her traditional teaching according to the lines laid down by Jules Isaac.

Notwithstanding the insolence of his ultimatum and of his virulent indictment of the Evangelists and of the teaching of the Fathers of the Church, which is founded on the very words of Christ himself, Jules Isaac received strong support from priests even in Rome and from many members of Amitié judéo-chrétienne.

On 23rd January 1965, the weekly paper, *Terre de Provence*, which is published at Aix, reported that Mgr. de Provenchères, Bishop of Aix, had given an address to the "Amitié judéo-chrétienne" on the occasion of the inauguration of the Jules Isaac avenue which took place that morning, and the following passage is taken from the article:

> "A large crowd had gathered in the Zironski amphitheatre to hear the address which Mgr. de Provenchères was to give on the subject of 'The Council decree on relations between Catholics and non-Catholics.'
>
> "The rural dean, Father Palanque, first of all recalled the moving ceremony that had taken place that morning in the presence of the Mayor, Mr. Mouret, and of Mr. Schourski and Mr. Lunel, president of the Friends of Jules Isaac. The latter's name would again be on their lips in connection with the third session on the Council schema of Vatican II. Mgr. de Provenchères would be able to give them the benefit of his knowledge which he had obtained at first hand when attending the Council.

"Mgr. de Provenchères told us how happy he was to describe his experiences since he had found the work at the Council very rewarding.

"Speaking of Jules Isaac, he told us that ever since he first met him in 1945 he had had a profound regard for him, which very quickly turned to affection. The Council schema appeared to be a solemn ratification of the points they had discussed together. It originated in a petition which Jules Isaac had addressed to the Vatican, which has been studied by more than two thousand bishops. The initiative which led to this event had been taken by a layman, a Jew. Mgr. de Provenchères then remarked that great events in history often began in this way, subsequently to be sanctified; the meeting between Jules Isaac and John XXIII had been a gesture of the Amitié judéo-chrétienne.

"Mgr. de Provenchères then gave a detailed account of the role played by Jules Isaac at Rome in the preparation of the Council, and the dean, Fr. Palanque, thanking Mgr. de Provenchères, outlined the work which the Bishop of Aix had done to ensure the successful passage of the schema."

While on the subject of Judaeo-Christian friendship it is instructive to note the haughty and contemptuous irony with which Joshua Jehouda, one of the spiritual leaders of contemporary Judaism, refers to it:

"*The current expression 'Judaeo-Christian' is an error which has altered the course of universal history by the confusion it has sown in men's minds, if by it one is meant to understand the Jewish origin of Christianity; for by abolishing the fundamental distinctions between Jewish and Christian messianism, it seeks to bring together two ideas that are radically in opposition.* By laying the accent exclusively on the 'Christian' idea to the detriment of the 'Judean' it conjures away monotheistic messianism—a valuable discipline at all levels of thought—and reduces it to a purely confessional messianism, preoccupied like Christian messianism with the salvation of the individual soul. If the term 'Judaeo-Christian' does point to a common origin, there is no doubt that it is a most dangerous idea. It is based on a '*contradictio in adjecto*' which has set the path of history on the wrong track. It links in one breath two ideas which are completely irreconcileable, it seeks to demonstrate that there is no difference between day and night or hot and cold or black and white, and thus introduces a fatal element of confusion to a basis on which some, nevertheless, are endeavouring to construct a civilisation. Christianity offers to the world a limited messianism which it wishes to impose as the only valid one. . . . Even Spinoza, who was further than any other thinker from the historic messianism of Israel, wrote: 'As for what certain churches say, that God assumed human nature, I must confess that this seems to me as absurd as saying that a circle assumed the shape of a square. . . .'

"The dogmatic exclusiveness professed by Christianity must finally end. . . . It is the obstinate Christian claim to be the sole heir to Israel which propagates anti-Semitism. This scandal must terminate sooner or later; the sooner it does, the sooner the world will be rid of the tissue of lies in which anti-Semitism shrouds itself."

(Joshua Jehouda: *l'Antisémitisme Miroir du Monde*, pp. 135-6)

The author's attitude would appear to be clear from the above, but let us illustrate it further:

"The Christian faith flows from a myth connected with Jewish history but not with the precise tradition which it has transmitted in the Law—both written and by word of mouth—as is the case with Israel." (Joshua Jehouda, ibid., p. 132)

"However, Christianity claims to bring to the world the 'true' messianism. It seeks to convert all the pagans including the Jews. But as long as the monotheistic messianism of Israel persists, and is present even though it does not manifest itself openly . . . Christian messianism appears as what it is in reality: an imitation which collapses in the light of the authentic messianism."

(Joshua Jehouda, ibid., p. 155)

It is the author's sincere hope that Christians who enter Judaeo-Christian circles of friendship are profoundly versed not only in the mysteries of their own faith but of that of the Jewish people, so that they understand their fundamental "contradictio in adjecto", and hence do not attempt to bring together two ideas that are radically in opposition.

However, when Jules Isaac and his associates went to Rome, they were careful not to mention these passages in their books; they spoke of Christian charity, of ecumenical unity, of common biblical filiations, of Judaeo-Christian friendship, of the struggle against racism, of the martyrdom of the Jewish people, and their efforts met with success, since 1,651 bishops, cardinals, archbishops and Council Fathers voted to reform Catholic teaching according to the desires of Jules Isaac, the B'nai B'rith and the World Jewish Congress.

Naturally, when they went to Rome to prepare the Council vote, Jules Isaac and the leaders of the Jewish organisations did not tell the Pope and the bishops:

"Your Evangelists are rank liars.

"Your Church Fathers are perverters and torturers who have spread throughout the world the hatred of the Jew and unleashed the savagery of the Beast.

"They are the precursors of Hitler and Streicher, and it is they who are veritably responsible for Auschwitz and the six million Jewish dead, victims of the Germans."

These accusations can be read in their complete and unabridged form in Jules Isaac's books, which are available in any bookshop, but apparently the Council Fathers have not read them, any more than they have read the works of Jehouda, Rabi, Benamozegh, Memmi and others.

No, Jules Isaac and the leaders of the great Jewish organisations did not say, in company with Joshua Jehouda, one of the masters of contemporary Jewish thought: Your monotheism is a false monotheism; it is a bastard imitation and a falsified version of the only true monotheism which is Hebrew monotheism, and if Christianity does not return to Jewish sources it will be finally condemned. (Joshua Jehouda, ibid., pp. 155, 260, 349)

They did not say in company with Benamozegh, who is one of the glories of contemporary Jewish thought: The Christian religion is a false, so-called divine religion. Its only hope of salvation, as for the rest of the world, is to return to Israel. (Elie Benamozegh: *Israel et l'Humanité*)

They did not say in company with Memmi:

"Your religion is a blasphemy and a subversion in the eyes of the Jews. Your God is to us the Devil, that is to say, the symbol and essence of all evil on earth."
(A. Memmi: *Portrait of a Jew*, pp. 188-9)

They did not say in company with Rabi:

"The conversion of the Jews to Christianity is treason and idolatry since it involves the supreme blasphemy, the belief in the divinity of a man."
(Rabi: *Anatomie du Judaisme français*, p. 188)

They took care not to arouse fears at Rome by unveiling their thoughts, and they succeeded in gaining a certain number of prelates to their cause.

All this is undoubtedly a strange story.

It may be true that there are a certain number of progressive bishops who, out of hostility towards traditional Catholicism, are perhaps prepared to use any weapons against it. But it is not unreasonable to imagine that they constitute a minority. How then does one explain their success?

It stems from two reasons:

Firstly, the vast majority of the Council Fathers are unaware of the role played by the Jewish organisations and Jules Isaac in the preparation of this vote: they had not read the latter's works;

And secondly, in general, the Council Fathers are not well informed on the Jewish question and they readily accept Judaic arguments, which are skilfully presented by formidable debaters such as Jules Isaac.

However that may be, the manœuvre was carried out with the utmost adroitness and it succeeded. The vote itself is there in witness to this fact.

One thousand six hundred and fifty-one Council Fathers considered that Jules Isaac's version of the Passion was preferable to St. John's and to St. Matthew's.

One thousand six hundred and fifty-one bishops, archbishops and cardinals admitted that the teaching of St. John Chrysostom, of St. Augustine, of St. Gregory the Great, of St. Ambrose and of St. Agobard should be purified and rectified to conform with the injunctions of Jules Isaac, whose *Jésus et Israel* was recently described by the Jewish writer, Rabi, as "the most specific weapon of war against a particularly harmful Christian doctrine", that is to say, the doctrine codified by the above-mentioned Fathers of the Church. (Rabi: *Anatomie du Judaisme français*, p. 183)

The modification of the Good Friday liturgy and the suppression of, among others, the prayer of the Impropria by the 1,651 bishops is an admission that Jules Isaac was right when he said, describing the Impropria

> "It is difficult to say which is more striking; its beauty or its iniquity." (Jules Isaac: *Genèse de l'Antisémitisme*, p. 309)

Apparently the bishops considered that the iniquity of this prayer prevailed over its beauty.

In brief, the vote of 20th November 1964, apparently taken in the spirit of Christian charity and in the desire for reconciliation between the Churches and for ecumenical unity, in fact represented a step away from traditional Christianity.

After discussing the intricate question of Judaeo-Christian friendship—Jules Isaac's masterpiece, warmly supported by the Cardinals

Feltin, Gerlier and Liénart—let us return to the heart of the subject, the part played by Jules Isaac and Jewish organisations in the Council vote.

We have reproduced long extracts from Jules Isaac because he is the theoretician and spokesman in this campaign against Christian teaching, but he is not alone in this field. Powerful organisations such as the B'nai B'rith and the World Jewish Congress have lent their support.

On the 19th November 1963, *Le Monde* published the following article:

> "The Jewish international B'nai B'rith organisation has expressed the desire of establishing closer relations with the Catholic Church. It has just submitted to the Council a declaration asserting the responsibility of the whole of humanity for the death of Christ.
>
> "Mr. Label Katz, President of the International Council of the B'nai B'rith, said that 'if this declaration is accepted by the Council, Jewish communities will explore ways and means of co-operating with the authorities of the (Catholic) Church to ensure the realisation of its purpose and projects.'
>
> "The declaration was approved by the Executive Committee of the International Council, the co-ordinating mechanism of the 475,000 strong B'nai B'rith organisation, which has members in forty-two countries.
>
> "Mr. Paul Jacob of Mulhouse, the President of B'nai B'rith in Europe, said that the approval of this declaration would strike a blow at the roots of anti-Semitism in many European countries.
>
> "Rabbi Maurice Eisendrath, President of the Union of Jewish Congregations in America, appealed on Saturday to the 4,000 delegates of the forty-seventh general assembly of American Reform Judaism to revise their judgment on Christianity and erroneous view-points about Christ."

Important personalities, leaders of contemporary Jewish thought, such as Joshua Jehouda in his book *L'Antisémitisme, Miroir du Monde*, have advanced similar arguments on the need to reform and purify Christian teaching:

> "Christianity obstinately refuses to recognise Israel as its spiritual equal.... The belief that Christianity offers 'the fullness' of Judaism, that it is its culminating peak, that Judaism has been fulfilled by Christianity, vitiates the very roots of universal monotheism, weakens the foundations of Christianity itself and exposes it to successive crises. If Christianity is to overcome its present

crisis it must raise itself spiritually to authentic monotheism. *The hour is coming when it will be necessary to cleanse the Christian conscience by the doctrine of universal monotheism.*
(Joshua Jehouda, ibid., pp. 10, 11)

"It cannot be denied that anti-Semitism constitutes the chronic disease of Christianity. It must be studied in terms of the crisis in Christian civilisation and not in terms of the qualities or defects of the Jews, which bear no relation to it.
(Joshua Jehouda, ibid., p. 14)

"In the field of anti-Semitism, it is the attitude of Christians which is determinative above all else. The Jews are only its innocent victims.
(Joshua Jehouda, ibid., p. 13)

"Over the centuries Christianity has incurred a debt of honour towards Israel. Whether this debt of honour has fallen due is the question implicitly propounded by this book. On a negative or affirmative answer to this question depends the spiritual evolution of Christianity, or, to put it more clearly, peace between the peoples."
(Joshua Jehouda, ibid., p. 15)

Joshua Jehouda, Jules Isaac, the B'nai B'rith, the World Jewish Congress: from their evidence it is clear that world Judaism has for years been carrying out a carefully prepared and concerted campaign which resulted in the recent vote at the Council.

In reality, under the guise of ecumenical unity, religious reconciliation and other plausible pretexts, its object is the demolition of the bastion of traditional Catholicism, which is described by Joshua Jehouda as "the decrepid fortress of Christian obscurantism".

According to Jehouda, there have been three attempts to "rectify Christianity", three attempts "aimed at purging the Christian conscience of the miasmas of hatred", three attempts "to amend the suffocating, paralysing effects of Christian theology", and "three breaches have been opened in the decrepid fortress of Christian obscurantism"—that is to say, three important stages have been accomplished in the work of the destruction of traditional Christianity, and they are:

The Renaissance;
The Reformation;
The Revolution of 1789.

Although he does not say so in as many words, it is quite plain, as several extracts will serve to make abundantly clear, that what

Jehouda finds so admirable in these three great movements is the work of dechristianisation to which each, in different ways, made a powerful contribution.

"The Renaissance, the Reformation and the Revolution constitute three attempts to rectify Christian mentality by bringing it into tune with the progressive development of reason and science . . . and as and when dogmatic Christianity relaxes, the Jews gradually free themselves from control."

Speaking of the Renaissance, he informs us that:

"We can say that if the Renaissance had not been deflected from its original course for the benefit of the Greek world, the world would have doubtless been unified by the creative thought and doctrine of the Cabala."

(Joshua Jehouda: L'Antisémitisme, Miroir du Monde, p. 168)

And this is what he says about the Reformation:

"With the Reformation, which broke out in Germany fifty years after the Renaissance, the universality of the Church was destroyed . . . (before Luther and Calvin) John Reuchlin, the disciple of Pico de Mirandola, shook the Christian conscience by suggesting, as early as 1494, that there was nothing higher than hebraic wisdom. . . . Reuchlin advocated returning to Jewish sources as well as ancient texts. Finally, he won his case against the convert Pefferkorn, who loudly demanded the destruction of the Talmud. The new spirit which was to revolutionise the whole of Europe . . . became apparent with regard to the Jews and the Talmud. . . . However, one is astonished to find that there were as many Protestant as Catholic anti-Semites."

In short, Jehouda concluded, "the Reformation marks the revolt against the Catholic Church, which is already a revolt in itself against the religion of Israel".

(Joshua Jehouda, ibid., pp. 169-72)

As for the French Revolution:

"The third attempt to amend the Christian position, after the failure of reformed Christianity to unite, took place under the impetus of the French Revolution . . . which marked the beginning of atheism in the history of Christian peoples. Declaredly antireligious, this Revolution continues, through the influence of Russian Communism, to make a powerful contribution to the dechristianisation of the Christian world."

(Joshua Jehouda, ibid., pp. 170-2)

Finally, the work of the "rectification of Christian mentality" was crowned by Karl Marx and Nietzsche, for

> ". . . in the nineteenth century two new attempts were made to purify the mentality of the Christian world, one by Marx and the other by Nietzsche". (Joshua Jehouda, ibid., p. 187)

Thus "the profound meaning of history, which remains unaltered in every epoch, is that of a veiled or open struggle between the forces working for the advancement of humanity and those that cling to coagulated interests, obstinately determined to keep them in existence to the detriment of what is to come". (Joshua Jehouda, ibid., p. 186)

In the eyes of these thinkers, the reforms proposed by the Council ought to represent a new stage in the abandonment, resignation and destruction of traditional Catholicism.

We are in fact witnessing a new struggle in the millenary confrontation between Jews and Christians. Jehouda, Rabi, Benamozegh and Memmi depict it in the following terms:

> "Christianity", says Jehouda, "obstinately refuses to recognise Israel as its spiritual equal . . . the belief that Christianity offers the 'fullness of Judaism', that it is its culminating peak, that Judaism has been fulfilled by Christianity, vitiates the roots of universal monotheism, weakens the foundations of Christianity itself and exposes it to successive crises . . . the hour is coming when it will be necessary to cleanse the Christian conscience by the doctrine of universal monotheism.
> (Joshua Jehouda, ibid., pp. 10-11)

> "Christian anti-Semitism, while proclaiming itself messianic, also claims to replace the messianism of Israel with faith in a crucified God who will secure the salvation of the souls of all the faithful. By lowering Jewish messianism to the level of paganism, Christianity tends to convert all the Jews to a reduced form of messianism. . . . But as long as the monotheistic messianism of Israel persists . . . Christianity appears as what it is in reality: an imitation which collapses in the light of the authentic messianism . . . (and) anti-Semitism will persist as long as Christianity refuses to face its real problem, which may be traced back to its betrayal of monotheistic messianism."
> (Joshua Jehouda, ibid., pp. 154-60)

And again:

> "It is the obstinate Christian claim to be the sole heir to Israel which propagates anti-Semitism. This scandal must terminate

sooner or later; the sooner it does, the sooner the world will be rid of the tissue of lies in which anti-Semitism shrouds itself."

(Joshua Jehouda, ibid., p. 136)

Now let us hear Elie Benamozegh, one of the masters of Jewish thought today:

"If Christianity consents to reform itself upon the Hebrew ideal it will always be the true religion of the gentile peoples.

(Elie Benamozegh: *Israel et l'Humanité*, p. 18)

"The religion of the future must be based on some positive and traditional religion, invested with the mysterious prestige of antiquity. But of all the ancient religions Judaism is unique in claiming to possess a religious ideal for all humanity (for) . . . the work (of Christianity) is only a copy which must be placed face to face with the original . . . since it (Judaism) is the indisputed mother (of Christianity), it is the more ancient religion which is destined to become the most modern.

"As opposed to Christianity . . . with its claim to divine origin and infallibility . . . and in order to replace an authority which proclaims its infallibility and which only begins at year one of the Christian era or of the Hegira . . . another, much more important infallibility must be found which, taking its origin from the history of man on earth, will only end with him.

(Elie Benamozegh, ibid., pp. 34-35)

"The reconciliation dreamt of by the early Christians as a condition of the Parousia, or final coming of Jesus, the return of the Jews to the bosom of the Church, without which, as all the Christian communions agree, the work of Redemption is incomplete, this return we say will take place not in truth as it is expected to happen, but in the only genuine, logical and lasting fashion possible, and above all in the only way in which it will benefit the human race. It will be a reunion between the Hebrew religion and the others that have sprung from it and, according to the last of the Prophets, the Light of the Seers, as the Doctors call Malachi, it will be 'the return of the children's heart to their fathers'."

(Elie Benamozegh, ibid., p. 48)

Rabi has this to say:

"There is", he tells us, "an irremediable difference between Jews and Christians. It is to do with Jesus. If we take it that he did exist in history, for the Jew he was neither God nor the son of God. The most extreme concession the Jew can possibly make was expressed by Joseph Klauzner, according to whom Jesus, whom he said was neither the Messiah, nor a Prophet, nor a lawgiver, nor the founder of a religion, nor Tanna, nor rabbi, nor pharisee, 'is considered as a great moralist and artist in the use of parables by the Jewish nation . . . the day when he is cleared of the stories of his miracles and mysticism, the Book of the Morality of Jesus will become one of the most precious jewels of Jewish literature of all time'.

(Rabi: *Anatomie du Judaisme français*, p. 204)

"Sometimes I see in my mind the last Jew alive standing before his creator in the last century as it is written in the Talmud: 'The Jew, bound by his oath, remains standing since Sinai.' What, I imagine, will this last Jew, who will have survived the outrages of history and the appeals of the world, what will he say then to justify his resistance to the usury of time and the pressure of men? I hear him say: 'I do not believe in the divinity of Jesus.' It is quite understandable that the Christian is scandalised by this profession of faith. But are we not scandalised by the Christian's profession of his faith?

" 'For us, he says, " 'conversion to Christianity is necessarily idolatrous because it involves the supreme blasphemy, the belief in the divinity of a man'." (Rabi, ibid., p. 188)

The above was written in the last ten years. Let us now go back two thousand years and re-read the account of the Passion.

"And they that had laid hold on Jesus led him away to Caiaphas the high priest, where the scribes and the elders were assembled. . . .

"Now the chief priests and elders and all the council sought false witness against Jesus, to put him to death; but found none: yea, though many false witnesses came, yet found they none. And at last came two false witnesses, and said. This man said, I am able to destroy the temple of God and to rebuild it in three days. And the high priest arose and said unto him: Answerest thou nothing? What is it which these witness against thee? But Jesus held his peace. And the high priest answered and said unto him: I adjure thee by the living God, that thou tell us whether thou be the Christ, the Son of God. Jesus saith unto him: Thou hast said it; nevertheless I say unto you, hereafter ye shall see the Son of man sitting on the right hand of power, and coming in the clouds of heaven.

"Then the high priest rent his clothes, saying: He hath spoken blasphemy; what further need have we of witnesses? Behold, now ye have heard his blasphemy, what think ye? They answered and said: He is guilty of death."

(The Gospel according to St. Matthew xxvi. 57-66)

St. Luke describes the trial as follows: Jesus is being interrogated by the chief priests before the scribes and elders:

"Art thou the Christ? Tell us. And he said unto them: If I tell you, you will not believe, and if I also ask you, you will not answer me nor let me go. Hereafter shall the Son of man sit on the right hand of the power of God.

"Then said they all: Art thou then the Son of God? And he said unto them: Ye say that I am. And they said: What need we any further witness, for we ourselves have heard of his own mouth?" (The Gospel according to St. Luke xxii. 67-71)

St. Mark's account is very similar to St. Matthew's.

After two thousand years the situation—one of unyielding opposition between Jews and Christians—still remains unchanged.

In conclusion it may not be amiss to relate a strange event which happened recently, involving the barrister, Hans Deutsch, an important and respected member of the Jewish Community in Germany. It was he who had intervened with Pope Paul VI in support of Jules Isaac's thesis in favour of the Jews, which brought about the Council vote.

On 3rd November 1964 a bolt fell from the blue. Hans Deutsch was arrested at Bonn, charged with swindling the German Government.

Four days later the following account appeared in Le Monde under the heading: HANS DEUTSCH PLAYED AN IMPORTANT PART IN CLAIMING INDEMNITIES DUE TO THE VICTIMS OF NAZISM:

"The arrest at Bonn of Professor Hans Deutsch on the 3rd November seems to have aroused lively reaction at Berne, Vienna and other centres concerned with German compensation to the Jewish victims of Nazism. . . . The news was announced on the 4th November by a spokesman for the Public Prosecutor of the Federal Republic at Bonn. Professor Deutsch is accused of having embezzled nearly 35,000,000 marks and of having induced third parties to make false statements.

"The personality of Professor Deutsch and the circumstances of his arrest throw a disquieting light on an affair destined to create a sensation . . . Mr. Deutsch is of Austrian origin. He left Vienna after the Anschluss and went to Palestine, from whence he returned to Europe after the war. A lawyer, he undertook to fight for the restitution of Jewish properties confiscated by the Germans, notably for those of the Austrian branch of the Rothschild family. His professional fees amounted to a considerable personal fortune, which increased with investment so that he was able to donate large sums to aid the cultural arts.

"The Professor had been received in audience by Pope Paul VI, whose aid he had requested in launching an appeal to fight prejudiced people who aggravate relations between Jews and Christians. The Pope agreed to give his support to this project, which had been inspired by the example of Jules Isaac.

"The charge brought against him has astonished the city of Vienna, where many circles have expressed their sympathy for Mr. Deutsch, in view of his cultural activities. Some reports say that Professor Deutsch was in Germany to discuss methods of raising the maximum amount of indemnities payable to the Jewish victims of Nazism."

Paris-Presse published two articles on the 8th and 13th November following the *Le Monde* story, from which the following passages have been taken:

"The Hatvany collection—one of the most superb collections of European paintings that exists—is the cause of the downfall of the Jewish Austrian barrister, Professor Hans Deutsch, who is accused of having improperly collected several million marks in the names of the victims of Nazi plundering.

"Former SS Chief, Hauptsturmführer Frederick Wilke, who is now a trouser manufacturer in Frankfurt, joined Deutsch in prison at Bonn. His evidence would have enabled the barrister to pull off the swindle of which he is accused.

"Baron Hatvany, the 'Sugar King' of Hungary, had built up a collection of 800 pictures including Rembrandts, Goyas and Degas. It disappeared during the war. The Baron died in 1958 and his three daughters instructed Professor Deutsch to obtain an indemnity from the Bonn Government. Proof was still not available that the collection had actually been stolen by the Nazis. This is where Wilke came in. He had stated before the commission of enquiry that the pictures had been removed by SS General von Pieffer-Wildenbruch and taken to Bavaria. The Bonn Government had no alternative but to pay the indemnity. After lengthy discussion the total indemnity to be paid to the Hatvany heirs was fixed at 35,000,000 marks. Deutsch received half of this sum forthwith. It was later discovered that the collection had indeed been taken but it had not been stolen by the Nazis, but by the Russians in 1944. And this is why Deutsch was arrested when he arrived in Bonn last week to collect the balance of his 35,000,000 marks.

"He is perhaps the most accomplished crook of the century.

"The Deutsch affair is now in the hands of expert investigators. Chemists and graphologists are carefully examining in their laboratories every particle of the bulky dossier which Professor Deutsch had just submitted.

"Preliminary investigations suggest that the Professor had already spent some 20,000,000 marks preparing this dossier; for the forgeries which he produced and the attestations of witnesses etc., are veritable masterpieces. 'If our suspicions are proved correct', said a German lawyer who is closely connected with the Public Prosecutor at Bonn, 'the Deutsch affair will turn out to be one of the most gigantic swindles that have ever been seen in Germany'. For the moment Hans Deutsch had lost none of his self-confidence. 'My whole life,' he said, 'bears witness for me. Pleas for the people of Israel, literary foundations, schools, the struggle to bring together Jews and Christians, not to mention the rest—these things just cannot be imagined. I can prove,' he said, 'that I have spent the whole of my life in the service of great causes.' But was he giving with the left hand what he received with the right? Was Mr. Hyde working for Dr. Jekyll or was the Doctor only a cover for Mr. Hyde?"

PART II

THE PROBLEM OF THE AGES

"It is no accident that Jews have been the precursors and makers of many revolutions of thought and spirit."
Lord Sieff, Vice-President of World Jewish Congress in article THE MEANING OF SURVIVAL.
Jewish Chronicle, 22nd July, 1966

4

THE COMPLEXITY OF THE JEWISH PROBLEM

As soon as one begins to examine the Jewish problem a major difficulty is encountered, namely its extreme complexity.

The Jews are not only the adherents of a religion; despite the dispersion they belong to a distinct community in which the factors of race, religion and nationality are so closely interwoven that it is impossible to separate them.

But one must beware of misunderstanding these terms, for with the Jews they bear a completely different meaning from that attributed to them in ordinary language. To be precise, let us say that the definition of the Jewish race does not correspond to the usual definition of the word race; that the Jewish religion bears no similarity to any other religion; and that the concept of the Jewish nation is inapplicable to any other nation and without precedent in the history of the world.

Furthermore, the Jews confuse the realities of the problem by adopting ambiguous arguments, and at the same time many Jewish people occupy prominent positions of responsibility among the societies of the nations they have entered.

This explains why the Jews are obstinately and fanatically opposed to the Jewish question being discussed in broad daylight.

In his classic work, *The Hapsburg Monarchy*, written before the First World War, Henry Wickham Steed, a remarkably well-informed person, discussing this point, said:

> Their ideal "seems to be the maintenance of Jewish international influence as a veritable *imperium in imperiis*. Dissimulation of their real objects has become to them a second nature, and they deplore and tenaciously combat every tendency to place the Jewish question frankly on its merits before the world."
>
> (H. W. Steed: *The Hapsburg Monarchy*, p. 179)

We will now attempt to depict in broad outline the difficulty and complexity of the problem by resorting to the best informed writers on the question.

"The Jewish question is universal and elusive. It cannot be truly expressed either in terms of religion, nationality, or race. The Jews themselves seem destined so to arouse the passions of those with whom they come into contact that impartiality in regard to them is rare. Some Jews, indeed, regard the very recognition of the existence of a Jewish question as a confession of anti-Semitism. . . .

"Yet it may safely be said that no question deserves more earnest study. It assumes a hundred forms, reaches into unsuspected regions of national and international life, and influences, for good or evil, the march of civilisation. The main difficulty is to find a starting-point from which to approach it, a coign of vantage high enough to command a view of its innumerable ramifications. Is it a question of race or religion? It is both and more. Is it a question of economics, finance and of international trade? It is these and something besides. Are the peculiar characteristics that form at once the strength and weakness of the Jews a result of religious persecution, or have the Jews been persecuted because these characteristics have rendered them odious to the peoples that have harboured them? This is the old question whether the hen or the egg should take genealogical precedence."

(H. W. Steed, ibid., pp. 145-6)

More recently Doctor A. Roudinesco has written that:

"The destiny of the Jewish people appears to the historian as a paradoxical, incredible and almost incomprehensible phenomenon. It is unique and unequalled in the history of humanity."

(Dr. A. Roudinesco: *Le Malheur d'Israel*, p. 7)

"For the whole history of the Jewish people is unique and without exception in the world. Even today it is an insoluble enigma for sociologists, philosophers and statesmen. Every culture is original and individual, but Jewish culture, the product of Jewish history, is absolutely exceptional."

(Daniel Pasmanik: *Qu'est-ce que le Judaisme?*, p. 83)

"The Jewish people alone among the peoples of the world has subsisted for two thousand years without a historic fatherland, without a State, without a home, without a normal economy, without a central coercive power; for many centuries it has been the sport of other nations, it has suffered humiliation and persecution at their hands, and in spite of all this it has kept itself intact—surely this is one of the great enigmas which can only be explained by the thesis of the idea of the chosen people?

Whether it will always remain this way is another question. For our part, we are convinced that national values cannot be preserved indefinitely without national dignity. Only the future can solve this problem decisively." (Daniel Pasmanik, ibid., p. 73)

"The people of Israel has a peculiar place in history, *for it is at one and the same time religion and nation, and these two factors are absolutely inseparable*, which is not the case with any other people. Obviously Israel is a race, but not in the biological sense, as the racists claim, but in an ethical, historical sense." (Joshua Jehouda: *L'Antisémitisme, Miroir du Monde*, p. 209)

The Rev. Bonsirven, S.J., emphasises the racial aspect of the Jewish religion in his book on Judaism in Palestine:

"Jewish nationalism . . . exists, ardent and uncompromising, in the form of a national religion, or to put it more exactly, in the form of a racial religion. This expression does not seem to make sense because it links two terms and concepts that are directly opposed to each other: the concept of religion, which is of its nature supranational and universal, and the concept of nation and race, which includes exclusiveness. Such is the fundamental, constitutional paradox harboured by Judaism."
(Rev. Bonsirven, S.J.:
Le Judaisme Palestinien au temps de Jésus Christ)

Nahum Goldmann, President of the World Zionist Organisation, declared in 1961:

"It is totally undesirable to seek to define the Jewish people as a racial or religious community, or as a cultural or national entity. Its unique history has created a unique collective phenomenon to which none of the terms that are used in different languages to describe human groups can be applied. What matters is this: a Jew thinks of himself as an integral part of Judaism, whatever way he may describe the Jewish people."
(Quoted by Rabi: *Anatomie du Judaisme français*, p. 304)

Finally, two non-Jewish writers, one a Swiss and independent, and the other, J. Madaule, sympathetic to the Jewish people, both consider that the unity of the Hebrew people stems less from the idea of race, nation or religion than from common, essentially religious traditions:

"The difference between Judaism and every other contemporary religion is not a question of degree; it is a difference of species and nature which is fundamentally paradoxical. We are not dealing with a national religion but with a religious nationality."

(G. Batault: *Le Problème Juif*, p. 66)

"What is the exact nature of this Jewish nationality? On the one hand, it cannot be called purely religious in essence since a great number of Jews no longer practise their religion, and on the other, the other religions do not give rise to any attributes of nationality whatever. But if religion and nationality are perfectly distinct with the Jews, as they are with others, how can one explain this strange nationality unattached to any land? To the exception of all others, it is based on a common past, on common traditions which are religious in origin."

(J. Madaule: *Les Juifs et le Monde Actuel*, p. 155)

If further proof were wanted of the complexity of the Jewish problem, it is to be seen in the difficulty involved in the definition of a Jewish person in law.

Obliged to give an official answer to this question, neither Hitler, nor the Vichy Government, nor even the Israeli Government have succeeded in elaborating a clear and satisfactory definition.

By the Law of Return, the fundamental law of the new Jewish State, promulgated at Tel-Aviv in 1948, Israel gave the freedom of the country to all Jews of the Diaspora, whatever their origin. Once this had been done, the government had to work out a legal definition as to who was and who was not a Jew. Unable to find a legal formula which took into account the three factors of race, religion and nationality, the government of Tel-Aviv was obliged to have recourse to the religious criterion. A Jew is someone who belongs to a Jewish community of religion or religious traditions and who is not converted to another religion.

One does not even have to be a believer:

"Present day Judaism is not identical with religious practice. One can be Jewish, and one can be considered as such . . . without as much as sharing the Jewish faith, and notably Jewish monotheism." (J. Madaule, ibid., p. 107)

Israeli legislation is based on the strictest religious intolerance.

Indeed, conversion to another religion, particularly Christianity, automatically excludes one from the Jewish community. A Christian or Moslem Jew cannot take advantage of the Law of Return without prior naturalisation, just like any other foreigner.

> "This was confirmed in December 1962 in a solemn judgment in the High Court of Israel, when the full rights of Israeli nationality were refused to a Jew converted to Christianity, who had long been living in Israel and wanted to be considered an Israeli, Father Daniel. Despite the recognised services which he has rendered the State, Father Daniel was not permitted to dispense with the formalities of naturalisation applicable in Israel to non-Jews. In other words, because he was a Christian he was not allowed to enjoy the benefit of the Law of Return to which he had appealed." (J. Madaule, ibid., pp. 65-66)

It would be the same as if an English Protestant, converted to Catholicism, ceased to be English.

In an article which appeared in *Aspects de la France* on 21st January 1965, Xavier Vallat quotes a no less typical example:

> "Perhaps you believe that it is easy for a half-Jew to become an Israeli citizen. Do not be deceived. The case of Mrs. Rita Eitani, municipal counseller of Nazareth, is instructive. Her father, a Polish Jew, was a Nazi victim. Her mother is a German Catholic, and she did not have her daughter immersed. By reason whereof the Minister of the Interior, Mr. Moshe Shapiro, requested Mrs. Eitani to give up her Israeli passport, *since she was not Jewish in the terms of the law, which stipulates that the child born to a non-Jewish mother is not considered Jewish unless converted to Judaism.* It is curious that Israel so rigorously applies the same method of discrimination for which it reproached the civil Statute on the Jews in France under the Vichy Government as the abomination of desolation."

Thus, paradoxical though it may seem, Israel, a lay State composed mainly of atheists and free-thinkers, is founded in law on theological concepts and religious institutions. Furthermore, not only has Hebrew, a sacred language, been made the national language, just as the Bible, a sacred book, has been made the national book, but a great number of religious practices have been preserved:

> "When you see a seven-branched candlestick in the kibbutz mapam, in other words belonging to a left-wing socialist party which professes atheism, you are told that it is a national symbol. During the pascal time, it is impossible to obtain unleavened bread in Israel. It is rather as if in a country where Catholicism was the dominant religion, restaurants could only serve meat on Fridays. If by chance you light a cigarette on the Sabbath in the dining-room of the King David at Jerusalem after your meal, a

waiter will discreetly ask you to put it out, as you could give offence to some other person in the room. . . . Jews are not allowed to smoke on the Sabbath."
(J. Madaule: *Les Juifs et le Monde Actuel*, pp. 68-69)

Finally, the Law of Return does not recognise civil marriage, civil divorce or civil funerals. What, from the point of view of the Statute, is the concern of the individual, is dealt with by the interior legislation of each faith.

A lay State, practising religious intolerance, Israel, which also claims to be a democracy, is yet one of the most racially conscious States in the world. Mixed marriages are forbidden:

"Mixed marriages between Jews and non-Jews are not possible in the new State of Israel, according to the law passed on the 28th of August, 1953."
(F. Lovsky: *Antisémitisme et Mystère d'Israel*, p. 116)

In this, Israeli legislation is merely ratifying the opinion of the Rabbinical consistory:

"The conference of European Rabbis which was held in 1960 in Great Britain passed the following motion: *We consider that it is our solemn duty to warn our communities and every son and every daughter of the Jewish people against the terrible evil of mixed marriages which destroys the integrity of the Jewish people and shatters family life.*"
(Rabi: *Anatomie du Judaisme français*, pp. 259-60)

In the State of Israel death itself does not bring peace:

"The non-Jewish husband cannot be buried in the Jewish cemetery beside his wife: apart from the case of a convert, *no space may be given or sold in a Jewish cemetery to a non-Jewish person.*

"In December 1957, Aaron Steinberg, the seven-year-old son of recent immigrants, died at Pardess Hanna in Israel. His father was Jewish, the mother Christian. According to Rabbinical law the child of an exogamous union takes the religion of his mother, but in canon law the child takes after the father. As a result the parents met with a refusal both from the Catholic cemetery at Haifa and the Jewish cemetery at Pardess Hanna. Although there are only religious cemeteries in Israel, a little place was secured for the body, but outside the wall."
(Rabi, ibid., pp. 261-75)

It is the same racial spirit of the Law of Return which in 1948 drove back into Jordan 900,000 Arabs from Palestine.

Finally, the trial of Eichmann has set a precedent in law which may well produce grave and long-term consequences.

At the end of the Second World War, Germany was condemned to pay to the State of Israel in compensation for the wrongs she had done to German and foreign Jews indemnities amounting to 2,000,000 marks a year, and these payments, which have been made regularly, have contributed considerably to the budget of Israel.[1]

In 1960 Adolf Eichmann, a German citizen who had taken refuge in Argentina, was kidnapped by Israeli secret agents, in contempt of the law of the country, and brought before an Israeli court for crimes committed, in the exercise of his office, against German and foreign Jews. He was condemned to death and executed.

By arrogating to itself the right to apply Israeli law to a German for crimes committed in Germany and which were answerable at law to the courts of his own country, the State of Israel has created a grave legal precedent.

Indeed, as Mr. Raymond de Geouffre de la Pradelle, a lawyer of international repute, pointed out in the *Figaro* on the 9th June 1960:

> "The tracking down (of war criminals) by the Allies, which began the day after the war ended, was based on the agreement of London of the 8th August 1945, and the declaration of Moscow of the 30th October 1943, to which the former document expressly refers.
>
> "The principle laid down is that war criminals shall be sent back to the country where they committed their crimes. Furthermore, the Statute of London of the 8th August 1945, set up an international Military Court to try those whose crimes were not confined to any precise geographical location.
>
> "The Statute of London was promulgated by the Allies after they had received the power to exercise German sovereignty contained in the unconditional surrender, which was handed to them on the 8th of May, 1945, by the head of the Reich Government, Grand Admiral Doenitz.
>
> "No international document authorises the State of Israel to

---

[1] In March 1965 *Le Monde* drew attention to the fact that on the expiration of the agreement which had been concluded with Israel in virtue of reparation for damages caused to the Jews, the government of Bonn will have paid out £336,168,000 (4,140 million new francs). Besides, Israel will have received goods and equipment to the value of 2,880 million N.F. (£175,392,000) from Germany. On top of this, Germany has paid indemnities to claims by individual Jewish victims which exceed the above figures.

try a foreign national to whom are imputed crimes against humanity or war crimes when these crimes were committed abroad. Furthermore, at the time when these crimes were committed, there was no question of the victims being of Israeli nationality, since the State of Israel had not then come into existence.

"The State of Israel is a sovereign power. Within the limits of the area under its jurisdiction Israel can, if she so desires, confer on herself whatever judisdictional power she thinks fit. But this law violates the general principles of law and of the international rule that competence to try crimes of an essentially international character is itself international, since, as the crimes were committed in Germany at a period when German law considered them permissible, they only constitute crimes from the point of view of international law."

Thus, in both the case of the indemnities paid by the Bonn government and of the trial of Eichmann, *it is the State of Israel which has come forward as the sole qualified representative of the Jewish community of the world, and as the sovereign State of the Jewish people throughout the world.*

Nothing could illustrate more clearly both the closeness and the ambiguousness of the ties which link the State of Israel and the Jews of the Diaspora.

The Jews have always claimed to be loyal citizens of the countries where they reside. But, as we have seen above, the indemnities and the trial of Eichmann prove that on the contrary the Jews remain strangers in the countries that receive them, and that they consider they are answerable at law, not to these countries, but to the State of Israel.

5

MOSAIC LAW AND THE TALMUD

WHEN one talks about the Jewish religion one thinks most commonly about the Mosaic law (or Pentateuch), codified in the Torah. Christianity cannot feel any particular animosity or mistrust with regard to the Pentateuch, which is one of its sacred books. It only considers that the Mosaic law has been transcended and superseded by the superior precepts of the Gospel; between the two there is consanguinity and continuity and not fundamental opposition.

> "Though Torah scrolls often were trampled underfoot by screaming mobs looting synagogues, or burned with the synagogue itself, such acts were never sanctioned by the Church, and the Torah was never officially condemned. Though Judaism was reviled as a blasphemy, though Jews were killed for being unbelievers, the Torah itself was looked upon with respect, for it was the Law of God. As one Pope expressed it, 'We praise and honour the Law, for it was given to your fathers by Almighty God through Moses. But we condemn your religion and your false interpretation of the Law'."
>
> (M. I. Dimont: *Jews, God and History*, p. 240)

But if some Jews have still remained faithful to tradition and the Torah, the majority have long since abandoned it in favour of the Talmud, a collection of commentaries on the Law compiled by the Pharisees and Rabbis between the second and the fifth century A.D. Many have become completely agnostic. Let us hear what Wickham Steed and eminent Jewish thinkers have to say about this delicate problem:

> "The Sadducees struggled for centuries against the tendency to wrap Judaism in an insulating mantle of precepts and commentaries, but the fall of Jerusalem decided the struggle definitely in favour of the Pharisees, who so multiplied commentaries upon the Law that codification became indispensable. A code named Mishna (Doctrine) was elaborated. From generation to generation the Mishna commentaries grew until their volume became un-

manageable. Once more codification proved necessary. Towards the middle of the fifth century A.D. a Mishna code was formed in Palestine and, at the end of the same century, a second code at Babylon. Both codes were called 'Talmud' (Research or Investigation). While the Palestine Talmud played an insignificant part in the subsequent life of Jewry, the Babylonian Talmud was regarded as a national possession. It has remained 'The Book' for Orthodox Jewry. It replaced the Torah as the fountain of all wisdom and as the guide in every detail of daily life. The Talmud, despite its character as a commentary upon a commentary upon a Law of uncertain origin, has not only preserved the Jewish Nation but has imbued it with a Pharisee spirit and separated it, perhaps for ever, from the main stream of human culture."

(H. W. Steed: *The Hapsburg Monarchy*, pp. 164-5)

Bernard Lazare confirms this view:

"It may be said that true Mosaism, purified and enlarged by Isaiah, Jeremiah and Ezekiel, broadened and generalised by the Judaeo-Hellenists, would have brought Israel to Christianity, but for Esraism, Pharisaism and Talmudism, which held the mass of the Jews bound to strict observances and narrow ritual practices....

"As the Book could not be proscribed, it was belittled and made subordinate to the Talmud; the doctors declared: 'The law is water, the Mishna is wine.' And the reading of the Bible was considered less beneficial, less conducive to salvation than the reading of the Mishna...." (Bernard Lazare: *Anti-Semitism*, p. 17)

"It was only after all this that the rabbis ultimately triumphed. Their end was attained. They had cut off Israel from the community of nations; they had made of it a sullen recluse, a rebel against all laws, foreign to all feeling of fraternity, closed to all beautiful, noble and generous ideas; they had made of it a small and miserable nation, soured by isolation, brutalised by a narrow education, demoralised and corrupted by an unjustifiable pride.

"With this transformation of the Jewish spirit and the victory of sectarian doctors, coincides the beginning of official persecution. Until that epoch there had only been outbursts of local hatred, but no systematic vexations. With the triumph of the Rabbinites the ghettos come into being. The expulsions and massacres commence. The Jews went to live apart—a line is drawn against them. They detest the spirit of the nations amidst whom they live, the nations pursue them. They burn the Moreh—their Talmud is burned and they themselves are burned with it."

(Bernard Lazare, ibid., pp. 18-19)

In his book *Le Malheur d'Israel*, Doctor A. Roudinesco shows how the Judaism of the prophets, universal in spirit, was to end in Christianity, and how the Judaism of the Law, founded on the Talmud, was to deviate and finally break from it:

"Modern orthodoxy is not the religion of the Bible and of the Prophets. It is a post-Biblical or Talmudic religion built up by the Pharisees and doctors of the Law between the second and fifth centuries after Jesus Christ, to preserve the small minority of Jews who had not followed Christ, and to consummate the definite break from triumphant Christianity.

"The universal, messianic, finalist Judaism of the Prophets ended with Jesus, and conquered the world in the Christian form.

"Legal, national Judaism kept its God exclusively in the community of its choice, which it has striven to protect from the dangers that constantly threaten it. It is based on an interpretation of biblical texts by oral, not revealed, traditions called Mischna, Gemara, Halaka and Hagada. This collection, known as the Talmud, was first conceived of in Jerusalem towards the end of the second century and completed in Babylon in the fifth century. The two Talmuds consist of eleven volumes in octavo and are twenty times the size of the Bible."

(Dr. A. Roudinesco: *Le Malheur d'Israel*, pp. 114-15)

"This imposing collection of rabbinical works has erected a rampart of laws around Judaism and stamped it with the rigidity and lack of mobility with which it is still distinguished today.

"It is in his religion that all the elements that are specifically Jewish must be sought. Sprung from its rigid and peculiar practices, his religion isolates the Jew and confers on him the character of a sort of foreign colony, unique in its kind, living in the midst of other nations. Despite the prevalence of heterogeneousness, inbreeding and the absence of any proselytism have finally created a sort of ethnic by a process of selection.

"In contrast to the religion revealed by Abraham, and legislated by Moses, based on a national God, stands the religion of the Prophets, inspired by a universal God who was just and good. With the Prophets, the idea of morality penetrates and is incorporated into their religion. Of necessity, the national God was egoistic; he was not merciful for 'he visited the sins of the fathers on their children and on their children's children unto the fourth generation' (Exodus xxxiv. 7). He ordered Moses and Joshua to destroy the other peoples pitilessly, and not to convert them. With the Jewish Prophets there appears for the first time in the history of humanity the idea of universal brotherhood.

(Dr. A. Roudinesco, ibid., pp. 125-26)

"As from the year 725 before the present era, Isaiah, Amos, Hosea, Micah, Deutero-Isaiah, Jeremiah, Ezekiel and Daniel created a new religion of a spiritual and moral elevation unknown before then. It is due to them that Yahve became a universal God; and it is also due to them that Israel maintained the cult of the one God. They saved both Judaism and monotheism. One must read the Prophets to find out how far the Jewish people had been carried away by idolatry. Uncircumcised in their hearts and stiff-necked, the people were returning to their idols as the dog to his vomit. It is not without reason that the memory of manifold gold calves has survived the ages. The leaders set the example: Solomon, despite his proverbial wisdom, worshipped Astarte and Milcom and built a temple at Kemosh and Moloc opposite Jerusalem (Kings xi. 5). Jeroboam the first set up golden calves 500 years after Aaron's, Tertullian said that the Jews only practised circumcision to check the tendency to idolatry and to remind them of their true God. Under King Manasseh false Gods were worshipped in the Temple itself, which had become a veritable Pantheon. Without the Prophets the worship of Yahve might perhaps have been engulfed." (Dr. A. Roudinesco, ibid., pp. 126-27)

The substitution of the Talmud for the Torah had two consequences which have never ceased to weigh heavily on the destinies of the Jewish people throughout the centuries.

Firstly, it exacerbated Jewish religious exclusiveness, which began to develop more and more into a national and political form, as F. Fejtö shows very clearly in his work, *Dieu et son Juif*:

"You above any other are the jealous people. That is your truth and your falsehood, it is your curse. . . .

"It is you who asked God not to deal with the other peoples, to repudiate all his other children.

"All or nothing was your motto, not his. Tyrannical children, you would have him all to yourselves. On the pretext of making him your only Lord, your only Master, your only King, you worked unceasingly to bring him down to your level, to dominate him, to make him the slave and instrument of your national expansion. . . .

"Nothing could be less generous or more possessive than your love of God....

"To put it quite simply, you wanted to be like him, to substitute yourselves for him, to take his place. Nothing less than that!

"The idea of sharing God with others was inadmissible to you. Equally insupportable was the thought of your inequality and inferiority with regard to him. Why should he have everything and you nothing? Why should he be all-powerful and you powerless? Why can he take everything that belongs to you if it pleases him: your wives, your mother, your sisters, your daughters, your flocks, your land, while you can only bow down before the expression of his will? It is unjust, you cry. It is not a covenant between equals, it is slavery. It is not a contract, it is dictatorship....

"And then there sprang up in your soul, from the depths of your collective conscience, that quarter where no man dares to venture once the night has fallen, this unutterable, monstrous dream, to make him disappear in one way or another and to substitute yourselves for him, to become like him, to be God.

"You didn't take long to transform yourselves from Adam to Cain and to kill Abel, the best among you, the one whose offering had been accepted....

"While proclaiming the existence of one God of the universe the Jew obstinately persists in seeking to capture this God for himself, and to exclude all others from the covenant...."

(F. Fejtö: *Dieu et son Juif*, pp. 104-109)

Bernard Lazare is no less explicit:

"With the law, yet without Israel to put it into practice, the world could not exist, God would turn it back into nothing; nor will the world know happiness until it be brought under the domination of that law, that is to say, under the domination of the Jews. Thus the Jewish people is chosen by God as the trustee of His will; it is the only people with whom the Deity has made a covenant; it is the choice of the Lord....

"Israel is placed under the very eye of Jehovah; it is the Eternal's favoured son who has the sole right to his love, to his goodwill, to his special protection; other men are placed beneath the Hebrews, and it is by mere mercy that they are entitled to divine munificence, since the souls of the Jews alone are descended from the first man. The wealth which has come to the nations, in truth belongs to Israel.

"This faith in their predestination, in their election, developed

among the Jews an immense pride. It led them to view the Gentiles with contempt, often with hate, when patriotic considerations supervened to religious feelings."
(Bernard Lazare: *Anti-Semitism*, pp. 13-14)

The second consequence of the transition from the Torah to the Talmud is equally important; contrary to an opinion which throws a completely false light on the problem of the relationship of Judaism and Christianity, neither faith any longer, since that date, rest upon a common book. Indeed, they have become more and more foreign to each other.

"Christianity cannot be called a little Jewish sect which had some success, as the rabbis claim. Christianity in all its true purity and grandeur fulfilled Judaism and, by denationalising it, made it universal and human, according to the expectations of the prophets. Jesus, the man of God, incomparable and unequalled, could have been accepted as the Messiah in accordance with the eschatology and messianism of Israel. Is it for the Jews to complain if the Christians recognised God himself in this son of Israel? For two thousand years Judaism had contained the seed of Christianity in spirit. Already prophecy had pointed to a Christianity in gestation. The birth of the child was a matter of time. Having rejected its own offspring, Judaism withered and withdrew into itself in morose, proud and sterile isolation. It completely abandoned proselytism and set itself up as the national religion of a small fraction of the Jewish people.

"Paradoxical though it may seem to both Jews and Christians, it is in Christianity that the true religion of Israel was realised. The modern Jew practises a religion which is posterior to the evangelical contribution established by the doctors of the Law, on a Bible interpreted on the edge of the Revelation. Whereas the Judaism of the prophets was enriched by the message of Jesus, the Judaism of the rabbis was engulfed in the Talmud."
(Dr. A. Roudinesco: *Le Malheur d'Israel*, p. 140)

"The Judaism of the Diaspora, hellenic Judaism as it was called, which represented nine-tenths of the Jews of the Empire, liberated from the constraint of the circumcision, denationalised, openminded and receptive, disappeared in about the fifth century, probably as a result of fusion with Christianity. Far removed from Jerusalem, it was not greatly affected by the catastrophes in the years 70 and 133. After the official creed of Jerusalem had passed away, the Palestine Jews looked upon the Jews of the dispersion as suspect from the point of view of strict orthodoxy. The rupture

MOSAIC LAW AND THE TALMUD

between the Judaism of the Diaspora and rabbinical Judaism was the work of the scribes, the doctors and the pharisees of the Law. As from the second century, the rabbis of Babylon and Galilee elaborated a religious, political and social code known as the Talmud. This book regulated the life of the Israelite in a different spirit from that of the prophets and the Bible. If serious divergences had existed between the Old and the New Testament, the Christians would not have kept the two texts, the one following on from the other. Having rejected the Gospel, the rabbis were obliged to re-interpret the text of the old Bible. They carried out this work by means of oral traditions more or less consistent with the old texts: the Mishna and the Gemara. The result of this compilation was a new Bible; the old remains with the Christians. The Talmud is composed of eleven thick volumes. This baneful book, for the most part unintelligible, a sad wreck of the Judaism of the prophets, does not enrich the human spirit (Salomon Reinach). The aim of the Talmud was to save what remained of Israel from being absorbed by Christianity . . . the old spiritual treasure of the prophets was abandoned by the rabbinites. . . .

"While Origen, Clement of Alexandria, St. Jerome and St. Augustine were enriching Christianity, Judaism was being impoverished by the Talmud.

"The imposition of the ideals of the Talmud on the new branch of Judaism has been the calamity of the Jewish people even to this day."

(Dr. A. Roudinesco, ibid., pp. 25-26)

6

THE MARRANOS

MEMBERSHIP of the Catholic Church is not based on race; it is solely a matter of religious faith. In the eyes of the Church, a Jewish convert is a Christian who shares to the full the privileges of membership of the Church.

"Baptism confers full membership of the Christian community without any reservations whatsoever. Conversion of the Jews was not only thought desirable but actively sought after. Once converted, they were received with joy; conversion put an end to all segregation. At the present time, however, the Jew is neither wanted nor sought after; national and racial antisemitism is much more discriminating."
(Dr. A. Roudinesco, *Le Malheur d'Israel*, pp. 42-43)

"Having recognised certain rigidly defined characteristics in each nation, modern nationalism has refused to see the Jew in any other light than that of a stranger in the land, a stateless and cosmopolitan person. No distinction at all is made between the assimilated Jew and the Jew who is conscious of his national traditions. Modern antisemitism is more illogical than that of the Middle Ages which was based on indisputable religious objections and not on unproved hypotheses and nebulous ideas.

"In as much as he is a stranger the Jew should be rejected because nationalism also harbours a hatred of foreigners."
(Dr. A. Roudinesco, ibid., p. 76)

The Christian attitude in mediaeval times is well summed up in the following appeal to the Jews made by the Bishop of Clermont-Ferrand, Saint Avit:

"Remain among us and live like us or depart as quickly as possible. Give us back this land to which you are strangers; spare us your presence here, or, if you wish to remain here, share in our faith."
(F. Lovsky: *Antisémitisme et Mystère d'Israel*, p. 182)

THE MARRANOS

The Jews who did not want to leave and who obstinately resisted conversion retorted by having recourse to underhand methods which led to great bitterness and caused profound uneasiness. The practise of Marranism, which was carried to great lengths in Spain, permanently envenomed relations between Jews and non-Jews.

Massoutié, a writer who has devoted two extremely interesting books to a study of the Jewish problem, has the following comment to make:

> "Judaism reacted to other religions in many different ways, but the most extraordinary reaction of all . . . is undoubtedly what we will call the *phenomenon of Marranism*. This is what Werner Sombart has to say on the subject (p. 385): 'The sudden increase in the numbers of pretended conversions of Jews to paganism, to the Moslem religion, to Christianity, is such an extraordinary phenomenon, such a unique event in the history of mankind, that we cannot fail to be astonished and dumbfounded every time we come to study it.'
> (L. Massoutié: *Judaisme et Hitlérisme*, pp. 97-99)

> "The Marranos were Spanish Jews in semblance converted to Christianity. It was from 1391 onwards and, according to Graetz, following religious persecution, that many Jews in Spain decided to adopt the Catholic faith. There was nothing new in this because, long before them, their ancestors of the dispersion had already had recourse to this ruse, either to escape religious persecution, or for motives of sheer material gain."
> (L. Massoutié, ibid., pp. 97-99)

> "However that may be, while they ostensibly practised Catholicism the Marranos all the while secretly followed the rites of Judaism to which they had remained deeply attached. The Spanish people were not deceived as to the sincerity of the religious beliefs of the new Christians. With good reason the Spaniards were suspicious of them and called them Marranos, which means 'accursed, damned', or in popular language, 'swine'. An extraordinary aspect of the situation and one which I admit I fail to understand is that the Marranos were not satisfied with zealously submitting to the authority of the Church; they went much further still and carried their deceit to extreme limits. Thus it was that many of them, both men and women, did not hesitate to enter religious orders—which they were in no way obliged to do—and became monks or nuns. What is more, Marranos became priests and even bishops. If Jewish historians themselves had not told us this, we could hardly believe it.

"We can understand why the Spanish people became angry when this was discovered; it was following this discovery that the Spanish Inquisition was set up."

(L. Massoutié, ibid., pp. 100-101)

"The struggle between the Inquisition and the Marranos went on for several centuries in the dark, an unparalleled, unexampled struggle, Graetz tells us, in which all the techniques of deceit and doggedness of purpose were pitted against accusations and cruelty." (L. Massoutié, ibid., pp. 103-105)

"Protestantism had its Marranos, too. Secret Jews were numerous among the Protestant refugees of the seventeenth century at the time of the revocation of the Edict of Nantes, as Werner Sombart tells us. In Germany for instance, we can rate the famous poet, Henry Heine, as a Protestant Marrano. Amazing as it may seem, this is how Graetz refers to Heine and to his co-religionist, Louis Boerne, both of them converts to Protestantism. I quote from a passage in *Geschichte der Juden*, volume XI, page 368, which was omitted from the French translation by Moses Bloch:

"'They were divorced from Judaism only superficially, like fighting men who put on the armour and colours of their enemy in order to strike him down and destroy him with greater certainty and vigour. What can one make of such behaviour by the sensitive author of the *Intermezzo* and the lively writer of the *Reisebilder?*'
(L. Massoutié, ibid., pp. 103-105)

"In a passage of his *History of the Jews*, Graetz tells us of Spanish and Portuguese Marranos who, behind the mask of Christianity and in the habit of monks, 'jealously cherished the sacred flame of their paternal religion, and at the same time undermined the foundations of the powerful Catholic monarchy.'

"If it is only reasonable for a Jew not to give up his religion and even to preserve the worship of his race and ancestors secretly, all the while behaving as a loyal citizen in the land of his adoption, it is incomprehensible that he should take advantage of his French or German citizenship, for instance, to undermine the institutions and customs of his new fatherland; in other words, to overthrow everything. If the modern Jew was to carry out on a national level what the Marranos of old did in the field of religion, it would lead to countless disasters for Israel. Modern nations, thus irritated, would plunge into savage anti-Semitism and there would automatically arise a new Inquisition, of a different type to be sure, but one that would perhaps be more terrible than Torquemada's.

"In my opinion, if Israel wants to avoid the worst catastrophes, it is in her interest to work in the open. Unfortunately, dissimulation is an age-old habit of hers and even the most pro-Semitic writers, such as Anatole Leroy-Beaulieu, find themselves obliged to admit it."

(L. Massoutié, ibid., pp. 114-15)

7

ASSIMILATION

THE official modern attitude in the West with regard to the Jews is based on the assertion that they are loyal citizens of the countries in which they live, and that they become completely assimilated with their surroundings. A German, French or English Jew is considered a German, a Frenchman or an Englishman of Israelite religion.

But in point of fact the Jew does not assimilate himself, or only very slowly and with great difficulty. All the specialists who have studied this aspect of the problem, whether Jewish or not are unanimous about this, at least when they are in good faith, for the attitude of the leaders of Judaism is full of ambiguity. On the one hand they demand for their own people the full rights of citizenship, but at the same time they make the utmost efforts to preserve their own specific Jewish traits and integrity.

The very principle of assimilation and its corollary, mixed marriages, is held equally suspect in both camps. Many western people are fiercely opposed to cross-breeding by the introduction of Jewish blood into their race.

The conclusions of Wickham Steed and rabbi Alfred Nossig are not calculated to allay their apprehensions:

"That Jews have a remarkable faculty for external adaptation to environment is incontestable, but it remains to be seen whether, with all their pliancy and pertinacious direction of will toward their immediate object, they are capable of adapting themselves internally. Experience and observation now extending over more than twenty-one years, in Germany, France, Italy and Austria-Hungary, incline me to answer this question in the negative.

(H. W. Steed: *The Hapsburg Monarchy*, p. 170)

"The intensity of the Jewish race character is such that the Jewish strain will persist for generations in non-Jewish families into which Jewish blood has once entered. The strain may be pro-

ductive of beauty or genius, or it may, on the other hand, bring the mental derangement so common in the better-class Jewish families."
(H. W. Steed, ibid., p. 168)

Rabbi Nossig, who agrees with this opinion, wrote:

"We may talk about a biological judaisation of the civilised world . . . the minutest drop of Jewish blood influences the spiritual character of families over many generations."
(Nossig: *Integrales Judentum*)

The American Jewish writer, Ludwig Lewisohn, is, if possible, even more precise:

"The French revolution came and gradually, very gradually and sporadically, the gates of the Ghetto were opened. Contempt, servitude, restrictive laws, special taxes remained. Citizenship was not granted the Jews of England until 1832 nor the Jews of Prussia until 1847. But this gesture and similar gestures elsewhere earlier and later, more or less sincere, were supposed capable of obliterating the historic existence, consciousness, experience of a people that had been a people for three thousand years.

"This was the fallacy of the Gentiles; this is the fallacy of the unhappy assimilationist. Both he and the semibenevolent Gentile are deceived by the uniqueness of the Jewish nation. Nationhood is identified with land, armies, power. The continued existence of Jewry from the Babylonian captivity to the French Revolution, a period of roughly two thousand three hundred years, proves that there is one nation without the conventional attributes of nationhood.

"Like every other people, the English, the German, the French, the Jews are racially mixed. As Celtic, Saxon, Latin and pre-Aryan blood is found in all these peoples, or, to employ another method of differentiation, Nordic, Alpine and Mediterranean, so the Jews in their enormously long history have undergone racial intermixture. The historic process evidently transcends the question of race and shapes people by forces which we are not instructed enough to grasp. Jews differ among themselves as widely as a Tyrolese German differs from a Schleswiger, a Provençal from a Norman, a Creole from the Vermonter. They remain Jews, even as these others remain, beyond all local and racial differences, Germans, Frenchmen, Americans. A central and permanent approach to an outer and inner norm, type, group of characteristics persists. Wherever the perception of this plain fact is not arti-

ficially inhibited, it is as potent as ever. The few remaining Marranos of Spain, Spanish and outwardly Catholic for over four centuries, have applied to the Chief Rabbinate of Jerusalem for formal readmittance to Jewry. . . .
(Ludwig Lewisohn: *Israel*, pp. 33-35)

"It is assimilation that would be the miracle, the break in the eternal chain of causality . . . our assimilationist may never think a Jewish thought or read a Jewish book. In the essential character of all his passions as well as of all his actions he remains a Jew. . . .
(Ludwig Lewisohn, ibid., p. 36)

"No, *assimilation is impossible*. It is impossible because the Jew cannot change his national character; he cannot, by wishing it, abandon himself any more than the members of any other folk can do so. . . .
(Ludwig Lewisohn, ibid., pp. 38-39)

"What shall he do? Whither shall he turn? He is a Jew. He remains a Jew. The majority has discovered the fact, as it always does, sooner or later; he discovers it too. Gentile and Jew find that there is no escape. Both believed in escape. There is none. None. . . ."
(Ludwig Lewisohn, ibid., p. 41)

Yet more recently, Doctor Roudinesco has written:

"The struggle against anti-Semitism on the religious level ought to be encouraged. Is the world sufficiently Christian yet to hear such a message? The religious sentiment has persisted in certain countries, Spain, Ireland, Canada and Italy for example, where there are but few Jews. Unfortunately, the Jewish problem has long ago exceeded the religious sphere, and nationalist and racist anti-Semitism is constructed on foundations far more difficult to unsettle. Then again, union on the religious level is viewed with considerable suspicion by the Synagogue, which is still afraid of conversions."
(Dr. A. Roudinesco: *Le Malheur d'Israel*, p. 190)

"Legal emancipation and assimilation have failed. German Jews were the most assimilated Jews in the world, and it was in Germany that anti-Semite fury was carried to extremes.

"The problem of assimilation is a complex one. Is it even possible or compatible with upholding a religion and tradition whose character is both national and separatist? Opinions differ greatly among the Jews themselves.

"Finally there are certain cases which defy all classification. Assimilation has not disarmed anti-Semitism. Assimilated Jews are even less tolerated than the others. It was the total failure of assimilation which opened the way for Zionism."
(Dr. A. Roudinesco, ibid., p. 191)

In Soviet Russia assimilation has completely failed despite the strident propaganda put out by left-wing parties that only Marxism could provide a definite solution to the problem of anti-Semitism in the world. This has been confirmed by, amongst others, Jean Paul Sartre, in a work of unutterably poor quality called *Réflections sur la Question juive*:

"Anti-Semitism is a mythical *bourgeois* representation of the class struggle; in a classless society it could not exist. There would be no place for it in a society whose members are all interdependent, since they are all engaged in the same undertaking. It exhibits a certain mystic link between man and his 'goods' which is a product of the present system of property. Thus in a classless society founded on the collective ownership of the instruments of work, man, liberated from the delusions of the hither-world, will be able to devote himself to his task, which is to bring into existence the reign of humanity, and anti-Semitism will have no further justification; it will have been cut off from the roots."
(Jean Paul Sartre, ibid., pp. 184-5)

In actual fact nothing of the sort has happened, as Fejtö recognises in his work *Les Juifs et l'Antisémitisme dans les pays communistes*, in which he publishes the following letter sent by a Jew in Moscow to a New York newspaper about the Moscow festival:

"The theory advocated by those who believe in assimilation (people who are either mad or unscrupulous), according to which old Jewish traditions are dead and buried, and the Jews have completely mixed with the Russians, to the greatest material benefit of both parties, and thus no longer need their own culture, has exploded like an over-inflated balloon, though in truth nobody ever doubted that it was an insecure proposition.

"Are the Jews content with Russian culture, which they can enjoy freely and at will? Today, without fear of being contradicted one can answer; No. Aspirations to Jewish art, Jewish music and the Jewish language have not been stifled by twenty years of forced assimilation. This need can be seen in the desire to see and hear the Israeli delegation, to receive some souvenir of Israel, a flower, an emblem, a ticket, a box of cigarettes. . . .

"If you ask a Jew what he thinks will be the consequences of this Festival, he will without any doubt reply that reprisals are foreseen, though it is uncertain what form they will take. They dread doing rash things, and yet the Jews gather where the concerts are to be held, driven by a force which springs from every human heart; the yearning for their own national culture."
(F. Fejtö, ibid., p. 225)

At a conference on this question held by Fejtö in Brussels in September 1958, a young member of the audience got up and said:

"Assimilation—or in other words, integration with the socialist community on a basis of perfect equality—is becoming more and more difficult, if not impossible. Assimilation is a failure; from the outset it was an impossible aim to achieve; Communism would no more be able to impose it than *bourgeois* liberalism; the Jew's only salvation lies in Israel, in the return to the judaic traditions, the promised Land, the reconstruction of the nation. . . ."
(F. Fejtö, ibid., p. 253)

This failure is all the more remarkable considering that the Soviet régime owed its initial success to international Jewish revolutionaries and that Jewish leaders were the masters of Russia until they were progressively ousted from positions of control by Stalin and his successors.

A fatality as inexorable as the tunic of Nessus seems to cling to the Hebrew people; masters in the art of revolution, upheaval and destruction, they are powerless to create. Elie Faure depicts this trait in striking terms:

"The Jew's historic mission has been clearly defined, perhaps for all time. It will be the principal factor in every apocalyptic epoch, as it was at the end of the ancient world, and as it is now at the end, amid which we are living, of the Christian world. At these moments the Jews will always be in the forefront, both to ruin the old edifice and to mark out the terrain and materials for the new structure which is to replace it. It is this dynamic quality which is the mark of their extraordinary grandeur and perhaps also, it must be admitted, of their visible impotence.

"The Jew destroys every ancient illusion, and if he takes more share than anybody—St. Paul formerly and Karl Marx today, for example—in constructing the new illusion, precisely by reason of his eternal thirst for truth, which always survives the outcomes of political and religious struggles, he is fated to insert in the same illusion the worm which will undermine it. The patriarch who in former times agreed to lead the human conscience towards the promised land across the glowing stretches of knowledge is not ready to lay down his formidable burden."

(Elie Faure: *La Question Juive vue par vingt-six emminentes personnalités*, p. 97)

In another passage, the Jewish scholar concludes on this subject:

"Despite reasons for hope which he accumulated in silence, could the Jew be regarded as anything other than a destroyer armed with the corrosive doubt with which Israel has always opposed the sentimental idealism of Europe since the time of the Greeks?"

(Elie Faure, ibid., p. 91)

Is Zionism the solution to the problem? No, answers Dr. Roudinesco:

"The national home in Palestine does not resolve the Jewish problem. In reality it represents a new danger for Judaism. It is a cruel disappointment to the idealism of liberal Jews who, since Moses Mendelssohn, have made so many attempts at assimilation as well as for all the Jews who have poured out their blood on the battle-fields in proof of their loyalty towards their countries of adoption.

"Having fought against nationalism and racism, in Israel the Jews proclaim themselves a nation and a race apart. Triumphant Zionism is consolidating everything which modern nationalist and racist anti-Semitism has erected in the past century. It is the greatest error committed by Judaism since the denial of Christ. Henceforth every Jew will be supposed to have a country to which he can be sent back without being able to raise the slightest valid protest. To claim the Holy Land as their real fatherland is even more illogical, since history tells us that hardly one out of ten Jews can claim to be descended from Palestinian Jews, and that from the remotest ages the Promised Land has only sheltered a small fraction of the Jewish population of the world. Had it been a question of a purely spiritual home, Jerusalem could have represented for the faithful what Vatican Rome represents for Catholics.

"The Israeli Government has set itself up as the protector of the Jews of the whole world. It attacked the Czecho-Slovak legation during the Slansky trial. It demonstrated in front of American buildings in favour of the Rosenbergs. . . . It asserts its rights over all Jewish nationals living outside its tiny frontiers without consulting them and in spite of their wishes. It practises a policy of racial discrimination against 150,000 Arabs living in

Israel in a special quarter, contrary to the stipulations of the Balfour Declaration, which laid down that the rights of non-Jewish communities living in Palestine were not in any way to be infringed.

"The Zionist solution does not resolve any of the difficulties of the Jewish problem; it inflicts an enormous injury on Judaism of the dispersion, and is grist to the mill of the anti-Semites."

(Dr. A. Roudinesco, *Le Malheur d'Israel*, pp. 182-5)

"The future of the little Palestinian State is forbidding. Every historian knows that the Holy Land is the most neuralgic spot in the world. It was there that the greatest drama in the history of humanity took place. All the empires fought each other for the sacred places. The Cross and the Crescent have confronted each other there for centuries. The crusaders came and left their bones and only the Venetian traders profited from it. The greatest powers in the world have got their eyes on this strip of land, on which the most important commercial and strategic routes in the world converge, across the most hotly disputed oil-fields."

(Dr. A. Roudinesco, ibid., p. 185)

"The Jewish question is not only confined to the moral order, it it a social and political problem with infinite repercussions. The Dreyfus affair rent and weakened France. Without anti-Semitism, Hitler would not have triumphed in Germany and the Second World War, which cost the lives of sixty million men, could have been avoided.

"Despite every expectation, legal emancipation, assimilation, and Jewish blood poured out on the battle-fields have all proved ineffectual. Anti-Semitism has persisted and become intensified. Israel's destiny remains sealed in misfortune."

(Dr. Roudinesco, ibid., p. 177)

In practice, despite noble professions of democratic faith, assimilation runs into almost unsurmountable difficulties.

Furthermore, the spiritual leaders of World Judaism fiercely oppose each and every different essay at assimilation: national integration, mixed marriage, conversion. . . .

Thus, in his book *Qu'est-ce que le Judaisme?* Dr. Pasmanik wrote:

> "You must choose between life or death. Death is conscious, systematic and deliberate assimilation. But a whole people would never decide to proclaim death as their vital aim. Especially when they know that their national values have preserved their vitality."
>
> (Dr. Pasmanik, ibid., p. 97)

In a recent study on Anti-semitism, Joshua Jehouda is equally categorical:

"Assimilation led to the collective suicide of Israel. It has turned the Jewish people, to use Andre Spire's expression, into 'individuals of dust', unquestionably destined to vanish even without the massive blows of anti-Semitism. If political Zionism, which sprang from the reaction against anti-Semitism, had not awoken the old messianic nostalgia of Israel, emancipated Judaism would have disappeared in anonymity amidst the peoples. Once again the messianism which the Jewish people carries in its breast has saved it from total disaster. Assimilation is the gradual process of detaching the Jews from the spiritual patrimony of Israel. It stems from a false interpretation of the French Revolution, which gave the Jews the dignity of man without abolishing ostracism with regard to the religious doctrine of Judaism."

(Joshua Jehouda: Antisémitisme, Miroir du Monde, p. 255)

And again:

"The conference of European rabbis held in Great Britain in 1960 passed the following motion: 'We consider it is our solemn duty to warn our communities and every son and daughter of the Jewish people of the terrible evil of mixed marriages which destroy the integrity of the Jewish people and shatter Jewish family life'." (Quoted by Rabi in Anatomie du Judaisme français, pp. 259-60)

This ban on assimilation extends to every detail of daily life, as we are told by J. Madaule, President of the Amitiés Judéo-Chrétiennes Internationales:

"A Jew may only adopt the clothing and language of the people amongst whom he is spread on condition that he remains a Jew in his heart and does not renounce the mysterious peculiarity which distinguishes him from other men."

(J. Madaule: Les Juifs et le Monde Actuel, p. 23)

In March 1964 Dr. Goldmann, President of the World Zionist Organisation, drew the delegates' attention to the dangers of assimilation.

The following article by André Scemama appeared in Le Monde:

"Jerusalem, 17th March 1964. On Monday Dr. Nahum Goldmann made his first speech at Jerusalem in his capacity as a citizen of Israel. As a matter of fact, the man who for many years has presided over the destiny of the world Zionist movement, had just the week before acquired Israeli nationality on landing as an immigrant at Tel-Aviv airport.

"On Monday he opened the first session of the Zionist action committee, the sub-commission of the World Zionist Organisation. Once again he emphasised that the gravest danger which menaced the Jewish people as such today was neither anti-Semitism nor economic discrimination, but the liberalism of our times, which made it possible for Jews to be assimilated into the surroundings in which they lived.

" *'Since we left the ghettos and the mellahs assimilation has become an immense danger,'* Dr. Goldmann declared."

In December 1964 the Twenty-sixth Congress of the World Zionist Organisation took place in Jerusalem. Again Dr. Goldmann warned his audience against the danger of assimilation. The following extracts are taken from André Scemama's report, *Le Monde's* special correspondent:

"Jerusalem, 31st December 1964. The World Zionist Organisation, which gave birth to the State of Israel, is holding its Twenty-sixth Congress in Jerusalem; 540 delegates representing the Zionist federations of thirty-one countries have gathered here.

". . . As opposed to two and a half million Jews living in Israel, nearly thirteen million are scattered throughout the world in communities.

". . . The strange part about this meeting is that 350 of the 540 delegates are Zionists who have not chosen to live in Israel.

"The real concern of the Zionist leaders is no longer, as formerly, with attracting the Jews of the dispersion to Israel, but with preserving the existence of the Jewish personality, which threatens to vanish in the comfort of an exile which is considered too liberal. In his opening speech, Nahum Goldmann, President of the World Zionist Organisation, spoke of this danger in these terms:

" 'We are living in an age when many of our people, especially our young people, are being threatened by a process of disintegration, not the product of a theory or of a deliberate ideology, but through their daily life and the lack of a faith to keep alive the Jewish conscience and inform each one why he must remain Jewish. If this process is not halted, it will represent a greater threat to perennial Jewish existence than persecution, the inquisition, pogroms and exterminations have been in the past'."

(*Le Monde*, 1st January 1965)

8

A STATE WITHIN A STATE

BY their refusal to be converted, and since they cannot really be assimilated, nor want to be, the Jews, taken as a whole, wherever they live as a minority in the heart of nations constitute a State within a State, "a veritable *imperium in imperiis*", as Wickham Steed described it in *The Hapsburg Monarchy*, (p. 179) even when they enjoy full rights of citizenship:

> "It is not just today but since the beginning of their existence that *the Jews have been considered as a foreign body, a thorn in the flesh of humanity. In the course of thousands of years it has been as impossible to eliminate them by brutality as it has been to assimilate them by gentleness.*"
> (Memorandum of the *Commission Théologique de l'Ocuvre Evangelique suisse*, October 1938 quoted by Jules Isaac in *Genèse de l'Antisémitisme*, p. 29)

> "The Diaspora Jews, though dispersed over three continents and in three civilisations, represented but one people, bound by one religion, one language, and one law. They were organised as 'states within states' with the permission of the various Gentile governments of the countries in which they lived."
> (M. I. Dimont: *Jews, God and History*, p. 262)

Thus, incapable of taking root, Israel lives among the peoples as a stranger, and the Judaism which it professes separates it from the world by its religion, its nationalism and its traditions:

> "'Thus, by its own nationalism Judaism cuts itself off from the exterior world. It automatically creates its own culture and ethnical ghetto. *This is why it is impossible to be both Jewish and the citizen of another nation at the same time.* One cannot pray "Next year Jerusalem" and yet remain at London or elsewhere'."
> (Koestler, quoted by J. Jehouda, in *L'Antisémitisme, Miroir du Monde*, p. 268)

We will now give three concrete examples from widely different points in history of the determination of the Jews to live on the fringe of nations.

Let us first open the Bible at the Book of Esther. The scene takes place in the fifth century B.C. At chapter xiii. 4-5 we read the letter sent by King Artaxerxes (Assuerus) to all the governors of the provinces:

> (And Aman) ". . . told me that there was a people scattered through the whole world, which used no laws, and acted against the customs of all nations, despised the commandments of kings, and violated by their opposition the concord of all nations."

In his book *Antisémitisme et Mystère d'Israel*, F. Lovsky quotes the same passage from the Bible of Jerusalem:

> ". . . Aman denounced us as a rebellious people, scattered throughout all the tribes of the world, in opposition with all nations by reason of our laws, and constantly despising royal commands to the extent of becoming an obstacle to the government for which we vouch to the general satisfaction."

And he continues the quotation from the Bible:

> "Considering that the said people, unique in its kind, is everywhere in conflict with the whole of humanity, that it differs from the rest of the world by a system of foreign laws, that it is hostile to our interests, and that it commits the worst misdeeds even so far as to menace the stability of our kingdom;
>
> "For these reasons we command that all (Jewish) persons . . . shall be radically exterminated . . . so that . . . absolute stability and tranquillity may henceforth be assured the State."
>
> (*Book of Esther* xiii. 4-7)

> "Lengthy commentary is useless", added Lovsky; "Have we not heard similar talk and read the same explanations less than twenty years ago?"
>
> (ibid., p. 97)

Let us advance 1,000 years to the Merovingian era. St. Avit, Bishop of Clermont-Ferrand, said to the Jews:

> "Stay with us and live as we do, or depart as quickly as possible. Return us our land in which you are strangers; free us from contact with you or, if you stay here, share our faith."
>
> (F. Lovsky, ibid., p. 182)

Let us advance a further 1,500 years, to Soviet Russia. The fatherland of Marxist internationalism, in the origin of which members of the Jewish race played such an important role, Soviet Russia cannot tolerate this particular form of nationalism, which in fact camouflages a rival internationalism claiming to escape the Soviet laws:

"The totalitarian State is particularly 'allergic' to every 'international' thought and connection which escapes its control. Thus the Soviet leaders find it is absolutely inadmissible that Jews of the U.S.S.R., whether assimilated or not, feel at one with foreign Jews, and that foreign Jews believe that they have a right to demand explanations from the Soviet Government as to the treatment of their Soviet co-religionists.

"The two prime causes of anti-Jewish policy since Stalin have not been eliminated:

"Firstly, there is always a tendency to consider the Jew as a foreign nationalist in all the Republics which form part of the Soviet Union—while pretending to believe that he has been assimilated.

"And in the second place, an atmosphere of suspicion surrounds Soviet Jews, especially because of their sentimental connections with Israel and with the rest of World Jewry."

(F. Fejtö: *Les Juifs et L'Antisémitisme*, pp. 31, 263)

If we can rely on what Fejtö says, and his remarks are based on various evidence published in the book referred to above, we realise that although the Soviet constitution is not explicitly anti-Semite, in practice the U.S.S.R. applies a statute to the Jews which is coming more and more to resemble the one which used to be enforced by the Christian monarchies in Europe, with this difference, that formerly discrimination was almost entirely religious, whereas today it is both racial, cultural and national: racial by virtue of the word Yevrei (Jew) stamped on the passport and identity card; cultural by virtue of the fact that certain universities are closed to Jews; and national by virtue of the fact that it is difficult for Jews to obtain high positions of responsibility.

Alongside this discrimination, tension is growing in Russia and the satellite countries between the native populations and the Jews, who are considered foreigners.

So far integration has completely failed in the mother-country of Socialism; the Jews refuse to assimilate and did not settle in Birobidjan, the province in northern Mongolia offered to them by Lenin. On the other hand Soviet Russia seems unwilling to allow them to emigrate to Israel, which they are more and more coming to accept as their cultural fatherland.

Thus throughout a period of 2,500 years, under different races, different customs, different attitudes and different religions, under the pagan Persians, under Catholicism in the early Middle Ages, and under the totalitarian anti-Christian State of the twentieth century, the Jewish problem has remained and remains to this day identical in form ever since the dispersion of Israel among the nations.

A stranger among the peoples, resisting conversion and assimilation, constituting a State within a State, the Jew untiringly applies himself to judaising the nations.

In his book *Les Juifs et le Monde Actuel*, J. Madaule shows how Luther, at the beginning of the Reformation, at first defended the Jews, but was not long in changing his attitude towards them, for, as he says:

"It was not the Jews who were becoming Protestants but the Protestants who were becoming judaised."

(J. Madaule, ibid., p. 171)

Karl Marx went even further and said:

"The Jew emancipated himself in Jewish fashion, not only by making himself master of the money-market but because owing to him and through him money has become a world power, and the practical Jewish spirit has been adopted by the Christian peoples. *The Jews set themselves free in proportion as the Christians became Jews.*

"Thus they contributed considerably to making money the means, the measure and the end of all human activity."

(Quoted in Salluste: *Les Origines Secrètes du Bolchevisme*, p. 285)

Alfred Nossig claims that the Jews have a historic mission to fulfil:

"The Jewish community is more than a people in the modern political meaning of the word. It is the trustee of an historic world mission, I would even say cosmic mission. . . . The conception of our ancestors was to found not a tribe but a world order destined to guide humanity. . . . *Gesta naturae per Judeos*, this is the formula of our history. And the hour of its accomplishment is approaching."

(A. Nossig: *Integrales Judentum*, pp. 1-5)

Elsewhere, Elie Faure has written on this subject:

"Sooner or later they must get the upper hand over and against all men. Later if need be, and in the dark and silence, provided that the triumph, an insatiable triumph, comes at the end. Later, what does it matter? At the extreme end of time."

(E. Faure: *La Question Juive*, p. 82)

Max I. Dimont concludes his book, *Jews, God and History* in these terms:

". . . two thirds of the civilized world is already governed by the ideas of Jews—the ideas of Moses, Jesus, Paul, Spinoza, Marx, Freud, Einstein."

(ibid., p. 419)

We would only draw the distinction that they themselves have denied, and continue to deny, Christ, and at the same time glorify Marx, Freud and Einstein.

The Jew often retains only the purely temporal aspect of the promises of the Covenant and the Prophets on which, even as an agnostic, he has been brought up, and which encourage him to pursue earthly happiness for immediate enjoyment. This is what the Church has called the "carnal" character of Israel and it is opposed to the spiritual character of Christianity. This quasi exclusive interpretation of the Covenant from the outset drew up the Synagogue against the church.

"The oldest form of Judaism knows nothing of another world. So, weal and woe can come only in this world. If God desires to punish or to reward, He must do so during man's lifetime. The righteous therefore is prosperous here, and the wicked here suffer punishment."

(W. Sombart: *The Jews and Modern Capitalism*, pp. 214-15)

"The ideal of Hebrew monotheism is the happiness of men on earth. The Bible never speaks of future life and we know what little value Homer's heroes attached to 'Hades'. Both want to achieve happiness on earth: the former through justice and fraternity, the latter through beauty and liberty. . . ."

(Dr. Pasmanik: *Qu'est-ce que le Judaisme*, pp. 18-29)

"The beyond does not exist for it," Elie Faure tells us. "Whatever may have been said, Israel has never believed in the beyond, except just at its decline, and except perhaps also in the bosom of esoteric Cabbalism reserved to a few initiates. Did Israel even ever think about it? Everything is natural in the world, including God, who ends in becoming the Spirit. The pact of the Covenant is a bilateral contract, obstinately precise and positive. If the

Jew obeys, the world will be his empire. That is his way of doing things. He lends at heavy interest. Israel is fiercely realistic. It is here below that it wants a reward for those who lead a good life and punishment for those who follow evil ways. None of its great prophets differ on this point. Elias, Isaiah, Jeremiah and Ezekiel wrathfully call down justice on earth, and if it does not descend it is because man is not worthy of it. It took St. Paul's conjuring-trick to remove it beyond death."

(E. Faure: *La Question Juive*, pp. 83-84)

"The philosophy of the Jew was simple . . . having but a limited number of years allotted to him, he wanted to enjoy them, and he demanded not moral but material pleasures, to embellish and make comfortable his existence. As there was no paradise, he could only expect tangible favours from God in return for his fidelity and piety; not vague promises, good for those seeking the beyond, but actual results, producing an increase of fortune and well-being. . . ." (B. Lazare: *Anti-Semitism*, pp. 278-9)

Convinced that they are the chosen people destined to possess the whole world as their empire in which to implant their ideal of life, the Jewish people dream of a terrestial reign in which they will control the social, economic and political life of the nations. And while Christianity dispenses its universal spiritual message to all peoples and at the same time respects their legitimate traditions, culture and customs, Judaism seeks to impose itself as the sole standard and to reduce the world to Jewish values, as has so truly been pointed out by George Batault:

"Essentially unadapted, and to a certain extent unadaptable, to the nation to which in law they belong, the Jews tend fatally and instinctively to reform and transform national institutions in such a way that they become adapted as perfectly as possible to themselves and to the ends which they pursue; ends which are practical at first, but also and above all, messianic. The final, 'imperial' objective, notwithstanding failures and trials always remains the triumph of Israel and its reign over a world subdued and pacified: it is the prophesy of Isaiah interpreted to the letter. . . .

"They are instinctively sympathetic to everything which tends to disintegrate and dissolve traditional societies, nations and countries.

"The Jews have a feeling and love for Humanity, taken as an aggregate of individuals as abstract and similar to each other as possible, released from 'the routine' of tradition and liberated from the 'chains' of the past, to be handed over, naked and uprooted, as human material for the undertakings of the great architects of the Future, who will at last construct on principles of Reason and Justice the messianic City over which Israel will reign.

"*The power of the Jews is in inverse proportion to the power of the States who receive them*, and thus they instinctively work to ruin the power of the State until, in one form or another, they succeed in enslaving and dominating it."

(G. Batault: *Israel contre les Nations*, pp. 107-109 and 75)

Jewish messianism, Batault shows, which claims to be universal in spirit, is in fact only a disguised form of imperialism:

"This form of universalism is absolutely identical with imperialism: the ideal propounded is panisrealism and panjudaism. In this sense, one could argue that pangermanism, for example, which aimed to subject the world, 'for its own real benefit', to the ideals of the Kultur, is also a doctrine with universal tendencies. But the other is, I repeat, purely and simply political, social and religious imperialism."

(G. Batault: *Le Problème juif*, p. 135)

"To be quite sure," Batault continues, "we have only to follow Isidore Loeb's guide to the description of messianic times in Deutero-Isaiah:

" 'The nations will gather to pay homage to the people of God: all the fortunes of the nations will pass to the Jewish people, they will march captive behind the Jewish people in chains and will prostrate themselves before them, their kings will bring up their sons, and their princesses will nurse their children. The Jews will command the nations; they will summon peoples whom they do not even know, and peoples who do not know them will hasten to them. The riches of the sea and the wealth of nations will come to the Jews of their own right. Any people or kingdom who will not serve Israel will be destroyed. . . .' (Isidore Loeb: *La Littérature des Pauvres dans la Bible*, pp. 219-20)

"As for the final result of the messianic revolution, it will always be the same: God will overthrow the nations and the kings and will cause Israel and her King to triumph; the nations will be converted to Judaism and will obey the Law or else they will be destroyed and the Jews will be the masters of the world.

"The Jews' international dream is to unite the world with the

Jewish law, under the direction and domination of the priestly people . . . in a general form of imperialism, which does not prevent Loeb, Darmesteter, Reinach or Lazare and so many others calling this conception universal fraternity."

(G. Batault, ibid., pp. 133-5)

Imbued with a messianic role, they are nevertheless unable to impose their will *openly* on the old Christian nations. They cannot be classed with the knights of medieval chivalry, with the du Guesclins, with St. Louis or St. Francis of Assisi or Richard the Lion Hearted. Yet in certain fields they possess exceptional qualities and powers, as shown in the following remarkable passage:

"His pitiless power of analysis," says Elie Faure, "and his irresistible sarcasm have acted like vitriol.

"From Maimonides to Charlie Chaplin the trail is easy to follow, although the circulation of the Jewish spirit was so to speak ethereal and its power of disintegration was not perceived until after its passage. . . .

"Freud, Einstein, Marcel Proust and Charlie Chaplin have opened in us, in every sense, prodigious avenues which overthrow the dividing-walls in the classical, Greco-Latin, catholic edifice, in the bosom of which the ardent doubt of the Jewish soul has been waiting for five or six centuries for an opportunity to unsettle it. For it is a remarkable fact that it seems to have been his sceptical role which was the first to emerge from the complete silence which enveloped the action of the Jewish spirit in the Middle Ages, a silence which was broken by a few voices as from the Renaissance and which masks such a vast uproar today. Lost in the depths of the masses of Western Christian societies, what could the Jew have done, reduced, moreover, to silence for fifteen centuries, but deny, within the frontiers and the hierarchy imposed by these societies—Christianity for Montaigne, cartesianism for Spinoza, capitalism for Marx, newtonianism for Einstein and if you like, kantism for Freud—waiting until from this very negation there began to appear little by little a new edifice profoundly stamped by an intellect for ever bent on driving away the supernatural from man's horizon and on searching, amid the ruins of morality and immortality, for the materials and means for a new spiritualism? Despite reasons for hope which he accumulated in silence, could the Jew be regarded as anything other than a destroyer armed with the corrosive doubt with which Israel has always opposed the sentimental idealism of Europe since the time of the Greeks? . . .

"In truth, they have brought everything into question again: metaphysics, psychology, physics, biology, the passions. . . .
(E. Faure, *La Question Juive*, p. 90)

"*The Jew's historic mission has been clearly defined, perhaps for all time. It will be the principal factor in every apocalyptic epoch, as it was at the end of the ancient world, and as it is now at the end, amid which we are living, of the Christian world.* At these moments the Jews will always be in the forefront, both to ruin the old edifice and to mark out the terrain and materials for the new structure which is to replace it. It is this dynamic quality which is the mark of their extraordinary grandeur and perhaps also, it must be admitted, of their visible impotence. . . .

"The Jew destroys every ancient illusion, and if he takes more share than anybody—St. Paul formerly and Karl Marx today, for example—in constructing the new illusion, precisely by reason of his eternal thirst for truth, which always survives the outcomes of political and religious struggles, he is fated to insert in the same illusion the worm which will undermine it. The patriarch who in former times agreed to lead the human conscience across the glowing stretches of knowledge is not ready to lay down his formidable burden."
(E. Faure, ibid., p. 97)

9

ANTI-SEMITISM

It may seem paradoxical at first sight that the people who were the first to spread the idea of the one God, whence Christianity proceeds, and who in their history as "the People of God" numbered so many prophets and remarkable men, should have been the object of such general and permanent repellence, and even hatred, which is known as anti-Semitism.

Throughout the whole history of the confrontation of Judaism and Christianity, the Jews have not failed to place the responsibility for this attitude on Christianity:

> "Christian anti-Semitism", as Jules Isaac tells us, "from the fact that it is supported by the Church, bears an official, systematic and coherent character which former pagan anti-Semitism has always lacked. It attends on theology and is nourished by it.... It also differs from pagan anti-Semitism, which invariably takes the form of a spontaneous reaction, exceptionally well commanded and organised, in that it pursues a most precise objective—which is to make the Jews hateful—and it owes its success in this achievement to a plan of action which has proved infinitely more harmful than that of pagan anti-Semitism."
>
> (J. Isaac: *Genèse de l'Antisémitisme*, p. 129)

This is also the opinion of Joshua Jehouda, who writes:

> "It is the obstinate Christian claim to be the sole heir to Israel which propagates anti-Semitism. This scandal must terminate sooner or later; the sooner it does, the sooner the world will be rid of the tissue of lies in which anti-Semitism shrouds itself."
>
> (*L'Antisémitisme, Miroir du Monde*, p. 136)

However, for those of us who are endeavouring to understand the Jewish problem in all its complexity throughout the ages, it would be vain to attempt to reduce it to such a view, over-simplified, partial and suggestive of contempt, for all historians, whether Jewish or not, agree that anti-Semitism existed long before Christianity.

Thus Doctor A. Roudinesco writes:

"The hatred of the Jew is very ancient; it appeared before the Christian era, from the very first moment the Israelites made contact with other peoples. *Anti-Judaism has flourished in all climates and in every epoch; it is the only historical phenomenon which has resisted the usury of time.* The word anti-Semitism is modern and comprises an ethnic idea." (*Le Malheur d'Israel*, p. 11)

"Anti-Semitism dates back well before Christianity", says the learned French social anthropologist, Vacher de Lapouge; "when one considers that it existed at least fifteen centuries before the present era, it is difficult to see in the agony of Christ the unique cause of the hatred with which they (the Jews) have been pursued by the Christians. . . ."
(*Les Sélections sociales*, cours professé à l'Université de Montpellier, 1888-9, pp. 465-7)

Indeed, many sociologists consider that other causes, inherent in the very character of the Hebrew people themselves, are at the root of the phenomenon of anti-Semitism.
This is demonstrated very clearly by the two Jewish writers, Bernard Lazare and Elie Faure:

"*An opinion as general as anti-Semitism, which has flourished in all countries and in all ages, before and after the Christian era, at Alexandria, Rome and Antioch, in Arabia, and in Persia, in medieval and in modern Europe, in a word, in all parts of the world wherever there are or have been Jews—such an opinion, it has seemed to me, could not spring from a mere whim or fancy, but must be the effect of deep and serious causes.*"
(B. Lazare: *Anti-Semitism*, Preface)

"Wherever the Jews settled after ceasing to be a nation ready to defend its liberty and independence, one observes the development of anti-Semitism, or rather anti-Judaism; for anti-Semitism is an ill-chosen word, which has its *raison d'être* only in our day.. . . .
"If this hostility, this repugnance had been shown towards the Jews at one time or in one country only, it would be easy to account for the local causes of this sentiment. But this race has been the object of hatred with all the nations amidst whom it ever settled. *Inasmuch as the enemies of the Jews belong to divers races; as they dwelled far apart from one another, were ruled by different laws and governed by opposite principles; as they had not the same customs and differed in spirit from one another, so that they could not possibly judge alike of any sub-*

ject, it must need be that the general causes of anti-Semitism have always resided in Israel itself, and not in those who antagonised it.
(B. Lazare, ibid., pp. 7-8)

"Which virtues or which vices have earned for the Jews this universal enmity? Why was he ill-treated and hated alike and in turn by the Alexandrians and the Romans, by the Persians and the Arabs, by the Turks and the Christian nations? Because everywhere, up to our own days, the Jew was an unsociable being.

"Why was he unsociable? Because he was exclusive, and his exclusiveness was both political and religious, or rather, he held fast to his political and religious cult, to his law."
(B. Lazare, ibid., p. 9)

"Anti-Semitic persecution", writes Elie Faure, "has never abated. It sprang from exterior causes, and not only from the too often quoted theocratic action, the accusation which preceded the Jews everywhere, that they had crucified the God they gave to Europe whom they did not want. They are possessed of an eternal anguish, which alienates them from all the peoples of the earth; they upset their habits, they devastate their well-worn paths, and they dislocate their ancient moral structures. . . .

"Their anguish is expressed in constant dissatisfaction, in stubborn recrimination, in a need to convince which gnaws at them like a prurient and which was only permitted them when they could not lay claim to political domination, and in intellectual restlessness; and thus they are led to criticise everything, to judge everything, to speak ill of everything, which automatically draws upon them the double tyranny of persecution and exile. This did not happen but yesterday. Nor does it date from the time of Christ. They so exasperated the Egyptians that they had to flee *en masse* from Egypt, and the Persians were so tired of them that they encouraged them to return home. The Romans, who were not interested in moral problems and whose firm tolerance kept religious peace everywhere, slit their throats and drowned their furious protests and passionate anathemas in blood. Pilate delivered Christ up to them in order to rid himself of them.

"Let it be said: they have annoyed the whole world. But therein perhaps lies their greatness. They refused silence and the slough of torpor. Everywhere they have with invincible obstinacy denied their surroundings, whether, dragged from captivity to captivity or sent away into exile after exile, they were forced into them or adopted them of their own free will. And this obstinacy will not I imagine die out before the last of them is gone. . . .

"It is not surprising then that from the earliest times until today, the Jew has awoken almost everywhere a frank or veiled hostility which has been expressed in almost every degree from purely speculative anti-Semitism to the most atrocious massacres...."

(E. Faure: *La Question juive*)

Renan, who can hardly be described as a man with a "Christian complex", or mentally unwell in terms of modern psychiatry, as apparently is the case, according to Joshua Jehouda, with all who do not admire the Jewish people, (*L'Antisémitisme, Miroir du Monde*, pp. 72-73), is no less explicit on this point:

"Hatred of the Jews was, moreover, so generally diffused a feeling in the ancient world that there was no need to spur it. This hatred marks one of the trenches of separation which, perhaps, will never be filled up in the human species. It is due to something more than race. It cannot be without reason that poor Israel has spent its life as a people in being massacred. When all nations and all ages have persecuted you, there must be some motive behind it all.

"The Jew, up to our own time, insinuated himself everywhere, claiming the protection of the common law; but, in reality, remaining outside the common law. He retained his own status; he wished to have the same guarantees as everyone else, and, over and above that, his own exceptions and special laws. *He desired the advantages of the nations without being a nation, without helping to bear the burdens of the nations. No people has ever been able to tolerate this.* The nations are military creations founded and maintained by the sword; they are the work of peasants and soldiers; towards establishing them the Jews have contributed nothing. Herein is the great fallacy inspired in Israelite pretensions. The tolerated alien can be useful to a country, but only on condition that the country does not allow itself to be invaded by him. It is not fair to claim family rights in a house which one has not built, like those birds which come and take up their quarters in a nest which does not belong to them, or like the crustaceans which steal the shell of another species."

(E. Renan: *The Antichrist*, pp. 126-7)

Anti-Semitism—and it should be noted that the term "anti-Semitism" is, properly speaking, incorrect in itself, since many Semite peoples, such as the Arabs or Egyptians, are or have been "anti-Semitic" in the customary use of the word—anti-Semitism, as we have shown, has existed for more than 3,000 years under many different forms:

1. There was anti-Semitism in Egypt, as the Bible relates;
2. There was anti-Semitism in Persia, as described in the Book of Esther;
3. There was anti-Semitism in Greece;
4. There was anti-Semitism in Alexandria, with the celebrated controversialist Appio at its head;
5. There was anti-Semitism at Rome, which numbered among its ranks some of the Eternal City's most famous sons: Cicero, Tacitus, Seneca, Juvenal and others.

"How glorious for anti-Semitism to be able to inscribe on its honours list the names of Seneca, Juvenal and Tacitus . . ." writes Jules Isaac in his *Genèse de l'Antisémitisme*. "Tacitus is unquestionably the most noble flower of all time in the crown of anti-Semitism." (ibid., pp. 114-15)

There was thus a general form of pagan anti-Semitism.
Religious anti-Semitism has been equally diverse. The world has seen:

1. Zoroastrian anti-Semitism;
2. Gnostic and Manichean anti-Semitism;
3. Orthodox anti-Semitism;
4. Moslem anti-Semitism;
5. Protestant anti-Semitism.

Of the latter form, nobody, perhaps, has used more violent language than Luther.

But among the Protestants, the most redoubtable adversary the Synagogue has ever had to face was, according to Massoutié, John Andrew Eisenmenger (1654-1704), professor of oriental languages at the University of Heidelberg. For it is from Eisenmenger's book, *Judaism Unmasked*, that

"Anti-Semites in Germany and other countries in turn have to this very day obtained most of their arms against the Synagogue. . . .
"Eisenmenger is bent on showing above all in his work at how many points Judaism and Christianity differ, two religions which originally only differed from one another in the lightest shades of meaning."

(L. Massoutié: *Judaisme et Hitlerisme*, pp. 138-9, 141)

But what is perhaps even more extraordinary is the fact of the phenomenon of political and philosophical anti-Semitism. The pages of history bear witness to:

1. Rationalist anti-Semitism, led by Voltaire;
2. Socialist anti-Semitism, under Toussenel;
3. Racial anti-Semitism under Hitler;
4. Nationalist and patriotic anti-Semitism in almost every country, and;
5. Economic anti-Semitism, which is similarly universal.

Finally today, most incredible of all, we are confronted with

1. Soviet anti-Semitism.

In short, every country and every epoch has in turn known anti-Semitism in one form or another, sometimes smouldering under the surface, sometimes prescribed by law, sometimes erupting in furious and bloody explosions.

And in the course of 3,000 years all possible and imaginable solutions have been tried in an endeavour to solve the Jewish problem:

1. Peaceful coexistence;
2. Conversion;
3. Segregation and the Ghetto;
4. Expulsion;
5. Pogroms;
6. Political emancipation;
7. Assimilation;
8. Mixed marriages;
9. The numerus clausus;
10. The spur and the yellow star;

and finally, the most recent solutions that have been attempted are:

11. Racism;
12. Marxism.

All these solutions have in the end proved inoperative.
Doctor Roudinesco records that:

> "Anti-Semitism appeared from the first moment when the Jews came into contact with the rest of the world; it has endured throughout the centuries to our own day. It has resisted political revolutions, social transformation and mental evolution. It is as active today as it has been in the past; it has assumed very varied forms according to the specific illusion of each epoch; it has often changed its name but its character has remained the

same. There is no reason to hope that it will disappear. If one measures its power by the number of its victims, one is obliged to recognise that it has become more intense. The carnage of Alexandria, the massacres of the Middle Ages, the Russian and Polish pogroms are insignificant compared with the recent exterminations under Hitler. . . .

"The Jewish question is not only confined to the moral order, it is a social and political problem with infinite repercussions. The Dreyfus affair rent and weakened France. Without anti-Semitism, Hitler would not have triumphed in Germany and the Second World War, which cost the lives of sixty million men, could have been avoided.

"Despite every expectation, legal emancipation, assimilation, and Jewish blood poured out on the battle-fields have all proved ineffectual. Anti-Semitism has persisted and become intensified. Israel's destiny remains sealed in misfortune."
(Dr. A. Roudinesco: *Le Malheur d'Israel*, pp. 173, 177)

The Jewish people tend to think of themselves as the innocent victims of the hatred of the world, but most of the defensive measures against them in the West—regarded by them as manifestations of prejudice, intolerance, hatred and anti-Semitism—have been borrowed from Jewish legislation and turned against its authors.

Religious intolerance was unknown in pagan society:

"Each people had its own particular gods and recognised the legitimate sovereignty of foreign deities over other countries."
(E. Benamozegh: *Israel et l'Humanité*, p. 21)

The Jews alone in antiquity professed uncompromising religious exclusiveness, as G. Batault explains in detail in the following passage:

"A certain apologetic school of history has for too long insisted on the idea that the pagans held the monopoly of intolerance and religious persecution. Nothing could be more false, and modern scholarship and impartial history prove that this assertion is more than fully justified. Intolerance, proceeding directly from the religious exclusiveness of the Israelites, is a purely Jewish invention, which was inherited by Christianity and so transmitted to the modern world.

"However the chosen people carried with it something which was to have an amazing destiny in the future in the heart of the western world, a strong and rigorous conception of the divinity, and a proud unshakeable and fanatical faith in an all-powerful, authoritarian, exclusive and jealous God, and in the height of virtuousness of a minutely-detailed, captious law.

"While the Alexandrine civilisation, the heir of both the Greek and all the Mediterranean civilisations, meted out to the world, under the aegis of the military and political genius of Alexander, the arts, the sciences, and the highest philosophical speculations, the Jews, who were beginning to spread over this immense sort of 'internation' which the hellenic world formed, presented it with jealous monotheism, exclusive ritualism and religious intoleration; ideas which were unknown until then, though their significance and influence were later to be unequalled. . . .

"Judaism was not only an exclusive belief which contradicted the pagans' profound convictions and feelings of tolerance, it was also an exclusive and tyrannical law which contradicted their habits, their customs, their manners and particularly their noble and touching sense of hospitality . . . Jewish exclusiveness made itself felt in the everyday commerce of daily life in a thousand and one little ways, by their refusal to eat with the pagans, or take part in their games and exercises, or serve under their standards, by their judicial autonomy and their separate marriages. Wherever rather numerous Jewish colonies became established, whether voluntarily or not, in the midst of Greek or hellenic peoples, the Jews inevitably adopted and kept a foreign appearance. In spite of the fact that they could talk and write Greek, and organise their life in the Greek fashion, their tight solidarity and their social and legal isolation, which by its malignancy exaggerated its significance and the consequences, placed them in opposition to life under the Greeks and the Romans, so that they were like strangers, 'more distant from us', said Philostrates, 'than Susa, Bactria or India'.

"To the minds of the ancients, so open, so comprehensive and so tolerant, Jewish exclusiveness was a monstrosity: intolerance, a Jewish invention and virtue, was completely incomprehensible to them. In the hellenistic period they were perfectly able to conceive of one God, worshipped everywhere under different names, and possessing different attributes, but they were quite unable to understand that this one God should be precisely and exclusively the God of the Jews. . . .

"Contrary to what one is too often led to believe, the Jews did not introduce to the world an international and universal or metaphysical conception of monotheism, which was derived quite normally from the political state of the time and from the speculations of Greek philosophy; but they did introduce the idea of the exclusive monotheism of Jahve, the jealous and tyrannical God.

"By a singularly ironical stroke of Fate, when upon two occasions, first with Christianity and later with Islam, the exclusive and jealous God of the Jews, with his inseparable companions intolerance and fanaticism, triumphed, he turned against the chosen people and added to their troubles."

(G. Batault: *Le Problème Juif*, pp. 60, 63, 64, 65, 85)

The intolerance which the Jews bitterly accuse Christianity of practising against them takes its roots, as we shall see, from essentially Judaic concepts:

"We can now see how the forces shaping Jewish history in the early Feudal Age began with two paradoxes. Not only were the Jews the only non-Christians left in the entire Christian world, but, ironically, they lived in freedom outside the feudal system, while the Gentiles were imprisoned within it.

"Why had the Jews not been converted or killed as had the other pagans and non-believers? Why had they received special exemption? Why did the Church protect them?

"The Church had manœuvred itself into this paradoxical impasse by the force of its own logic. Because the civilisation of the Middle Ages was religiously oriented, it was important that the Jews be converted to Christianity. . . .

"At first every conciliation was held out to the Jews as an inducement to accept Christianity. The Jews would not convert. . . . The Jew was an ambivalent figure in the Western world. He could neither be converted nor killed. . . . The Jew therefore was excluded from the feudal system. . . .

"Some of the laws enacted against the Jews in these centuries were not new. They were, in fact, patterned after Old Testament and Talmudic laws against non-Jews. Old Jewish laws forbade a non-Jew being appointed king of Israel, or holding a post from which he could govern Jews. To prevent too great an intermixing between Jews and Greeks, Palestinian law forbade a Jew to sell land to a non-Jew. The Christians enacted like laws against the Jews. These cannot be judged as good or bad in terms of today's society. They were an expression of society in those days."

(M. I. Dimont: *Jews, God and History*, pp. 218-19)

Let us take as a particular instance, the Inquisition, set up in the thirteenth century to put an end to the Albigensian heresy.

After the crusade against the Albigensians, which numbered a great many victims:

"The Papacy became alarmed at all this bloodshed, forbade the private hunting of heretics (as it was later to forbid the local hunting of Jews), and instituted the Inquisition (from the Latin *inquisitio*, meaning an 'inquiry') in order to determine whether an accused actually was a heretic. During the first centuries of its existence, the Inquisition had no power to deal with Jews, Mohammedans, or any other non-believers, only with Christians.

"As the Church abhorred the shedding of blood, it was decided that those convicted should be burned. Ironically, modern man looks with horror upon burning someone for his religious beliefs, yet sees nothing incongruous in shooting or hanging a man for his political convictions. Also, ironically, the authority for killing a heretic stems from the Old Testament itself, from Deuteronomy xvii. 2-5: 'If there be found in the midst of thee . . . man or woman, that does that which is evil in the sight of the Lord thy God in transgressing His covenant, and has gone and served other gods, and worshipped them . . . and it be told thee . . . then shalt thou bring forth that man or woman . . . thou shalt stone them with stones that they die.' Because only Christians could commit heresy in the eyes of the Church, this Mosaic law, with an updated punishment, was applied only to them. And thus came about the twist of fate which brought Jews comparative safety from the Inquisition while Christians burned one another at the stake."

(M. I. Dimont, ibid., pp. 224-5)

Doctor Roudinesco too agrees that the burden of intolerance must be divided among the Jews and the Christians:

"They were monsters, these men who burnt other men alive who were not of their faith. The sole ground for complaint against the Jews at this time was of a religious order. But the theological anti-Judaism of the Middle Ages is easy to understand. Religious tolerance did not exist. The Jews were as intolerant as the Christians. The former persecuted their heretics just as the Christians persecuted theirs. The Synagogue excommunicated as rigorously as the Church."

(Dr. A. Roudinesco: *Le Malheur d'Israel*, p. 40)

Again, it was the Synagogue which was the first to impose on Jews the duty of wearing a distinctive badge; and yet among the different measures which the Church has taken against the Jews to thwart their policy of infiltration and corruption, there is one against which they have always violently protested, considering it particularly defamatory, namely, the obligation to wear a distinctive badge, such as a spur, a hat or a star.

This measure, which was imposed by the 4th Lateran Council in 1215, and renewed by the bulls of Honorius III (1221), Martin V

(1425), Paul IV (1555), St. Pius V (1566) and Clement VIII (1593), was only reviving an old Jewish custom, which laid down that the Jews should distinguish themselves from other peoples by their dress. This was emphasised by Clement III when he made known the decision of the Council to the faithful:

> "All that we have to do," he said, "is to bring the Jews back again to the observation of the laws of Moses commanding them to wear distinctive dress."

St. Thomas Aquinas, writing to the Duchess of Brabant, makes the same comment on the decision:

> "It is what they are commanded in their own law, that is to say, to wear fringes on the four corners of their cloaks so that they may be distinguished from other peoples."
> (Quoted by Lovsky in
> *Antisémitisme et Mystère d'Israel*, p. 199)

Let us finally deal with the question of race.

The Jews protested vehemently against Hitler's racial régime; and yet they were the first people in history to exalt the idea of race, thinking of themselves as belonging to the "chosen race". In other words, they created a concept of race which other peoples, having long ignored, have borrowed from them, at times even to turn it against them.

It is opportune to remark here that the Jews are the only ethnic group who are naturally and fundamentally race conscious, since their ideas of race and religion are inextricably entwined. "The Semitic religions", wrote Kadmi-Cohen in *Nomades*, "are only the spiritualised deification of the race."

Thus it is not without a certain irony that we are now witnessing a flood of rage against a policy which in Germany revived the idea of race, turning it against its inventors.

In the *Revue de l'Histoire des Religions*, E. Dhorme wrote in 1934:

> "Judaism has made a powerful contribution in implanting in the world this concept of race, or more specifically of the seed . . . which should be traced back to great ancestors and endure without mixture throughout the ages. The persecutions which the Jews have suffered in Christian countries are due, in part, to the fusion of race and religion which marked out the children of Israel as a special category of unassimilable citizens. *Racism is a dangerous theory, but let us recognise that it was upheld by the Semites long before it was by the Aryans.*"
> (Quoted by Lovsky, ibid., p. 364)

All Jewish writers exalt the indestructibility and superiority of their race, which they regard as destined to exert a great influence on all others. Disraeli, the Prime Minister of Great Britain, wrote:

"Every generation they must become more powerful and more dangerous to the society which is hostile to them. Do you think that the quiet humdrum persecution of a decorous representative of an English university can crush those who have successfully baffled the Pharaohs, Nebuchadnezzar, Rome, and the Feudal ages? . . . No penal laws, no physical tortures can effect that a superior race should be absorbed in an inferior, or be destroyed by it. The mixed persecuting races disappear; the pure persecuted race remains. And *at this moment, in spite of centuries, of tens of centuries, of degradation, the Jewish mind exercises a vast influence on the affairs of Europe.*"

(Disraeli: *Coningsby*, pp. 226-7)

In *Notre Jeunesse*, Charles Péguy draws a very characteristic portrait of his friend Bernard Lazare, in which the word "race" recurs as the central theme, pregnant with meaning. We have taken the following extract from it:

"There was never a moment when every muscle and every nerve was not strained to answer his secret mission. Never was a man more conscious of his role as the leader of his race and of his people, nor more responsible for them; a man perpetually taughtened by an unatonable reverse and sub-tension. Not a sentiment, not a thought, not the shadow of a passion, but was not strained and governed by a commandment fifty centuries old; a whole race, a whole world he carried on his bowed shoulders, a race, a world of fifty centuries on round, heavy shoulders; and his heart was consumed with fire, with the fire of his race and of his people; his heart was on fire, his mind was passionate, and from his prophetic lips came forth live coals!" (C. Péguy:

Notre Jeunesse dans Oeuvres en prose 1909-14, p. 560)

In 1936 the Jewish author Kadmi-Cohen wrote a book called *Nomades* to glorify and indeed to deify his race which, according to him, has succeeded in preserving its unity and purity throughout its nomadic life. The extracts below have been taken from his work:

One cannot ignore the

"Extraordinary and absurd persistence of the Semite race and, within the race, the persistence of physical types. Sometimes one notices a striking resemblance in the cast of features between a Jew who has been completely westernised and the Arab Bedouin, from whom he is separated by a stretch of some 3,000 years.

"Besides, the perpetuity of certain manners is significant. Centuries of living amidst Slav and Nordic peoples have not lost the Jew his frenzy, his need to gesticulate nor his immoderate love of the highly-seasoned cooking of the Mediterranean.

"Examples of this stability, which is so surprising that one is compelled to call it survival, are so numerous that they embody the whole of Arab and Jewish life.

"There is in the destiny of the race, as in the Semitic character, a fixity, a stability and an immortality which are most striking. . . .

"I am what I am, says the Eternal. The Eternal, it is the race.

"One in its substance, not differentiated. One in time—stable—eternal." (Kadmi-Cohen : *Nomades*, p. 14)

"The unity of the Semitic concept is primarily and absolutely explained by the nomadic character of the Semites' way of life. A race of nomads, they were shepherds who roamed from pasture to pasture rather than farmers who tilled the land. They have remained nomads. The imprint is as indelible as a mark cut on the trunk of a tree, for as the trunk grows and expands the mark becomes protracted and disfigured, but it remains none the less distinguishable. (Kadmi-Cohen, ibid., pp. 115-16)

"Let it be fully recognised; the nomadic state, with the Semite, as opposed to the history of other peoples, has never partaken of a transitory character or of a stage in the preparation for a sedentary life. It takes its source from the depth of the Semite heart.
(Kadmi-Cohen, ibid., p. 19)

"That the nomadic life may by itself be a factor in the preservation of the race and of its ethnic purity is conceivable. A tribe which wanders thereby accepts isolation, and in spite of and even because of its migrations, it remains identical and true to itself.
(Kadmi-Cohen, ibid., p. 25)

"So the blood which runs in its veins has preserved its purity first and foremost, and the succession of the centuries will only serve to strengthen the value of the race.

> "The Semites and particularly the Jews provide natural and historical proof of this phenomenon. Nowhere has the respect for the blood been proscribed with equal intransigence. . . .
>
> "The history of this people such as it is recorded in the Bible, constantly insists on the danger of mixing with foreigners . . . and in our days, just as thirty centuries ago, the vitality of this racial characteristic is maintained and can be seen by the infrequency of mixed marriages between Jews and non-Jews.
>
> "Thus it is round this exclusive love and jealousy, one could say, of race, that the profound meaning of Semitism and of its ideal character is centred. The People constitutes an autonomous and autogenous entity, dependent on no country, not accepting the laws in force in the country where it resides, and energetically refusing the introduction of cross-breeding, fruitful though it may be. Without material or external support, it cultivates solely its own unity. . . .
>
> ". . . and it is . . . this formidable value, which is thus conferred on the race, which alone explains this unique phenomenon, absolutely without exception, that of all the innumerable peoples, one alone, the Jewish people, has survived on its own and remained from time immemorial, in spite of everything."
>
> (Kadmi-Cohen, ibid., pp. 26-28)

Practising an exclusive form of racial apartheid themselves, the Jews are equally uncompromising opponents of race when it is a question of rival ideologies of the German or other kinds. They urged fanatically for war against Hitler. In scarcely veiled terms, Leon Blum invited the democracies to destroy racial ideology in an article which appeared in *Paris-Soir* on 23rd March 1939:

> "The re-organisation, the reconciliation and the co-operation of all the States in the world that are attached to liberty and peace, and the stimulation and exaltation of the democratic system, and at the same time the systematic destruction of the racist ideology, that is the essential task incumbent on the great movements of public opinion, without which the governments would be impotent."

10

WORLD REVOLUTION

SIX million dead, such is the fearful figure with which the organisations of Jewry ceaselessly confront the world; it is the unanswered argument of which they availed themselves at the Council in order to obtain a revision of the Catholic Liturgy.

Le Monde of the 3rd January 1965 recently published an article *à propos* of this subject by Vladimir Jankélévitch, from which we have taken the following passage:

"This crime without name is a crime that is truly infinite, and the further it is analysed the further its inexpressible horror deepens. We ourselves, who should have so many reasons to know, are daily learning something new, some particularly revolting detail, some torture of special ingenuity, some Machiavellian atrocity of which one is compelled to say that only Germanic sadism could be guilty. It is not surprising that a fathomless crime should produce some sort of meditation that knows no exhaustion. The unheard of inventions of cruelty, the depths of the most diabolical perversity, the unimaginable refinements of hatred, all this leaves us dumb and at first baffles the mind. One will never plumb the depths of the mystery of this gratuitous wickedness.

"Correctly speaking, this grandiose massacre is not a crime on the human scale any more than are the splendours of astronomy and the light years. . . .

"Before infinity all finite dimensions tend to become equal, with the result that the punishment becomes almost a matter of indifference; what has happened is literally unatonable. We don't even know whom to blame or whom to accuse. . . .

"The methodical, scientific and administrative massacre of six million Jews is not a wrong *per se, it is a crime for which a whole people is accountable*. . . .

"What happened is unique in history and without doubt will never happen again, for nothing like it has been seen since the world began; the day will come when we will no longer even be able to explain it."

As one can see from the above, the Jews furiously repudiate the very idea of collective responsibility as far as they are concerned, but do not hesitate to hold the German people collectively responsible for the wrongs done to Israel under the Hitler régime.

However, it now appears that we cannot accept this figure of six million. A French writer, Paul Rassinier, has made a very penetrating study of this subject, which he has brought together in four large volumes, entitled: *Le Mensonge d'Ulysse, Ulysse trahi par les siens, Le Veritable Proces Eichmann ou les Vainqueurs incorrigibles* and *Le Drame des Juifs Europeens.*

Rassinier is a left-wing Socialist and an agnostic, who was himself deported to Buchenwald; he cannot therefore be suspected of being sympathetic to National Socialism. In Appendix II we give a résumé of these works, and of the author's conclusions.

Since the last war, the whole world has been inundated with a torrent of literature, for the most part unreasoning, and at the same time violently and axiomatically hostile to Germany under Hitler, in which all desire calmly and honestly to seek out the truth and face it, however unpleasant it may be, however unlike what it is pre-conceived to be, appears to have been thrown to the wind. "The first law of history", wrote the great Pontiff, Leo XIII, "is not to say what is false; next, not to fear to say what is true." It is appropriate therefore, at this stage, to recall a few sober facts about the last war, which are not as well known or remembered as others.

Firstly, Hitler's Germany did not only attack the Jews; if we count all the losses suffered during the war, more non-Jewish deportees and prisoners of war and others died than Jews.

At the outbreak of war there were about 300,000 French Jews and 170,000 foreign Jews in France. Rather less than 100,000 were deported, of whom the majority were foreign Jews. We recognise that this is a very great number but we are far away from the legendary six million figure.

On the other hand, at the Liberation about 105,000 Frenchmen were assassinated by other Frenchmen in the name of the Resistance; 95 per cent of these were good men whose only fault was that they were anti-Communist and not pro-Gaullist. No one seems to care about this. The universal conscience is only interested in Jewish victims.

Paul Serant has described the purges which took place in France and other European countries after the liberation, and which in France went on for years:

"As soon as the commissions began to bring out of prison those who could not be reproached with anything, people began to demand that the purge be maintained.

"They were not all Communists. It was in a paper of a mainly conservative readership, l'*Ordre*, that Mr. Julian Benda demanded the most harsh enforcement of a purge against those who were beginning to talk of clemency. The government, in his opinion, must agree to be the government of a party, the patriotic party. It doesn't matter if all Frenchmen are not represented since those who are not patriots ought not to count. Here is a good reason to refuse them appeasement: 'It is perfectly false to maintain that reconciliation of the type you preach is vital for a nation. The Russian government is a one-party government of patriots and it pitilessly exterminated that class of citizens which thirty years ago, itself hoped and worked for the victory of the enemy. One cannot exactly say that the Russian nation is no longer in existence as a result. . . .' One could hardly put it more briefly or more precisely."

(Paul Serant: *Les Vaincus de la Libération*, p. 234)

The Allies themselves have heavy responsibilities to bear.

Take, for example, the handing over to the Soviets of the whole of Wlassow's army by the Anglo-American authorities. In their zone the Americans were perfectly free to do what they liked and they must have known that they were handing these men over to certain death.

At the outset of the invasion of Russia by the German army in 1941, many thousands of Russian officers and soldiers deserted and threw in their lot with the Germans in order to fight with them against the tyranny of Stalin. One of them, General Wlassow, former Commander of the 2nd Soviet Army, a national hero of the U.S.S.R. and very popular in the army, was put in command by German officers of various Russian units which had been formed to fight to liberate their country from the Soviet yoke.

A first Wlassow army, a crack unit 40,000 strong, commanded by Colonel Boudnitchenko, occupied Prague, replacing the German SS units. At the approach of the Russian troops, this division withdrew towards the American army which had entered Czechoslovakia and which compelled them to hand over their arms. When the American troops retreated the division found they were surrounded by the Soviets. Many committed suicide and the rest were taken prisoner; the officers were shot and the non-commissioned officers and soldiers were sent away to concentration camps. But beforehand many were used by Beria for propaganda purposes. Manacled, they were piled into lorries with posters on them which read: "This is the fate which Americans reserve for those who put their trust in them", and paraded in front of unit after unit. Few of them survived.

A second Wlassow division, commanded by General Meandrov, was interned by the Americans at Platting in Bavaria; in February and March 1946 they were handed over to the Soviets in the most disgraceful fashion. Awoken at dawn, the men were penned up like animals, herded to the station and crammed into trucks to the blows of rifle butts, while jazz music blared to stifle their cries. Many committed suicide, and a few succeeded in escaping.

The cavalry units under Wlassow formed an autonomous corps and were in Italy at the time of the German collapse. Moving up to Bavaria to rejoin Wlassow, they were halted at Linz by the British authorities, who invited the Cossack leaders to dine with them. Among them were General Prince Bekovitch Tcherkassy, General Krasnov, his nephew Colonel Semione Krasnov and others. When they arrived in full evening-dress they were arrested by the British, who took them to Berlin and handed them over to the Soviets. They were all hanged.

General Wlassow himself was captured by a Soviet unit and hanged at Moscow.

The Americans also handed over to the Soviets General Troukhine, Wlassow's deputy-in-chief, General Malychkine, his Chief of Staff, and several other high-ranking officers.

Two of Wlassow's envoys, who had been sent to negotiate the internment of his troops in Western Germany, for which they had obtained safe-conducts from the Americans, were nevertheless arrested on their arrival and held prisoner. Captain Lapine refused to commit suicide and was handed over to the Soviets. Captain Bykadorov was released.

The Americans continued handing over the remains of Wlassow's units little by little until June 1947. At that date an important Wlassow detachment was put on board ship for Russia, not without having first fought a veritable battle with the Americans.

No forcible repatriations took place in the French zone of occupation. But under the first Gaullist government, the Soviet State Security was authorised to set up a camp at Beauregard, whence former Soviet citizens interned in the camp were forcibly repatriated to the U.S.S.R. Furthermore, this body was given a free hand to operate in broad daylight in Paris itself, happily only for a short period; on several occasions its agents entered the flats of former émigrés and took away former Soviet subjects who did not want to be repatriated and had taken refuge there. Between March and April 1946, Lieutenant Laptchinski, a young Russian, was removed from the flat of Count Ivan Tolstoy, the grandson of the great writer, who had been sheltering him.

In 1947 the Beauregard camp was closed.

And after the death of Stalin the survivors of Wlassow's army were released from the concentration camps.

Let us now turn to Soviet Russia.

The number of the victims of Marxist terrorism reaches apocalyptic proportions. In Russia and in the satellite countries as well, there have been millions of deaths of every category; by assassination, by famine, by shooting in street-fighting and massacres by the Tcheka ... and tens of millions of people have been deported. Up to quite recently, it has been estimated that the camps of political deportees, particularly those in the far North of Siberia, had held sometimes as many as fifteen million prisoners, many of whom had died of misery, exhaustion and illness. It is enough to recall the massive and pitiless deportation of the Russian Koulac peasants who were hostile to collectivisation:

"... according to Margaret Buber-Neuman, Navareno Scarioli, the Italian Communist who fled to Moscow in 1925 and experienced the Russian concentration camps between 1937 and 1954, painted a picture in the Rome magazine *Vita* on the 23rd November 1961 which surpasses in horror anything which could have been written by survivors of the German camps, even the most incredible stories."

(Rassinier: *Le Véritable Procès Eichmann*, pp. 9-10)

Under the heading "A Yugoslav review says that the U.S.S.R. committed the crime of genocide before Hitler", *Le Monde* of the 7th February 1965, analyses an account by Mr. Mihajlov, an undergraduate of the University of Zadar, Dalmatia, of a trip he made the summer before to the Soviet Union, published in the literary review, *Delo*, from which the following extract is taken:

"... this piece of writing is going to cause trouble. It consists of a series of reflections and notes on the concentration camps in the Soviet Union in which, up to 1956-57, between eight and twelve million people were interned....

"The great majority of those who have been rehabilitated and who had the luck to survive, do not want to keep silence any more, writes Mr. Mihajlov....

"Another passage ... deals with the 'death camps'. It is symptomatic, writes Mr. Mihajlov, that the Soviet Press makes less and less mention of Nazi camps and avoids comparing them with her own. The first death camp was not organised by the Germans but by the Soviets; it came into operation in 1921 at Holmogor near Archangel. It worked 'successfully' for years.

"Recalling the terror in the first years after the revolution and the execution without trial in Crimea, 1920-1, of 120,000 prisoners, Mr. Mihajlov states that a certain Vera Grebnjakov, known under the alias of Dora, is still remembered there. She did her 'work' at Odessa and with her own hand is said to have killed and tortured 700 prisoners.

"Hitler was not the first to commit the crime of genocide, says the writer. On the eve of the Second World War, the peoples along the frontiers of Turkey and Iraq were deported to northernmost Siberia where, being unaccustomed to the cold, they died like flies."

(*Le Monde*, 7th February 1965, front page)

In the last war, one and a half million people from Poland and the Ukraine were deported by the Soviet Union:

"Interrogated at Nuremberg on 21st March 1946, by General Rudenko, the Russian prosecutor, Field-Marshal Goering replied that 'one million people from Poland and the Ukraine were deported from territories occupied by the Soviet Union and taken to the East and Far-East' (C.R. des débats, vol. IX, p. 673) but he was not allowed to quote references or to proceed further. The first Polish government of London has however published a document according to which the number of Poles deported was between 1,000,000 and 1,600,000 of whom 400,000 died on the journey; among the dead were 77,834 out of 144,000 children according to information provided by the American Red Cross ... the Russians extended the process to the Baltic States, whence they deported 60,940 Esthonians, 60,000 Latvians and 70,000 Lithuanians...."

(Rassinier, *Le Véritable Procès Eichmann*, p. 44)

A further 12,000 officers of the 1939 Polish army were massacred to a man by the Russians; 4,000 of their corpses were identified in the Katyn Forest graves.

Of the 100,000 German prisoners captured at Stalingrad only 5,000 came back alive, the others died in the camps.

Between 1st July 1945 and 1st January 1947, approximately 7,300,000 people were sent back from Silesia to Germany by the Russians, according to Rassinier (ibid., p. 107). Jammed into cattle-trucks, they were left without food on a journey of four to five days. In the *Revue des Deux Mondes* on 15th May 1952, Mr. Jean de

Pange stated that more than four million of these unfortunate people died.

Hideous scenes of massacre and violence accompanied the capture of Berlin and the invasion of Germany by the Soviet armies, for on the Eastern Front it was a veritable war of extermination, conducted on both sides with atrocious savagery.

Finally, one must not forget the bloody repression of the popular uprising in Hungary in 1956.

Until the death of Stalin, terror has always been an essential part of the Soviet régime, and in the realm of revolutionary terrorism, and the development of Marxism as a revolutionary doctrine, the names of outstanding Jewish leaders readily come to mind: Karl Marx, Lassalle, Kautsky, Liebnecht, Rosa Luxembourg, and others. It is a modern form of messianism, always read to overthrow everything. On the subject of Marx, this is what Bernard Lazare has to say in his celebrated work, *Anti-Semitism*:

> "The descendant of a long line of rabbis and teachers, he inherited the splendid powers of his ancestors. He had that clear Talmudic mind which does not falter at the petty difficulties of fact. He was a Talmudist devoted to sociology and applying his native power of exegesis to the criticism of economic theory. He was inspired by that ancient Hebraic materialism which, rejecting as too distant and doubtful the hope of an Eden after death, never ceased to dream of Paradise realised on earth. But Marx was not a mere logician, he was also a rebel, an agitator, an acrid controversialist, and he derived his gift for sarcasm and invective, as Heine did, from his Jewish ancestry."
> (pp. 315-16)

On the other hand, this is what Rabi says in his *Anatomie du Judaisme français*:

> "There is always a chosen people in the Marxist vision but henceforward it is the proletariat. There will be catastrophes, such as the prophets have foretold, but these are the normal results of the inevitable class struggle. There is also a finality in the historical process, its destiny is sealed, victory is inexorable, the proletariat lives and struggles in the path of history, and history, if not God, is on the side of the proletariat. With Marx, socialism became a secular version of Jewish messianism. The idea was born in Palestine and has now taken root in Moscow and Peking."
> (p. 250)

The following passage is taken from the revolutionary Jewish writer, A. Rosenberg, who was a leader of the German Communist

Party between 1917 and 1927. It is of capital importance since it clearly reveals the essentially revolutionary and destructive nature of Marxism, camouflaged behind the slogan of the liberation of the proletariat.

"It was not an overwhelming consciousness of the necessity for freeing the proletariat from its hunger and misery that caused Marx to regard revolution as the sole means to achieve that aim. He did not proceed from the proletariat to revolution. Indeed he chose a path proceeding in a directly contrary direction . . .; it was in his search for a means by which to achieve this revolution that Marx discovered the proletariat.
(Arthur Rosenburg: A History of Bolshevism, p. 3)

"In 1848-9 Marx and Engels published in Cologne the Neue Rheinische Zeitung as 'a mouthpiece of democracy'. It proved to be the most daring and most influential newspaper at the disposal of German democracy. . . .
"It was not a workman's paper in the customary meaning of the word. Indeed the various occupational and class interests of the workers received scant attention in its pages. . . .
(Arthur Rosenberg, ibid., p. 12)

"The Party organisation was looked upon by Marx and Engels simply as a medium through which they could better influence the working class as a whole. . . .
"On 13th February 1851, Engels gave open expression to these views in a letter to Marx. He wrote:
"'Have we not pretended for many years that Krethi Plethi was our Party, although we had no Party there, and those whom we at least officially recognised as members of our Party . . . did not comprehend the very ABC of our movement? What have we to do with a Party that is nothing more than a herd of asses, and that swears by us because its members look upon us as their equals?' . . . .
"It may be discerned clearly from this," Rosenberg added, "how in those days Marxism was introduced into the working classes as something extraneous to them."
(Arthur Rosenberg, ibid., pp. 14-15)

Similarly, the principal leaders of Soviet Russia until the advent of the dictator Stalin were of the same enigmatic race:

"I earnestly desire to avoid writing one single line which might tend to inflame a festering wound", wrote Sarolea in 1924. "But it is no use denying that the festering wound is there. . . . That the Jews have played a leading part in the Bolshevist upheaval and are still playing a leading part in the Bolshevist Government is a proposition which no one will deny who has taken the trouble to study Russian affairs at first hand. I am quite ready to admit . . . that the Jewish leaders are only an infinitestimal fraction. But it is none the less true that those few Jewish leaders are the masters of Russia, even as the fifteen hundred Anglo-Indian civil servants are the masters of India. For any traveller in Russia to deny such a truth would be to deny the evidence of his own senses."

(Charles Sarolea: *Impressions of Soviet Russia*, pp. 158-9)

Their dictatorship fell not only upon Russia but upon every country in Central Europe when Bolshevism attempted to implant itself by a bloody reign of terror; under Bela Kuhn and Szamuelly at Budapest, Liebnecht and Rosa Luxembourg at Berlin, and Kurt Eisner and Max Lieven at Munich.

In this, it is worth noting that their deeds are absolutely consistent with their words, and in support of this contention we quote below from the foremost Jewish theoreticians of Bolshevik terrorism: Karl Marx, Engels, Leon Trotsky and Neumann.

First, let us take a passage from Marx written only two years before his death, which puts in clear relief his ideas about dictatorship and violence. In a letter to the Dutch Social-Democrat, Domela Nieuwenhuys, Marx wrote on 22nd February 1881:

"A socialist government cannot put itself at the head of a country if adequate conditions do not exist to enable it immediately to take the requisite measures to terrify the *bourgeoisie* and so achieve the first step for the unfolding of its policy."

(*Pravda*, 14th March 1928; quoted by Leon de Poncins in
Le Plan Communiste d'Insurrection armée, p. 17)

This is Engel's judgment on the commune:

"The revolution is undoubtedly the most authoritarian thing in the world. Revolution is an act in which one section of the population imposes its will upon the other by rifles, bayonets, guns, and other such exceedingly authoritarian means. And the party which has won is necessarily compelled to maintain its rule by means of that fear which its arms inspire in the reactionaries. If the commune of Paris had not relied upon the armed people as against the *bourgeoisie*, would it have maintained itself more than twenty-four hours? Are we not, on the contrary, justified in reproaching the commune for having employed this authority too little? (p. 20)

"As long as the proletariat still needs the State, it needs it not in the interests of freedom, but in order to suppress its opponents."

(Engels, quoted by Lenin in
The Proletarian Revolution and Kautsky the Renegade, p. 24)

Trotsky, for his part, has written a whole book to justify the necessity of the red terror, called *Defence of Terrorism*, from which we have taken the following:

"The man who repudiates terrorism in principle, i.e. repudiates measures of suppression and intimidation towards determined and and armed counter-revolution, *must reject all idea of the political supremacy of the working class and its revolutionary dictatorship.* The man who repudiates the dictatorship of the proletariat repudiates the Socialist revolution, and digs the grave of Socialism. . . . (pp. 23-24)

"The Red Terror is a weapon utilised against a class doomed to destruction, which does not wish to perish. If the White Terror can only retard the historical rise of the proletariat, the Red Terror hastens the destruction of the *bourgeoisie*. This hastening —a pure question of acceleration—is at certain periods of decisive importance. Without the Red Terror, the Russian *bourgeoisie*, together with the world *bourgeoisie*, would throttle us long before the coming of the revolution in Europe. One must be blind not to see this, or a swindler to deny it.

"The man who recognises the revolutionary historic importance of the very fact of the existence of the Soviet system must also sanction the Red Terror. . . . (pp. 60-61)

"Concerning the destruction of which the Commune is accused, and of which now the Soviet Government is accused, Marx speaks as of 'an inevitable and comparatively insignificant episode in the titanic struggle of the new-born order with the old in its collapse'. Destruction and cruelty are inevitable in any war. Only sycophants can consider them a crime 'in the war of the slaves against their oppressors, the only just war in history' (Marx)."

(L. Trotsky: *The Defence of Terrorism*, p. 89)

Let us not forget that Trotsky describes as sycophants those who were horrified by the crimes of genocide committed by the Soviets on their countrymen.

Finally, Neumann, under the *nom de plume* of Neuberg, wrote a thick book called *L'Insurrection armée* as a guide towards the practical application of revolutionary terrorism, a résumé of which was published in Leon de Poncin's: *Le Plan Communiste d'Insurrection armée*, 1939.

In 1927 Neumann, who was regarded as an expert in the art of insurrection, was sent to China by Moscow with Borodin and Galen (General Blücher), both of whom were Jewish, to organise the Communist uprisings in Shanghai and Canton.

It was put down in blood by Chiang Kai-shek, and most of the Communist leaders were executed. Only Mao Tse-tung and two or three of the present rulers of Communist China escaped the massacre and undertook the famous retreat of "the long march" in order to avoid falling into the hands of the troops pursuing them. Neumann, Borodin and Galen fled to Russia, and after this failure Neumann's name went down in history as the "Butcher of Canton". Later he took part as a Soviet delegate in the Spanish civil war, and finally all three disappeared and were executed by Stalin at the famous Moscow trial.

When the Soviet armies began to invade Eastern Germany in their march upon Berlin, the celebrated Jewish journalist Ilya Ehrenburg proclaimed to the winds:

" 'Kill! Kill! In the German race there is nothing but evil; not one among the living, not one among the yet unborn but is evil! Follow the precepts of Comrade Stalin. Stamp out the Fascist beast once and for all in its lair! Use force and break the racial pride of the Germanic women. Take them as your lawful booty. Kill! as you storm onwards kill, you gallant soldiers of the Red Army!' "
(Quoted by Admiral Doenitz in:
Memoirs, Forty Years and Twenty Days, p. 431)

They were not only the theorists of the Red Terror; they were the principal agents in carrying it out.

"Unfortunately, not only have men belonging to the Jewish race played a very large part both in the beginning and in the development of the Bolshevist Revolution, but they have also been the chief participators in some of the worst crimes of that Revolution. In the annals of terrorism there are four names which stand out in sinister isolation—Jankel Yourowski, the monster who shot down the twelve members of the Imperial family in the cellars of the Elpatinski House in Yekaterinburg, including the four young daughters of the Tsar; Moses Uritski, the first executioner-in-chief of the Tcheka; Bela Kun, the butcher of Budapest and of the Crimea; Djerdjinski, the present Inquisitor-General of

the Tcheka. Of those four names there is not one who is a Russian. One of the four is a Pole; the three others happen to be Jews."
(C. Sarolea, *Impressions of Soviet Russia*, pp. 160-1)

And Sarolea concluded with these prophetic words:

"We have simply to admit the fact that the Bolshevist Revolution has been largely engineered by men belonging to the Jewish race. We have to face the further fact that the deeds committed by those men have roused fierce vindictive passions in the hearts of the Russian people. . . . (p. 159)

"The Bolshevist fever will burn itself out; but the anti-Semitic passion will grow as Bolshevism decreases. Already signs of the coming storm are visible all over Central Europe. . . . What, then, must we not expect in Russia? For not only is the anti-Semitic passion infinitely greater in Russia than in any other country, but it also affects very much larger numbers."
(C. Sarolea, ibid., p. 166)

A *propos* of the Spanish revolution the documents published in the Official Report of the Portuguese Government to the Committee of Non-Intervention provide a vivid illustration of the Communist plan for armed insurrection, from which the following extract has been taken:

". . . In the session on the 27th February the Komintern paid special attention to the question of the 'bolshevisation' of Spain. This organisation sent to the Peninsular two technicians, both well-known revolutionaries, to direct the work of the Communists: Bela Kun and Losovski. They were given ample financial resources and ordered to achieve the Communist objectives. . . .

"The agitator Bela Kun and his comrades Losovski, Janson, Riedal Priamo (or Primakoff), Berzine and Neumann arrived at Barcelona in March and set to work without delay. . . .

"The sight of their work must fill the organisers of the Spanish revolution with satisfaction. Spain is a sea of blood. The immense wealth, the masterpieces which all the gold in the world could not reconstruct and the historical relics which formed a patrimony common to many countries have been sacrificed and lost for ever. A great number of some of the highest moral, artistic and intellectual achievements lie shrouded in the eternal silence of death.

"All parts of the programme drawn up some months ago by the Komintern have been carried out in the territory subject to the Government of Madrid. If they have not been put into execution throughout the country, it is because the national reaction did not permit it.

"Everything had been foreseen from a distance and executed methodically."

Finally, the heads of the Soviet régimes installed by Moscow in the satellite countries after the war were Jewish: Rakosi in Hungary, Anna Pauker in Roumania, Slansky in Czecho-Slovakia and Jacob Berman in Poland.

For, as Arthur Bliss Lane, the former United States Ambassador to Poland (1944-7), said:

". . . the growing anti-Semitism, even our Jewish sources admitted, was caused by the great unpopularity of the Jews in key government positions. These men included Minc, Berman, Olszewski (whose real name was said to be Specht), Radkiewicz and Spychalski. Our Jewish friends said that the Jews in Poland had little regard for the government and resented the implication that the Jews in it were representative of their people. I told the Department of State that, from the reports received, I believed there was bitter feeling within the militia against the Jews because the Security Police, controlled by Radkiewicz, dominated the militia and the Army, and a Russian general, Kiziewicz, dominated the Internal Security Police (K.B.W.). It was known, furthermore, that both the U.B. and the K.B.W. had, among their members, many Jews of Russian origin."

(A. B. Lane, U.S.A. Ambassador to Poland, 1944-7, in
I Saw Poland Betrayed, pp. 250-1)

Since then, in Russia as in the satellite countries, they have been progressively eliminated from positions of control to be replaced by Russians and natives.

But before their eviction the chiefs of the terrible secret police were often of Jewish origin. The Jewish writer Fejtö, a convert of Hungarian origin, says in his excellent work, *Les Juifs et l'Antisémitisme dans les Pays communistes*:

"The highest placed amongst the Polish Communist Jews serving the Terror was Jacob Berman. . . . (p. 71)

and speaking of Hungary he tells us:

"Between 1945 and 1948 . . . the population did not seem to pay much attention to the fact that the higher ranks in the (Hungarian) régime were mainly composed of Jews (Rakosi, Gero, Revai, Vas, Antal Apro, George Lukacs, and others . . .). The country only became aware of this fact after 1948, at which date Communism changed its appearance and became increasingly sectarian and oppressive in its police measures. Several notorious agents of this oppression, notably Gabor Peter, the Hungarian 'Beria', Mihaly Farkas, Minister of Defence, and his son Wladimir, who was the foremost torturer of the political police, were likewise of Jewish origin. A good many Hungarian Jews already foresaw with terror that the people, enraged by the régime of penury and oppression which the popular democracy had become, would rise up against their tormentors. Once again, as in 1919 after the fall of Bela Kuhn, the Jews seemed predestined to pay the cost of a régime of which some of them appeared to be the principal beneficiaries." (p. 93)

During the present century there have been a number of world shattering political crimes in which men of Jewish race have been the principle instigators. The following are some of the best known cases:

Between 1905 and 1917 in Russia there was a continuous series of violent political crimes to which some of the highest dignitaries of the Czarist régime fell victim including the Czar's uncle, the Grand Duke Sergius, the Prime Minister Plehve, Stolypine and others. The two most prominent leaders of the terrorist organisations responsible for these murders were the Jewish revolutionaries, Guershouni and Azef in collaboration with Silberberg, Max Schweitzer and Routenberg. In 1907 a bomb was thrown at the State Bank in Tiflis killing a number of Cossack Guards, and a considerable quantity of money was stolen for the purpose of financing the Bolshevik agents. The following year, one of the principle organisers, Meyer Genoch Moisevitch Wallach, alias Finkelstein was arrested in Paris charged with being concerned in the theft of 250,000 roubles from the Tiflis Bank. He was deported from France and came to England where he lived under the aliases of Buchmann and Harrison, and on the outbreak of the First World War he was active in stopping recruiting among the Jews of the East End of London. With the assistance of two other Jewish revolutionaries from Moscow, Holtzmann and Fineberg he was concerned with the circulation of seditious literature on behalf of Germany. After the Bolshevik revolution in 1917 he subsequently became Soviet Ambassador to the Court of St. James in London, assuming the name of Maxim Litvinoff. Later he became President of the Council of the League of Nations.

The assassination, after the war of Count Stephen Tiza, Prime Minister of Hungary was at the instigation of three Jewish terrorists, Keri, Fenyes and Pogany.

Count Stürgkh, Prime Minister of Austria was murdered by the Socialist Jew Adler, son of the leader of the Austrian Socialist Democratic Party.

Hetman Petlioura was assassinated in Paris by the Jewish Communist Schwartzbart.

In 1938, the German diplomat, von Rath was assassinated in Paris by the young Jew Grynspan.

The British High Commissioner in Cairo, Lord Moyne was assassinated by Jewish terrorists.

The dynamite outrage on the King David Hotel in Jerusalem which killed a great many British officers was undertaken by a Jewish underground movement.

Both Count Bernadotte of Sweden, plenipotentiary of the United Nations and Colonel Sérot of France fell victim to Jewish assassins.

Finally, of recent years there was the murder of Lee Oswald, the assassin of President Kennedy by Jack Rubinstein.

Who sows the wind reaps a whirlwind. When you unleash revolutionary terror on the world it is not surprising if you fall victim to it yourself one day. It is the innate justice of history.

When terrorism is exerted in the revolutionary sense, described in school text books as "the sense of history", and when it is directed by Jews, it is a social experience "broad, human and generous", despite the millions of deaths it involves.

When revolutionary violence turns against its instigators and the victims are Jewish, then it becomes a "morbid cancer of civilisation", a "sadistic form of anti-Jewish hatred" and a "retrogression by humanity towards the dark ages of medieval obscurantism". The Jews become the innocent victims of anti-Semite barbarity and the martyrs of humanity.

II

ETERNAL ANTAGONISM

THE irreducible antagonism with which Judaism has opposed Christianity for 2,000 years is the key and mainspring of modern subversion—a position which, as we have attempted to show by quotations from learned and respected Jewish doctors and scholars, far from being preposterous, as it may at first appear, is quite understandable when one grasps that it flows naturally from the Judaic mind and spirit. For, as Darmesteter tells us, "the Jew championed reason against the mythical world of the spirit . . . during the intellectual night of the Middle Ages . . . and he understood as nobody else did how to find the vulnerable points in its doctrine. . . . He was the doctor of unbelief." (Quoted by A. Spire in *Quelques Juifs*, p. 233)

The advent of Christ was a national catastrophe for the Jewish people, especially for its leaders. Until then they, and they alone, had been the Sons of the Covenant; they had been its sole high-priests and beneficiaries.

The powerful empires which surrounded them either ignored or treated with scorn the obscure, rather sparsely populated nation of Israel.

In his *Genèse de L'Antisémitisme*, Jules Isaac describes what the Greeks and Romans thought about Israel.

After a time:

"The Greek world became more heedful of the Israelite nation, which it had hitherto regarded as insignificant . . . a singular, incomprehensible people, lacking everything which, in the eyes of the Greeks, gave human life meaning, light and beauty; lacking any visible civilisation or works of art; fanatically pious, but in an obscure faith whose abstract gods could not be formed by the sculptor's chisel and worshipped as images. And yet this nonentity of a people laid claim to everything: it stood up to radiant Hellas; more than that, it dared to preach to the latter, to set itself up as the master of prayer and the Chosen of the Divinity. What astounding incongruity and exasperating folly. The anti-Judaism engendered in certain Greek circles was primarily a reaction against claims that were considered intolerable and outrageous, a reflex of injured self-esteem, complicated by mistrust, ignorance and misunderstanding. It was destined to spread throughout the whole length and breadth of that world which had been more or less brought under the sway of the hellenes; but originally and essentially it was only one aspect of the violent antagonism which had just arisen in Palestine between the Judeans and Greeks, a mutual war of extermination, as Father Lagrange has said, which was to extend far beyond the borders of Palestine, to fester and subsequently break out into new and bloody conflicts, in which massacrers and massacred changed sides frequently, as the strongest side prevailed, and each opponent strained his utmost to mount a fresh pogrom." (p. 70)

The Romans adopted the same attitude:

"It was an unheard of thing to them that the pax Romana, Roman order and the imperial religion which was its symbol, should be disputed and shaken by a breed of indecent, superstitious Oriental agitators.

" 'The quarrel redoubled its fury, solely because the Judeans would not give up the fight,' wrote Tacitus. The scoundrels.

"This righteous anger surges throughout Tacitus." (pp. 120-1)

But Israel attached no importance to what the pagans might think or say. It did not feel it was being interfered with because the criticism came from outside. It touched neither Israel's interior cohesion, nor its immeasurable pride, nor its unshakeable belief in an imperial future:

"The little people of Israel, such as the prophets conceived of it, became the navel of the world. Jahve, its god, brought about every event, whether good or bad, and all were related to him. Israel became the centre of the universe and the centre of history. Nothing has existed, nothing does exist and nothing will exist except in terms of its own destiny. This view of prophetic mysticism, so naïve in its vanity and so proud, leads to a veritable religious imperialism. According to the prophets, Israel, by the grace of Jahve, its god, is destined to govern the world; when the people of the servants of Jahve conform to the divine ordinances, the time will come when Israel shall reign over all the earth." (G. Batault: *Le Problème Juif*, pp. 69-70)

But suddenly there arose up among them a prophet—man or God —who was indeed the son of the royal race of David, and also the son of the Covenant, heir to the Promise. He claimed that he had been sent from above by God his Father, to carry out and complete the promise of the Covenant. "I am not come to destroy the Law, but to fulfil it." (Matthew v. 17). And in proof of his mission he performed a number of unheard of wonders; the multitudes, subdued, followed him.

But—and this is the most serious point about his mission—he interpreted the Promise in a new and entirely different sense, which threatened to overturn and destroy the whole proud Judaic edifice, by rendering it spiritual and universal.

The realisation of the Promise was transferred from the material to the spiritual level; it overflowed beyond national limits and was no longer reserved to the Jews as its sole beneficiaries, but extended to include the whole world.

> "The idea of a celestial fatherland common to all souls replaced that of Jerusalem of the Jews; it no longer conceived of the flowering of one race nor of the triumph of one nation, for the chosen people was lowered to the level of just one among the peoples. This was something to which neither the pride nor the religious nationalism of the Jews could consent, it was contrary to the Law and the Prophets, and contrary to the messianic promises. The time was to come when the kingdoms would submit to Israel."
>
> (G. Batault, ibid., p. 91)

The chief-priests and the pharisees, unable to tolerate such a blasphemy and infringement of their privileges, delivered the dangerous agitator to the Romans, in order to be rid of him, and had him put to death.

But Christ rose from the dead and his teaching spread like a train of powder across the ancient world. His disciples were denounced to the Roman authorities as rebels against the emperor, and they were pursued, fed to the beasts, tormented and crucified. However, the flood rose unceasing, penetrated the higher spheres of Imperial power, and suddenly the world swung in favour of the Church of Christ:

> "On 28th October A.D. 312, the battle of Milvian Bridge took place. Constantine was victorious against Maxentius, who was believed to have drowned in the waters of the Tiber.
>
> "One battle sufficed to change the face of the world and its religious countenance. . . .
>
> "Constantine's victory is rightly considered as the starting-point of a new era, that of the Christian empire. It is true that its immediate result seems to have been the establishment of the

liberty and equality of creeds (313). . . . Thenceforward, for reasons which have not been completely clarified, the victorious Constantine united his destiny with the Church of Christ, and the latter had won the game. The Church conquered and retained imperial favour, it took a privileged position within the State, and began to move towards even greater and more perilous heights, where the Church was closely linked with the State and became, in other words, a State Church. A great and a surprising revolution, deplored by some and praised by others, one of the most important revolutions in History, to which the reign of Constantine was only a prelude, since it reached its completion in the extraordinary and chaotic fourth century. But the unheard of success of the Church was to bring in its wake the misfortune of the Synagogue, for which the fourth century was a fatal epoch, marking the commencement of a future of anguish, sorrow and catastrophes."

(Jules Isaac: *Genèse de l'Antisémitisme*, pp. 155-6)

The Jews did not then, and they do not now, accept this defeat. The rupture between Judaism and Christianity is total. The position is one of mutual, unyielding antagonism. It could hardly be stated more clearly than in the following remarkable passage from the Jewish convert, Fejtö:

"If the Jew is right, Christianity is only an illusion.

"If Christianity is right, the Jew is, in the most favourable hypothesis, an anachronism—the image of something which ought no longer to exist.

"Christianity, for the Jew, means the renunciation of a monopoly and of a 'nationalist' if not to say racialist interpretation of 'the election'; it means opening oneself to human fraternisation and at the same time a great 'amen' to God and all that God decides; it means accepting suffering and death, and it means renouncing one's pride, one's love and one's distrust of Self.

"I know of no other people that has been submitted to such a difficult trial by Christianity.

"Since for no other people has the change to Christianity signified, in the short or long run, the disappearance of the people itself as such. No other peoples' religious traditions, which faith in Christ demanded they should abandon, were so intimately connected with all the conditions of their civil existence.

"For the other peoples of the Roman empire, religion was in effect a 'superstructure' or an embellishment. It could be replaced without shaking the edifice. But for the Jew, religion was the infrastructure, the *raison d'être*, the base of his being. But the apostles invited them to sell all their goods, for Heaven was at hand and the gates beyond were wide open. The Jew said: no, it is not true, it cannot be true that God wants me to do this. Prove it to me.

"And it is at that point that we reach the other reason (or pretext) which justifies the Jew saying 'no' to Christ—that he did not correspond to the idea—whether true or false—which the Jew had developed of the Messiah, and of his own salvation."

(F. Fejtö: *Dieu et Son Juif*, pp. 34, 190-2)

"By claiming to be the true 'Israel'—Israel according to the 'spirit' and not according to the 'contemptible' flesh—Christian theology intends to permanently replace Israel. Unfortunately, Israel has not disappeared and does not want to do so."

(J. Jehouda: *L'Antisémitisme, Miroir du Monde*, p. 50)

The irremediable difference is to do with Jesus:

"If we take it that he did exist in history, for the Jew he was neither God nor the son of God. The most extreme concession the Jew can possibly make was expressed by Joseph Klauzner, according to whom Jesus, whom he said was neither the Messiah, nor a Prophet, nor a lawgiver, nor the founder of a religion, nor tanna, nor rabbi, nor pharisee, 'is considered as a great moralist and artist in the use of parables by the Jewish nation . . . the day when he is cleared of the stories of his miracles and mysticism, the Book of the Morality of Jesus will become one of the most precious jewels of Jewish literature of all time'.

"*Christianity is essentially preoccupied with the individual salvation of man. Judaism only contemplates the salvation of the House of Israel, which alone can permit the salvation of the seventy nations of the universe. For centuries this has been the constant objective of the talmudists and cabbalists.* They have one fundamental aim: to maintain one community on which the salvation of the whole world depends. Only by virtue of his rite is the Jew allowed to integrate with his community."

(Rabi: *Anatomie du Judaisme français*, pp. 203-204)

"The steps by which the Christian faith conquered its independence were to lead it rapidly and inevitably into a merciless war against Israel 'according to the flesh', the new Church proclaiming itself the true Israel of God and the only Israel 'according to the spirit'. But was the gravity of such a claim fully realised? It amounted to something much worse than a slander on the Jewish people; it was an attempt to make away with its spark of life, with its sacred fire, one could even say with its soul; and even more—so closely are the spiritual and temporal elements linked to each other—it was an attempt to make away with its place in the sun, with its privileged status in the Empire."

(J. Isaac, *Genèse de l'Antisémitisme*, p. 150)

Christianity was on the ascendance for fifteen centuries, and throughout the whole of the medieval period Judaism was powerless to influence the destinies of nations. Profiting from the tolerance of the authorities and from the protection of the Popes, it could only live on, waiting for an opportunity to penetrate the monolithic Christian structure from within. It looks upon this period as one of dark obscurantism and barbarity, for Israel tends to judge the world in relation to itself, itself being the salt of the earth and the measure of all things.

Then, with the Renaissance and the Reformation, the unity of the Faith was broken. Judaism advanced through the breach which had thus been opened and thenceforward threw its weight behind every movement which weakened and unsettled Christianity—the Renaissance, the Reformation, the Revolution of 1789 and Marxism.

Throughout the whole of this period, Darmesteter tells us:

"The Jew championed reason against the mythical world of the spirit. It was with him that thought took refuge during the intellectual night of the Middle Ages. Provoked by the Church, which sought to persuade him, having in vain attempted to convert him by force, he undermined it by the irony and intelligence of his arguments, and he understood as nobody else did how to find the vulnerable points in its doctrine. He had at his disposal in this search, apart from the wisdom of the sacred scriptures, the redoubtable wisdom of the oppressed. *He was the doctor of unbelief; all who were mentally in revolt came to him, either secretly or in broad daylight. He was at work in the vast laboratory of blasphemy under the great emperor Frederick and the princes of Swabia and Aragon. It was he who forged all that deadly arsenal of reasoning and irony which he bequeathed to the sceptics of the Renaissance and the libertines of the grand siècle* (the reign of Louis XIV); Voltaire's sarcasm, for example, was nothing more than the resounding echo of a word murmured six centuries previously in the shadow of the ghetto, and even earlier (in the Counter-Evangelists of the first and second centuries) at the time of Celsus and Origen at the very cradle of the Christian religion."

(Quoted by A. Spire in *Quelques Juifs*, p. 233)

Bernard Lazare, for his part, depicts Jewish anti-Christian action in the eighteenth century:

"In like manner we would have to inquire what was the importance, I will not say of the Jew, but of the Jewish spirit throughout the period of fierce revolt against Christianity which characterised the eighteenth century. We must not forget that in the seventeenth century, scholars like Wagenseil, Bartolocci, Buxtorf and Wolf, had brought forth from oblivion old volumes of Hebrew polemic, written in refutation of the Trinity and Incarnation and attacking all dogmas and forms of Christianity with a bitterness entirely Judaic, and with all the subtlety of those peerless casuists who created the Talmud. They gave to the world not only treatises on questions of doctrine and exegesis, like the *Nizzachon* or the *Chizuk Emunah*, but published blasphemous tractates and pseudo-lives of Jesus, of the character of the *Toldoth Jesho*. The eighteenth century repeated, concerning Jesus and the Virgin, the outrageous fables invented by the Pharisees of the second century; we find them in Voltaire and in Parny, and their rationalist satire, pellucid and mordant, lives again in Heine, in Boerne and in Disraeli; just as the powerful logic of the ancient rabbis lives again in Karl Marx, and the passionate thirst for liberty of the ancient Hebrew rebels breathes forth again in the glowing soul of Ferdinand Lassalle." (B. Lazare: *Anti-Semitism*, pp. 306-307)

According to Jehouda:

"The Renaissance, the Reformation and the Revolution (of 1789) constitute three attempts to rectify Christian mentality by bringing it into tune with the progressive development of reason and science.

"As dogmatic theology began to yield its oppressive control over man's conscience, the Jews began to breathe more freely.... The three breaches opened in the decrepid fortress of Christian obscurantism extend over roughly five centuries, in the course of which the Jews were still considered as the pariahs of history....

"If the Jews were still removed from all the intellectual and social activity of the Christian peoples, nevertheless, despite the ostracism to which they were subjected, their thought played a preponderant though unacknowledged role in the Renaissance, the Reformation and the Revolution, which are all indirectly stamped with its mark . . . and it is certainly not by chance that these attempts (to rectify Christian mentality) were inspired by the assiduous study of Jewish sources at a time when the Jews were still looked upon with suspicion and mistrust."

(J. Jehouda: *L'Antisémitisme, Miroir du Monde*, pp. 161-2)

Jehouda gives us concrete examples of the part played by Jewish proselytizers such as Pico de Mirandola and John Reuchlin in this transformation of Christianity.

Pico de Mirandola, who died in Florence in 1494, was a hebraiser who devoted himself to studying the Cabbala under the direction of Jewish masters such as Jehuda Abravanel:

"It was in the princely house of Pico de Mirandola that the Jewish scholars used to meet. . . . The discovery of the Jewish Cabbala, which he imparted to various enlightened Christians contributed far more than the return to Greek sources to the extraordinary spiritual blossoming which is known as the Renaissance. About half a century later, the rehabilitation of the Talmud was to lead to the Reformation . . . Pico de Mirandola had understood that the indispensable purification of Christian dogma could only be effected after a profound study of the authentic Jewish Cabbala. . . .
(Joshua Jehouda, ibid., p. 164)

"With the Reformation, which broke out in Germany fifty years after the Renaissance, the universality of the Church was destroyed. A new age began. The Renaissance had not succeeded in purifying Christian dogma, and the Reformation finished by complicating even more 'the problem' of Christianity, evident though it was. It may be summarised as a question of how to overcome its fundamental dualism, the contradictory two-fold origin in Jerusalem and Athens to which Rome succeeded. It is indeed a well-known fact that the Reformation was achieved by Luther (1483-1546), Calvin (1509-64) and Zwingli (1484-1531), but it is not so well-known that previously John Reuchlin (1455-1531), Pico de Mirandola's disciple, shook the Christian conscience by suggesting as early as 1494 'that there was nothing higher than hebraic wisdom'. And when in 1509 a renegade Jew, Joseph Pfefferkorn, had the Talmud seized and finally obtained, after several previous attempts, the definite condemnation of this collective compendium which contains a thousand years of Jewish wisdom, John Reuchlin did not shrink from exposing himself to every menace and danger in order to defend before the Emperor and the Pope the extraordinary value of the Talmud, whose veritable meaning he had fathomed.

"Reuchlin advocated returning to Jewish sources as well as to ancient texts. Finally, he won his case against the convert Pfefferkorn, who loudly demanded the destruction of the Talmud. 'The new spirit which was to revolutionise the whole of Europe became apparent with regard to the Jews and the Talmud', wrote the historian Graetz. However, the Reformation, which made known the bare text of the Bible, proved even more incapable than the Renaissance of purifying Christianity of its congenital anti-Semitism. One is astonished to find that there were as many Protestant as Catholic anti-Semites. The Reformation, finding itself in an intellectual impasse, adopted the principle of fideism, thus excluding all possibility of it reasoning its faith. . . .

"The Reformation itself submitted to the irresistible attraction of the 'Greek miracle', which splits thought by separating it from faith and by adopting, albeit it imperceptibly, the pagan laicism which prepares the ground for atheism. The French Revolution marked the beginning of atheism in the history of Christian peoples and, declaredly anti-religious, it continues, through the influence of Russian Communism, to make a powerful contribution to the dechristianisation of the Christian world. . . .

"The third attempt to amend the Christian position, after the failure of reformed Christianity to unite, took place under the impetus of the French Revolution.

"Although the French Revolution and the Russian Revolution which followed it liberated the Jew in the social and political fields, they both hold the monotheistic religion of Israel in the same contempt as Christian theology. . . .

"Laicism, to which the Revolution gave birth, confers on the Jew his dignity as a man, but Christian theology has not yet abolished its spiritual contempt for him. This accounts for the twofold attitude of the modern world with regard to the Jew and for the successive outbursts of anti-Semitism. . . .

"Thus anti-Semitism, the foot-and-mouth-disease of Christianity, is still rebellious even after the three attempts to purify Christian dogma. But, notwithstanding all the successive purgings, Christianity remains firmly fastened to its mythical dogmatism which inevitably engenders anti-Semitism. The affirmation that Christianity holds out to Judaism the last phase of its spiritual future must in the end be completely rethought from top to bottom in the interests of Christianity itself, and thus of western civilisation. . . . (Joshua Jehouda, ibid., pp. 169, 170, 172-4)

"Whoever looks deep into the meaning of universal history, in order to see it as a whole, discovers that from antiquity until the present day it has been penetrated and fashioned unceasingly by two contrary currents, known under various names: messianism and anti-Semitism. . . .

"But the profound meaning of history, which remains unaltered in every epoch, is that of a veiled or open struggle between the forces working for the advancement of humanity and those that cling to coagulated interests, obstinately determined to keep them in existence to the detriment of what is to come.

"For messianism and anti-Semitism constitute the two opposite poles of the progress of humanity. Anti-semitism is the negative pole of messianism. . . ." (Joshua Jehouda, ibid., p. 186)

Today the attack is renewed under the banner of ecumenism and the war is being carried into the very interior of the Church itself. Supported by progressive parties, the spiritual leaders of World Jewry are asking for a reconsideration of the Church's traditional doctrine on Judaism, as we showed in the first three chapters of this work.

We are told that reconciliation is possible and desirable. We are the first to agree that it is desirable, but it is far more difficult to defend the proposition that it is possible. For people of the Jewish faith, steeped in the Talmud, reconciliation, as we have demonstrated, means nothing less than the abandonment by Christianity in its entirety of everything that constitutes the essence of its doctrine, and its integral return to Judaism, which for its part intends to yield nothing, and firmly maintains its position of intransigence.

All the Jewish thinkers, the rabbis and the leaders of Judaism are unanimous on this point. Hear what Andre Spire has to say, speaking about Darmesteter:

"Beyond every confession, above every dogma, he (the Jew) has remained anchored to the spirit of the Scriptures. By an original twist of thought, he incorporates the most attractive features of Christianity into Judaism and, leading the Church back to the synagogue, reconciles the mother with her daughter in an ideal Jerusalem. But it is the daughter, as one would expect, who recognises her wrongs and confesses her errors."

(A. Spire, *Quelques Juifs*, p. 255)

Joshua Jehouda writes:

"A modern prophet once exclaimed: 'Shame and curse on you Christian peoples if you obstinately persist in stifling the monotheistic tradition of Israel. For without the renewal of monotheistic messianism there is no hope of salvation for you and the rest of the world.'"

(J. Jehouda: Antisémitisme, Miroir du Monde, p. 349)

Rabi makes the following comment:

> "It is not the cross which will repair the schism between the Jewish people and the rest of the nations, as Lovsky believes. It will only become possible when the world truly accepts the Jewish idea of common filiation. Man need seek no other moral and history no other end."
>
> (Rabi: *Anatomie du Judaisme français*, p. 186)

Elie Benamozegh, one of the most eminent Jewish thinkers, who is known as "the Plato of Italian Judaism", wrote an important introduction to his work *Israel et l'Humanité* which perfectly summarises Jewish thought on this subject, of which we give a brief account here.

After describing the religious crisis in the world, Elie Benamozegh thinks that the only way to resolve it is by reaching religious unity and he examines the conditions under which agreement should be reached.

In the view of this rabbi, a fervent cabbalist, the religion of the future could not be rationalism, which, issuing solely from the human mind, only clings to intelligible and changing things. For religion, the act of adoration and worship of the Absolute, surpasses our senses and faculties and implies a truth founded upon Revelation.

Only the religions that have sprung from the Bible and tradition, only Judaism, Christianity and Islam fulfill these conditions.

But among them, Judaism occupies a pre-eminent position. The first-born of the children of God, the guardian of messianism, it is to Israel that the priestly function belongs by right in the great family of the nations, for in antiquity the first-born:

> ". . . was the priest of the family who carried out the orders of his father and took his place in his absence. The sacred things were in his charge, he officiated for the family, he taught them, he gave them his blessing. In recognition of his services, he was given a double share of the paternal inheritance and the consecration or imposition of hands. . . . Such was the Jewish conception of the world. In heaven, one sole God the father of all men, and on earth one family of peoples among whom Israel is the first-born, charged with the priestly function of teaching and administering the true religion of humanity."
>
> (E. Benamozegh: *Israel et l'Humanité*, p. 40)

Thus Judaism is to become the religion of the human race and the Jewish conception of the world is to prevail over every other.

Christianity, issued from Hebraism, is to return to the older and more authentically divine tradition which formed it, in spite of its own venerable and antique tradition. The excessive number of Christian sects, its errors and discords and the obscurity of its dogmas, no longer corresponds to the needs of modern times. In order to continue to exist, it must reform its defects by accepting the ideal that Judaism is based on man and on society and by returning to the primitive faith in God and in his revelation. On this condition, it will preserve its messianic character, it will unite with Judaism in order to secure the religious future of humanity, and it will remain the religion of the Gentiles:

> "The reconciliation dreamt of by the early Christians as a condition of the Parousia, or the final coming of Jesus, the return of the Jews to the bosom of the Church, without which, as all the Christian communions agree, the work of Redemption is incomplete, this return we say will take place not in truth as it is expected to happen, but in the only genuine, logical and lasting fashion possible, and above all in the only way in which it will benefit the human race. It will be a reunion between the Hebrew religion and the others that have sprung from it and . . . 'the return of the children's heart to their fathers'."
> (E. Benamozegh, ibid., p. 48)

The defence of the traditional Christian standpoint penned in answer to these criticisms, with which we conclude this chapter, is taken from *Le Malheur d'Israel* by the Jewish writer, Dr. Roudinesco:

> "The persistence to our day of this small community in the face of unheard of persecution and suffering has been described as a Jewish miracle. Their survival is not a miracle; at best it may be called a misfortune. The veritable Jewish miracle is the spiritual conquest of humanity by Christianity. The mission of the chosen people has long since terminated. Those of the Jews who hope to complete Christianity one day by a renewed messianism ignore the fundamental laws of the evolution of humanity."
> (pp. 197-8)

12

"PORTRAIT OF A JEW"

IN 1962 a Jewish writer from Tunis, A. Memmi, who had been living for many years in France, published a book called *Portrait of a Jew*.

This work is highly instructive for it does in effect present us with a portrait depicting, with the utmost clarity, the profound reactions of a Jew confronted with the old Christian civilisation of a nation such as France, a reaction which is typical not of France alone but of every Christian country.

Memmi's discomfort and apprehension as soon as it is a question of anything to do with France's past history is conspicuous in the following passages, which in a remarkable way confirm and summarise the points we have been making in the previous chapters of Part II of this work.

> "No Gauls, please. Enough of Celts, ancient Romans and conquering Arabs! For then, I find myself naked and alone: my own ancestors were neither Gauls, Celts, Slavs, ancient Romans, Arabs, or Turks. . . .
>
> "I have never been able to say 'We' in referring to those historical pedigrees on which my fellow-citizens pride themselves. I have never heard another Jew say 'We' without wincing, without vaguely suspecting him of an inadvertent blunder, of complacency or of a slip of the tongue."
>
> (A. Memmi: *Portrait of a Jew*, p. 199)

Thus there is racial and national antagonism between the Jews and the nations, but, deeper still, there is religious antagonism:

> "When, several years ago, I left Tunisia to come to France, I knew that I was leaving a Moslem country, but I did not understand that I was going to a Catholic country. A few weeks were enough to impress that fact on me. . . .
>
> "I quickly discovered that French reality is an inextricable mixture of liberalism and Catholicism, clericalism and anti-cleri-

calism at the same time . . . but the common Christian background is everywhere—sometimes more or less buried, other times more or less obvious. . . .

"France remains a profoundly Catholic country just as America is a Protestant country. . . .

"When I travel in the interior of this country, what do they show me with righteous pride? What do I ask myself spontaneously to see because I know that they are worth seeing, if not churches, chapels, baptisteries, statues of Virgins, objects of worship and very few other things. I have verified the accuracy of those descriptions by orthodox writers: the villages are crowded around their churches, around bell-towers that can be seen from afar and that really do seem to protect them.

"Is this only so in France? By no means. I was stunned, outraged, and then wryly amused, when I read in the Italian newspapers the solemn declaration of Togliatti, leader of the Italian Communists, encouraging and blessing 'the Communist communicants'. I am well aware that it was only a matter of *strategy*: but if there must be strategy, there is a reality to evade. Now the reality of the Italian people is profoundly Catholic, like Polish reality, Spanish reality, etc.

"My religious situation is the result not so much of the degree of my profound religion, but of the fact that I do not belong to the religion of the men among whom I live, that I am a Jew among non-Jews. And this also means that my children, my relatives, my friends frequently find themselves in the same situation. I am always in a certain way outside of the religious world, the culture and the society to which I otherwise belong.

"The law of Christian countries is a law of thinly disguised and often proclaimed Christian inspiration; the law of Moslem countries is a Moslem law, taken for granted and openly acknowledged. . . .

"The religion of non-Jews is, in fact, everywhere—on the street as in institutions, in shop-windows and newspapers, in monuments, in conversations, in the very air itself: art, morals and philosophy are as Christian as law and geography. The philosophic tradition taught in the schools, the great motifs of painting and sculpture, are as impregnated with Christianity as are the laws of marriage and divorce. When I was on the Riviera last year I amused myself noting the villages that bear the names of saints: St. Tropez, St. Maxime, St. Raphael, St. Aygulf. Their number is astonishing. It is the same, for that matter, in the stations of the Paris Metro. My first irritation against Paris, a city I love so dearly in other respects, had a religious basis, if I remember correctly. Working for part of the day on a miserable job, I used to stay up late at night to get ahead in my studies. Every morning I was awakened—and to my exasperation several times in succession—by bells ringing at full peal, continuing at great length, pausing, and then returning to the charge just as I was dozing off again! True, I was living in a small hotel a few steps away from a church but in this city you are always two steps away from a church . . . those bells summoned men to duties they shared with other men and were a symbol of their origin; at the same time, for me they sounded the signal of my exclusion from that community. I was in a Catholic country; everyone must find those matin bells normal and perhaps pleasant—except me and those like me who were embarrassed and annoyed. A hopeless rebellion, however: the non-Jews, who were not annoyed, nor perhaps even awakened, represented numbers and power. Whatever concerns them, whatever they approve of, is lawful. Those bells are merely the familiar echo of their common soul. . . .

(A. Memmi, ibid., pp. 184-8)

"Do Christians realise what the name of Jesus, their God, can mean to a Jew? For a Christian, even an atheist, it evokes, or at least has evoked at some time, a being infinitely good, who offers himself as The Good, who desires at least to carry on the torch of all bygone philosophies and all morals. For the Christian who is still a believer, Jesus epitomises and fulfils the better part of himself. The Christian who has ceased to believe no longer takes that ideal seriously; he may even resent it, accuse the priests of incompetency or even of deception; but though he denounces it as an illusion he generally leaves no doubt as to the grandeur and beauty of that illusion. *To the Jew who still believes and professes his own religion, Christianity is the greatest theological and metaphysical usurpation in history; it is a spiritual scandal, a subversion and blasphemy.* To all Jews, even if they are atheists, the name of Jesus is the symbol of a threat, of that great threat that has hung over their heads for centuries and which may, any moment, burst forth in catastrophes of which they know neither the cause nor the prevention. That name is part of the accusation, absurd and frenzied, but so efficiently cruel, that makes social life barely liveable. That name has, in fact, come to be one of the signs, one of the names of the immense apparatus that surrounds the Jew, condemns him and excludes him. I hope my Christian friends will forgive me. That they may better understand, let me say that *to the Jews, their God is, in a way, the Devil, if, as they say, the Devil is the symbol and essence of all evil on earth, iniquitous and all-powerful, incomprehensible and bent on crushing helpless human beings.*

"One day in Tunis, an idiot Jew (we always had a certain number of them who haunted cemeteries and community gatherings) seeing a Christian funeral pass, was suddenly seized with an uncontrollable rage. Knife in hand, he flung himself on the funeral procession which scattered terror-stricken in all directions. But the idiot, paying no attention to the crowd screaming in terror, rushed straight at the acolyte . . . grabbed the cross out of his hands, flung it on the ground and trampled it furiously.

"I did not understand his action until later. Anxiety expresses itself as best it can; the idiot reacted in his own way to our common malaise before that world of crosses, priests and churches, those concentrated symbols of hostility, the strangeness of the world that surrounds us the moment we leave the narrow confines of the ghetto. . . ."   (A. Memmi, ibid., pp. 188-9)

"I am now convinced that the history of peoples, their collective experience, is a religious history; that it is not only marked by religion, but lived and expressed through religion. It was one of our greatest and most disastrous *naïvetés* to have believed, like our Leftists, in the end of religions. It was a great mistake, in our efforts to understand the past of nations, to try to minimise the part religion played. There was no need either to rejoice in it or to deplore it, only to note its extraordinary importance and to take it into account. . . ."   (A. Memmi, ibid., p. 190)

"During the Christmas week, scientific and political speeches on the radio and television all begin with the invocation: 'In these days when the hearts of all men are as a little child's. . . .' All men? Not mine certainly; I do not belong in that communion. One of General de Gaulle's first gestures on assuming power was an address to the Pope in which he asked him to bless France and the French. *Is the Jew a part of that France? If so, how would he like to have his country blessed by the Pope, and himself included in it?* In reality, the head of state acts as if the Jew did not exist. And it is true that he scarcely counts, that he dare not even count himself: otherwise why would he permit the chief of state, his representative, to appeal to the Church in his name? The Papal nuncio is the doyen of the diplomatic corps: by what right if not by an admitted pre-eminence of the Catholic religion, which is not his? . . .

"I realise, even as I am saying this, how unconvincing, how

ridiculous my rebellion may seem and how exorbitant my demand. Would I pretend to impose my law on the majority? Is it not normal for a nation to live according to the desires, customs and myths of the greatest number of its citizens? Perfectly normal, I admit immediately. I scarcely see how it could live otherwise...."
(A. Memmi, ibid., pp. 191-2)

"What is not normal in all this is my life, different for that reason, in the bosom of the nation. The Jew is the one who does not belong to the religion of the others. I merely wish to draw attention to the difference and those consequences I have experienced, and which are not part of that normality. It is clear that I must live a religion that is not mine, a religion that regulates and sets the rhythm for all collective life. I must take a holiday at Easter and not at Passover. Do not tell me that many non-Jewish citizens also condemn this contamination. Theirs is merely a theoretical condemnation: their daily life is ordered by the common religion, which is at least their own religion and does not tear them to pieces. 'The trouble with you', said one of my non-Jewish friends, half seriously, 'is that you have never been a Christian....'"
(A. Memmi, ibid., p. 193)

"I have written elsewhere that as adolescents and later as young men we refused to take seriously the persistence of nations. *We lived in enthusiastic expectation of a new age, such as the world had never known before, signs of which we thought we could already detect—the death (which had certainly begun) of religions, families and nations. We had nothing but anger, scorn and irony for the die-hards of history who clung to those residues.* Today I see more clearly why we expanded so much energy on cultivating those hopes. Certainly the impatient and generous nature of adolescents which drives them to free themselves, and the whole world, of all shackles, is particularly suited to revolutionary ideologies. But, in addition, we were Jews. I am convinced that this had much to do with the vigour of our choice. Beyond our desire to be accepted by the families, religions and nations of non-Jews who rejected and isolated us because we were Jews, we longed to be one with all men and so, at last, become men like others.

"Unfortunately, whether we were deluding ourselves, whether we may have relapsed since then into a period of regression, or whether it is simply that I have grown older, *I have to admit that those residues were as stubborn as weeds and persisted in remaining fundamental structures in the lives of nations*, essential aspects of their collective being. The post-war period saw an indisputable religious revival which swept the orthodox parties to power throughout Europe. Because they understood that situation, the Communists, who keep their fingers on the pulse of nations, extolled the 'Catholic communicants', offered their 'outstretched hands' to Christians and called themselves patriots and nationalists. The Socialists did not even need to resort to trickery. . .

"To all appearances we were doomed to religions and nations and for a long time. Once again I am not passing judgment, I am simply stating facts.

"What was going to become of us, of our adolescent hopes? What we felt confusedly, what we were trying to suppress by rejecting the society of those days, I neither can, nor do I wish to make a secret of any longer. The religious state of nations being what it is, and nations being what they are, the Jew finds himself, in a certain measure, outside of the national community. . . .
(A. Memmi, ibid., pp. 195-6)

"The history of the country in which I live is, to me, a borrowed history. How could I feel that Joan of Arc is a symbol for me? Would I hear with her the patriotic and Christian voices? Yes, always religion! But show me a way to separate national tradition from religious tradition. . . . *It is impossible for me to identify myself seriously with the past of any nation.*"
(A. Memmi, ibid., pp. 197-8)

Since the Jews are not of our race, being "neither Gauls, nor Celts, nor Slavs, nor Romans". (Memmi).

Since our national traditions are completely foreign to them.

Since our chivalry and the past history of its code of honour and self-sacrifice is looked upon by them as a hateful epoch.

Since our religion is "a blasphemy, a spiritual scandal and a subversion". (Memmi).

Since our God is in the eyes of the Jews "in a way, the Devil, that is to say, the symbol and essence of all evil on earth, which makes social life barely liveable". (Memmi).

Since the Evangelists are, according to Jules Isaac, liars and perverters of the truth.

Since our great saints and Fathers of the Church are, again according to Jules Isaac, scurrilous pamphleteers, venomous theologians full of hatred, torturers, the veritable forerunners of Hitler and Streicher, answerable, from a distance, for Auschwitz.

Since our gothic cathedrals are, according to H. Heine, "the most terrible fortresses of our enemies".

Since they take offence at our villages and metro stations named after saints.

Since the bells of our churches injure Jewish ears.

Since in their eyes it is inadmissible that

1. The President of the Republic should attend a Catholic reliligious ceremony in his official capacity (or Protestant ceremony in a Protestant country)
2. That the Pope should bless our country.
3. That the Papal nuncio should be doyen of the diplomatic corps by virtue of the very fact that he is the nuncio.

Since they find it intolerable that Christian and not Jewish feasts regulate holidays in the calendar.

Since they desire with all their might to see the death agonies of religions, nations and families—of others at least, for the Jewish religion, Jewish families and the Jewish nation preserve their own untouchable character.

And since in France they constitute a minority of scarcely half a million people in a country of fifty million inhabitants, and likewise in every other country in the world except Israel.

Then one is naturally led to ask whether it is lawful, useful, wise or opportune that Jews in our country are or have been:

Ministers and Presidents of the Council,
Ambassadors,
Members of the Académie Française,
Lord Chancellors of the Légion d'Honneur,
Generals,
Rectors of Universities and Inspectors of Public Instruction,
Keepers of the Bibliothèque Nationale,
Chiefs of Police and of the Information Service,
Examining magistrates,
Directors of national banks,
Directors of great national industries: the automobile industry, the aviation industry, etc.,
Directors of national theatres,
Authors of academic manuals on the History of France,

and likewise in regard to the other nations of the world.

After reading the works of Heinrich Heine, Bernard Lazare, J. Darmesteter, Kadmi-Cohen, Ludwig Lewisohn, Emil Ludwig, Walter Rathenau, Alfred Nossig, Leon Blum, Joshua Jehouda,

Edmond Fleg, Elie Benamozegh, Andre Spire, Elie Faure, Jules Isaac, Rabi, Max I. Dimont, and A. Memmi, one is inevitably led to the conclusion that it is perfectly legitimate and praiseworthy for Jews to defend and maintain their traditions and live in the different Western countries without being harassed or persecuted.

But it is quite inadmissible that they should be allowed to profit from this tolerant attitude in order to undermine, disintegrate and finally destroy our own religious, national and cultural traditions. They style the reactions against them "anti-Semitism", but they are in reality measures of defence to protect the community from a foreign influence, all the more dangerous since it is at work in the heart of our institutions, protected by fraudulent abuse of the term citizenship, calling itself French in France, English in England, German in Germany, and so on. . . .

Indeed, one can go so far as to ask whether it is legitimate, wise and consistent with the respect which the Church has always professed towards the Holy Scriptures, that an assembly of bishops, coming to Rome from all over the world to meet in Council, should seek advice from a Jewish writer, Jules Isaac, with a view to "rectifying and purifying" traditional Christian teaching with regard to Judaism.

Jules Isaac, about whom one of his co-religionists, Rabi, wrote:

> "His Jésus et Israel, published in 1948, is the most specific weapon of war against a particularly harmful Christian doctrine."
> (Rabi: Anatomie du Judaisme français, p. 183)

But, if one is to judge by the Council vote of November 1964, the desiderata of Jules Isaac, the B'nai B'rith and the World Jewish Congress weighed heavier in the minds of the 1,300 bishops and Council fathers than the Evangelists, than St. Augustine, St. John Chrysostom, St. Gregory the Great—and practically all the doctors of the Church and all the Popes—who elaborated the doctrine which is today denounced by Jules Isaac and others as particularly harmful.

PART III

THE COUNCIL'S SOLUTION

At the (Orthodox) Rabbinical Council of America, attended by 900 rabbis representing one and a half million Jews in the U.S.A. and Canada, Rabbi Dr. Joseph B. Soloveitchik, professor of Talmud at Yeshiva University, told the assembled rabbis:

"We are opposed to any public debate, dialogue or symposium concerning the doctrinal, dogmatic or ritual aspects of our faith.

"There cannot be any mutual understanding concerning these topics, for Jew and Christian will employ different categories and will move within incommensurate frames of reference and evaluation.

"We believe in and are committed to our Maker in a specific manner and we will not question, defend, offer apology, analyse or rationalise our faith in dialogues centred about these 'private' topics which express our personal relationship to the God of Israel."

(Reported in the *Jewish Chronicle*, 28th January, 1966, p. 40)

13

THE VATICAN VOTE

THE fourth and last session of the Council opened on 14th September 1965, and the schema on the Jewish question—"The schema on non-Christian religions"—was again submitted to the Council Fathers on 14th and 15th October.

After the Pope had refused to promulgate the vote taken in November 1964, the original text was profoundly reshaped by the conciliar commission in charge of the preparation of the schema. The new text submitted for the approval of the Council was distinctly less favourable to Jewish demands and more acceptable to conservative consciences; however, it still contained a few ambiguities which could be interpreted as promising a prudent revision, but a revision nevertheless, of the traditional Catholic attitude towards Judaism, which has remained unaltered for fifteen centuries.

Later we will study the new text, which regulates the position of the Church today with regard to contemporary Judaism, but let us begin with a rapid sketch of this historic vote.

Early in October 1965 the great battle on the Jewish question commenced, and from the start it took an extremely violent turn. In November 1964 the conservative minority had been taken entirely by surprise, but meanwhile it had had time to take stock of the situation, and, realising the extreme gravity of this vote for the Church, it energetically combated the Jewish-Catholic coalition, which was able to dispose of a Press almost entirely at its service.

At the fore in favour of the schema was Cardinal Bea, the theologian Fr. Congar, and papers such as *Le Monde* (H. Fesquet) and *Le Figaro* (Abbé Laurentin). Two arch-bishops and a Bishop led the conservative opposition: Mgr. de Proença Sigaud, archbishop of Diamantina in Brazil, Mgr. Lefebvre, Superior General of the Holy Ghost Fathers, and Mgr. Carli, Bishop of Segni in Italy.

The battle was fought with a relentless tenacity which rapidly spread into the heart of the Council and was echoed in the columns of the French daily Press. The following extracts demonstrate the bitterness of the struggle and the capital importance of the stakes.

On 14th October, 1965, *France-Soir* (whose director is P. Lazareff) launched the campaign with the following paragraph, under the heading: "Anti-Semitic tracts distributed at the Council".

"A tract signed 'Leon de Poncins' of anti-Semitic inspiration and drawn up in French has been sent to quite a number of the Council Fathers. On Thursday and Friday the Council is due to take a final vote on the text of relations with non-Christians and in particular with the Jews."

On 15th October, Abbé Laurentin wrote several columns on the vote in *Le Figaro* under the heading: "The Jews and Deicide: An inextricable vote." In it he said:

Rome, 14th October. "The vote on the question of the Jews and deicide has dominated the Council for the past eight days. The first poll took place this morning and the result will not be known until tomorrow.

"But it is a burning, complex question. There has been a spate of propaganda. Three vigorously anti-Semitic documents have been liberally distributed to the Fathers, in the following order:

"1. The first is a pamphlet by Leon de Poncins, printed in Italian—*Le Probleme des Juifs au Concile*. This is his thesis—'The text on the Jews voted on last year is the work of progressive or ignorant bishops who have ratified the themes of judaic hatred of the Christians. The Sovereign Pontiff refused to ratify it for this reason. This accounts for the profound modifications brought into the new text, the object of today's ballot.'

"2. The second pamphlet, also printed in Italian, is the work of Edoardo di Zaga. His thesis is that 'the declaration in favour of the Hebrews favours pro-Semite racism, and attacks the legitimate right of Christians and all peoples to defend themselves against the danger of Jewish hegemony.'

"3. Finally, they received two days ago directions for voting from *Coetus internationalis patrum*, the organ of the conciliar minority who are demanding the *non placet* on the whole of the schema and on the burning question concerning the Jews. Mgr. Carli, Bishop of Segni, one of its three signatories and directors, had published, in February 1965 in *Palestra del Clero*, the great review of the Italian clergy, a long article which maintained the following thesis: 'The Jewish people at the time of Jesus, as understood in the religious sense, that is to say, as a group professing the religion of Moses, was jointly responsible for the crime of deicide. Although only the leaders, followed by a small number of the people, materially consummated the offence, Judaism of subsequent times shares objectively in the responsibility of the deicide'."

Abbé Laurentin then devoted several columns to the modifications introduced into the schema between 1964 and 1965. According to him, the Fathers of a progressive tendency sharply regretted the reductions in the text of the previous year, and he concluded: "As is evident, the situation is full of ambiguities. On the one hand, the cardinal has acceded to the principal requests, either from Arab circles or from the group whose spokesman, Mgr. Carli, has expressed views hostile to the Jews. On the other hand, he firmly asserts that the intention and sense of the text remains unchanged. It would be difficult to deny that there has been a split between the dual purpose of the cardinal and of his secretariat. Nor could one deny that in the situation in which they found themselves, it was almost impossible to resolve this distortion. The problem confronting the Fathers was in a certain sense inextricable."

On 17th October the news of the Council vote occupied the front page of *Le Monde*, and the whole of an interior page, and the following is an extract:

FINALLY ADOPTED BY THE COUNCIL

The Declaration on the Jews evokes satisfaction, though not without reserves.

"The declaration on the Jews included in the schema on non-Christian religions was finally adopted on Wednesday by the Council. As *Le Monde* announced in its latest issue yesterday, the ballot on the text, in which 2,023 Fathers took part, produced the following results: 1,763 *placet*, 250 *non placet*, and 10 abstentions.

"Israeli circles and the American Jewish Committee—as well as Christian circles attached to the cause of reconciliation with the Jews—express satisfaction, tempered with regret that the text was finally sweetened, in several respects. On the other hand, the Grand Rabbi Kaplan deplored the fact that the term 'deicide' as applied to the Jews was not explicitly condemned.

"However, the majority of the reactions are that, now that the text has been adopted—and it still has to be promulgated by the Pope, it will be judged by its fruit, that is to say, by the way in which it is translated into religious teaching and by the attitude of Catholic circles with regard to the Jews.

"No reaction had yet been received by late Saturday morning

from the Arab countries, with the exception of a criticism from the orthodox Patriarch of Antioch."

From our special correspondent
HENRI FESQUET

Rome, 16th October. "The vote on the declaration on the Jews brings to an end the incredible number of advances, visits, letters, tracts, pamphlets and pressures with which the secretariat for unity has been assailed for more than three years. When the full details of the various attempts to frustrate or minimise the significance of the conciliar declaration become known, people will be amazed at so much passion, aberration, hatred and, in a word, ignorance and stupidity.

"On the other hand, several will regret with good cause that the last version of the text presented by the secretariat for unity had lost a little of its bite. It is especially sad that the real reasons for which these modifications were made have been more or less concealed behind pious motives. Roman diplomacy has once again triumphed over complete frankness. Many Fathers have said as much.

"But we must remember that the declaration, such as it was when voted upon, did rescue the essentials. The observers at the intersession who spread the most alarming rumours were heavily deceived. Vatican II has achieved the wish of John XXIII *grosso modo* by severely censuring anti-Semitism. The Church has implicitly recognised her past faults in the matter, and they are heavy, lasting and numerous. The new ecumenical mentality has overcome the prejudices of former times. In this connection, the vote on Friday inaugurates a fresh page in the history of relations between Rome and the Jews.

"Up to the last day the Catholic anti-Semites worked together in an attempt to muzzle the council. We have already drawn attention to the pamphlet in Italian by Mr. di Zaga. Another, from the pen of a Frenchman, Leon de Poncins, accuses the bishops who approved of the text last year of being 'ignorant (of the nature of their actions)'.

"*A declaration worthy of an anti-Pope.*

"But mention must above all be made of the four page tract which the bishops received. It is preceded by a paragraph as long as it is curious: 'No council, nor any Pope, can condemn Jesus, the Roman, Catholic and Apostolic Church, her pontiffs (the tract lists fifteen 'anti-Semitic' Popes, from Nicholas I in the ninth century to Leo XIII), and her illustrious councils. But the declaration on the Jews implicitly contains such a condemnation, and for this very good reason it should be rejected'."

On 22nd October, a long article filled almost the whole of the front page of the daily evening paper, *Paris-Presse*. It was much more objective than those in *Le Figaro* and above all of *Le Monde*, and despite its length we have quoted considerable extracts. The author of the article was well informed, since in fact the Holy Father did promulgate the schema on non-Christian religions (without change) on October 28th, although the date had been previously fixed for the end of November.

We quote *Paris-Presse*:

THE AFFAIR OF THE ANTI-JEWISH TRACTS AT THE COUNCIL

compels the Pope to promulgate the schema on non-Christian religions sooner than foreseen.

A violent corridor campaign aimed at Cardinal Bea.

(From our special correspondent, Charles Reymondon)

Vatican City, 21st October

"The Pope has decided to promulgate on 28th October the schema on non-Christian religions, that is to say, the schema which deals essentially with relations between the Jews and the Church.

"He intends thus to put an end to an anti-Semitic campaign which had acquired extraordinary volume in the heart of the Council, and which was accompanied by grave insinuations against Cardinal Bea.

"It is an event of considerable significance and has shaken this week at the Council, which in principle is committed to silence and to the work of the commissions alone.

"Last Friday, Pope Paul had announced that only four texts would be promulgated before All Saints day. But on the same day the vote on the most controversial schema of all, the one in question, took place. It revealed a strong enough minority, absolutely opposed to the schema: 250 fathers, 245 of whom totally refused the passage on the Jews, without there being any question of modifying or replacing it.

[Thus the opposition was much stronger in 1965 than in 1964 since, despite the indisputable improvement in the text, the number opposing it rose from 99 to 250—*Author's note.*]

"As in previous sessions no document had been promulgated with more than 10 per cent opposing, nobody believed on Friday, or even on Saturday, that the 'declaration on non-Christian religions' would be promulgated before November 18th at the earliest.

"Yet on Sunday, from his window overlooking St. Peter's Square, the Pope precipitated things.

"Why?

Unacceptable terms

"It is probable that a new element moved the sovereign pontiff. One should not try to find the explanation from the list of his visitors between times. Whether Paul VI was influenced or not, it is highly likely that he had become anxious at possible backwash, and that, by a swift stroke of authority, such as is his custom, he meant to put an end to campaigns of opinion that were dangerous while he equivocated.

"The critics of the actual project of the declaration on the Jews are strong. On the one hand there is the objection raised by the Arab world: that Jewish political intentions are behind this move (which is why chapters were finally added to the text, to balance it, on Islam, then on Buddhism, and then, yet again, on all other religions). The Eastern patriarchs had spoken unanimously last year: 'We don't even want to talk about this declaration; its terms are quite unacceptable to us.' Through diplomatic channels, the Arab states had threatened the Pope most clearly with reprisals against the Eastern churches, their missions and their schools. President Soekarno, representing the Moslem governments, had visited the Pope and told him the same thing. Finally, the Pope had received letters from Eastern Catholic hierarchies which informed him of the scandalised reaction of their flocks. They foreshadowed the risk of a schism on the part of these Churches to whom fidelity to Rome has already proved so costly in history.

Minority

"By contrast with the opposition from the East, which is explained by motives of expediency or political justice, the accusations arising from the rest of Christianity are much more serious, even though they are only representative of a small minority.

"They are based, indeed, in a much more disturbing manner, on the doctrinal level. They claim to demonstrate, by reference to authorities and documents, that there is an ignominious contradiction between what the Council proposes to say about the Jews, and holy scripture, the fathers of the Church, preceding Councils and some of the most eminent popes.

"But they go much further. Less and less indirectly, they are insinuating against Cardinal Bea, who is principally responsible for the text, the suspicion of simony. Simony is one of the gravest crimes which have poisoned the history of the Church, and one which the Pope recently told the correspondent of *Corriere della Sera* had completely disappeared today. The word comes from the Acts of the Apostles, where it is written how Simon the Magician offered money to St. Peter in order to receive spiritual powers from him. To be guilty of simony is to traffic in holy things: the sacraments, nominations to ecclesiastical positions, or the transformation of doctrine itself, all for a sum of money.

"Now, Cardinal Bea is accused of having accepted Jewish capital for the functions of his secretariat for unity. (The journeys necessitated by relations with the Orthodox and the Protestants are obviously costly.) He is accused of having imprudently promised, *per contra*, a declaration which would, as far as it concerns the Church, be the epilogue to the Nuremberg trial: that she should demand pardon from the Jews for all the persecutions which Christian doctrine has caused them throughout the centuries (deicide Jews, the people accursed by God, etc.).

"That denunciation is without proof. It is probable that if the Cardinal published his accounts, and the sources, that there would be silence at once. But it is inconceivable that a man in such an elevated position should lower himself to such a dispute.

"But the following extract, which is taken from a tract in Spanish circulated in the corridors of the Council, will give one an idea of the violence of the accusations which originated two years ago in a Latin-American country:

" 'We are ready to take the necessary steps to save the Church from such an ignominy. We appeal to the Council Fathers who have not yielded to Jewish pressure, or who have not sold themselves in simony to Jewish gold . . . to repel the perfidious declaration. . . .'

"The document is signed by twenty-eight organisations from the United States, Spain, France, Portugal, Germany, Austria and six Latin-American countries, Jordan and Italy. However, several leaders of these organisations, notably four out of five of the French, denied within the first twenty-four hours that they were signatories.

[In their issue of 21st October, *Le Monde*, which had already drawn attention to this document, announced that it was spurious, at least as far as the signatures were concerned—*Author's note.*]

"The whole affair constitutes an incredible hornet's nest. It is impossible here to get to the bottom of the thrilling, luminous and terrible 'Jewish question', for history has coloured its blood red. This part of the record can only serve to give an idea of the importance which the present decision of the Pope carries: throwing all his authority into the scales, he is free to modify the text himself before his final decision, in order to rally the opposition, a possibility which may not be ruled out."

We will now compare the 1964 and 1965 texts and examine the essential points of the schema, which are: the question of deicide, the collective responsibility of the Jewish people for the death of Christ, and anti-Semitism and persecution.

The 1964 text "deplored and condemned hatred and maltreatment *(vexationem)* of Jews", but the 1965 and final text "condemns all persecutions of any men" and "deplores manifestations of anti-Semitism".

These are the actual words of the latter text:

"The Church condemns all persecutions of any men; she remembers her common heritage with the Jews and, acting not from any political motives, but rather from a spiritual and evangelical love, deplores all hatred, persecutions and other manifestations of anti-Semitism, whatever the period and whoever was responsible."
(*De Ecclesiae*: Declaration on the Relation of the Church to Non-Christian Religions, Tr. by T. Atthill, C.T.S., 1966, p. 7)

The 1964 text was very dangerous—unacceptable, according to the conservatives—when examined in the light of Jewish demands, whose spokesman was Jules Isaac.

It put the Church in the position of the accused, guilty of the permanent, unjustifiable and unatonable crime of anti-Semitism for two thousand years.

It questioned the good faith and truthfulness of the Evangelists, of St. John and St. Matthew in particular; it discredited the teaching of the Fathers of the Church and of the great doctrinarians of the papacy by depicting them in distasteful colours; in short, it threatened to demolish the very bastions of Catholic doctrine.

We readily grant that the 1,651 Council Fathers who voted on this text were quite unaware of all that the vote implied, for a preliminary survey had convinced me that the vast majority of the Council Fathers had read none of the books of Jules Isaac, Joshua Jehouda and others whose demands, supported by the great world Jewish organisations—the B'nai B'rith, the World Jewish Congress, the American Jewish Committee, the Alliance Israelite Universelle —formed the basis of the schema submitted to them. The whole affair had been hatched in semi secrecy and with supreme skill by Cardinal Bea, Jules Isaac and a small group of progressives and Jewish leaders,[1] whose antagonism to traditional Christianity was veiled under appearances of Christian charity, ecumenical unity, and common biblical relationship. We have revealed the manœuvre in the first chapters of this book, and will not repeat it here, except to remark that it came very near to succeeding. In fact, it had already succeeded; but the Pope opposed it, in extremis, refused to promulgate the 1964 vote, and sent the text back to the commission to work on.

Let us return to the 1965 text, which formulates the official doctrine of the Church. What was the reaction of the Arab countries? They had reacted extremely violently to the 1964 text. In the course of an interview with *Le Figaro*, published in their issue of October 25th, the patriarch Maximos IV, who is himself of Arab origin, revealed their reaction to the 1965 text:

"Maximos IV being Arab himself, I asked him: 'What is the reaction of the Arab countries to the Council's declaration on the Jews?'"

This was his reply:

"In view of the notable amendments introduced into the new text of the declaration, the reaction of the Arab countries was semi-neutral this time. The new amendments will prevent political exploitation in favour of universal Zionism and the State of Israel, for it is now a purely religious text.

"Anti-Semitism is not Arabic for the Arabs are Semites. The unfavourable and often violent reaction of Zionist propaganda to the publication of the new text proves that Zionist circles are seeking something other than an appeal to forget the past and to universal charity. They wanted a declaration of a political tendency. And that the Council was bound to refuse them. As for the rest, we are the first to invite Christian charity among all peoples without distinction of race or religion. But Christian justice equally obliges us to claim the rights of the oppressed, the robbed and the refugees unjustly driven from their homes and reduced to living on international charity. If we reprove persecutions against the Jews, we must equally reprove persecutions and injustices done by the Jews."

[Several hundred thousand Arabs were brutally driven out of

---

[1] According to Fr. Weigel, S.J., professor of ecclesiastical history at Woodstock College, Maryland, who is on the staff of the review *America*, the declaration condemning anti-Semitism which was accepted by Cardinal Bea in 1964, was suggested by Zachariah Schuster, President of the American Jewish Committee.

Palestine by the Israeli Government, where they had been living for centuries, and they have been living in misery ever since in refugee camps—*Author's note.*]

"Thus since the Council text can no longer be used for political ends in favour of Zionism, the opposition of the Moslem peoples no longer has any basis."

Passing from the content matter of the various texts, we now come to the question of deicide.

An early text, elaborated in 1963, declared that it is an error and an injustice *(injuria)* to describe the Jewish people as deicide.

The 1965 text suppressed this clause. the question of deicide was withdrawn from discussion and the Church remains at the *status quo*.

In February 1965, Mgr. Carli ended a long article on this subject, published in the Italian review *Palestra del Clero* (15th February), with the following passage:

"We must now draw a general conclusion from the preceding biblical excursus. It seems to me that it may be summed up thus: for textual as well as for authoritarian reasons, the thesis according to which Judaism should be considered as responsible for deicide, and reproved and accursed by God, in the meaning and within the limits outlined above, is still legitimately defendable or at least legitimately probable.

"For this reason, a prohibition by the Council tending to put an end to free discussion one way or the other seems to me inopportune. Indeed, it would be more in harmony with the nature of the Council and with the practice adopted with regard to other schemas to leave it to the study and discussion of theologians and exegetes. . . .

"In any event, customary charity and Christian prudence ought to dictate the most suitable means and occasion for announcing a truth which, although displeasing—as one may well understand —to the parties concerned, does not merit for that reason alone to be consigned to absolute silence if, as many consider, it is effectively to be found in the deposit of divine Revelation."

Thus Mgr. Carli's conclusion was accepted by the conciliar commission when it withdrew the discussion on the motion of deicide.

This decision aroused the wrath of the Grand Rabbi, Joseph Kaplan. Interviewed by "Europe I", he said:

"I want it to be recognised that in 1965 the word deicide has no meaning and that furthermore it has an odious resonance. But precisely by reason of all the harm which this false accusation has done to the Jews for seventeen centuries, the schema should have clearly proclaimed that the accusation ought no longer to be brought against the Jews because it has no meaning and because it has an odious resonance. But the schema did not mention it. One can perceive the open determination of those who modified the text last year not to wash the Jews of the accusation of deicide and that is extremely serious."

(Reproduced by *Le Monde*, 17th October 1965)

Likewise, the Chief Rabbi of Rome, Elio Toaff, violently protested on 4th April 1965, when the Pope delivered a homily on the Passion, in the course of which he said:

"It is an extremely solemn and sad page which recalls for us the meeting between Jesus and the Jewish people. This people was predestined to receive the Messiah and had been waiting for him for thousands of years and was completely absorbed in this hope and certitude, but at the very moment, that is to say when Christ came and spoke and showed himself, not only did they not recognise him, but fought him, slandered him, abused him and finally put him to death." (*Osservatore Romano*, 7th April 1965)

Dr. Toaff and Dr. Sergio Piperno, President of the Union of Italian Jewish communities, sent the following telegram to the Vatican:

"Italian Jews express their sorrowful amazement at charge Hebrew people in death of Jesus contained in Sovereign Pontiff's homily, delivered shortly before Easter Roman parish Our Lady of Guadalupe and reported official Vatican Press, thus renewing deicide accusation, secular source tragic injustices towards Jews, to which solemn affirmations Vatican Council seemed to terminate for ever." (*Il Messagero de Roma*, 8th April 1965)

The 1964 text practically absolved the Jews of all responsibility for the death of Christ. The 1965 text formally recognises the responsibility of the Jewish leaders and their followers for the death of Christ but does not extend this responsibility to the whole Jewish people living in Christ's time, still less to the Jewish people of today.

The following is the relevant passage from the text concerning the collective responsibility of Israel:

"Even if the Jewish authorities, together with their followers, urged the death of Christ (cf. John xix. 6), what was done to him in his passion cannot be blamed on all Jews living at that time indiscriminately, or on the Jews of today. Although the

Church is the new People of God, the Jews should not be presented as rejected by God or accursed, as though this followed from Scripture. Therefore all must take care that in instruction and in preaching the Word of God, they do not teach anything which is not in complete agreement with the truth of the gospel and the spirit of Christ." *(De Ecclesiae,* ibid., pp. 6-7)

In the final version, therefore, in 1965, the Council did not follow Jules Isaac on this point, for Jules Isaac denies the responsibility of the leaders of Judaism and throws it all upon the Romans, but it yields on another point by absolving the Jewish people of any responsibility for the decision of their leaders.

The 1965 motion before the Council absolutely conforms with historical truth such as it appears from the accounts of the Evangelists—it is the leaders of Judaism and their followers who are responsible for the death of Christ. Strictly speaking, one can say that the whole of the Jewish people was not consulted and does not carry the direct responsibility for it, but the question of collective responsibility is very complex.

In fact, the decisions of leaders always involve the collective responsibility of peoples, even if the latter have taken no part in the decision, and in the last resort it is the peoples who undergo its consequences. History is full of examples of this sort. Take the last war, for example. Hitler's leaders did not consult the German people as far as the outbreak and conduct of the war is concerned, but it lead finally to murderous bombardments, the destruction of whole towns, the invasion of their country, the violation of millions of their women, massive deportations and millions of deaths. Similarly, Churchill did not consult the British people before involving his country in war with Germany.

Do the legal principles accepted by the Western peoples recognise collective responsibility in law? Yes, to a certain extent they do, if one is to judge by the Nuremberg trial.

As far as Judaism is concerned, the Council's decision raises thorny problems: numerous and eminent doctors of the Church, for example, have upheld the principle of the collective responsibility of Israel. On this point, in the course of two resounding articles which he devoted to the Jewish problem in the Italian review *Palestra del Clero* (15th February and 1st May 1965), Mgr. Carli quoted some striking authorities, and concluded one of the articles with these words:

"Can one call the Jews deicide?
"It has been said that one ought not to speak of 'deicide' be-

cause, according to etymology, God cannot be put to death. But it is easy to reply that the murder of Jesus Christ, the true son of God, merits the name of deicide in strict (exact) theological terminology.

"The real question is whether the whole Jewish 'people' should be considered as guilty of 'deicide'. The 1964 declaration says no in an indisputable fashion.

"However, the numerous scholars and exegetes who clearly find evidence in the Old Testament—despite Ezekiel xvii—of the principle of 'collective responsibility' for good as well as for evil, seem to me to be right. The whole history of Israel is woven on a doubly polarized canvas: on the one hand, there is God with his collective gifts and punishments, and on the other, there is the 'chosen people' which accepts or refuses. The whole people is considered responsible and subsequently punished for faults officially committed by its leaders, even when they are unknown to a great part of the people.

"Examples of such an attitude may be found in the New Testament"—Mgr. Carli quotes a great number of extremely striking passages, which unfortunately we have not the space to reproduce here—and then goes on to add:

"Without the doctrine of collective responsibility all this would remain in undecipherable mystery.

"To conclude, I consider that one can legitimately assert that the whole Jewish people at the time of Jesus, as understood in the religious sense, that is to say, as a group professing the religion of Moses, was jointly responsible for the crime of deicide, although only the leaders, followed by a small number of the faithful, materially consummated the crime.

"These leaders were not, of course, elected democratically by universal suffrage, but according to the legislation and attitude of mind then in force, they were considered by God himself (cf. Matthew xxiii. 2) and by public opinion, as the legitimate religious authorities, the officials responsible for the acts which they took in the name of religion itself. But it is precisely by these leaders that Jesus Christ was condemned to death; and he was condemned precisely because he claimed to be God (John x. 33; xix. 7), and yet he had given sufficient proof to be believed (John xv. 24).

"The sentence of condemnation was taken by the Council (John xi. 49 et seq.), that is to say, by the highest authority of the Jewish religion, appealing to the Law of Moses (John xix. 7), and laying the motive for the sentence upon an action in defence of the whole people (John xi. 50) and of religion itself (Matthew

xxvi. 65). It was the priesthood of Aaron, the synthesis and principal expression of the theocratic and hierocratic policy of the Old Testament, which condemned the Messiah. Consequently, one may attribute deicide to *Judaism*, when considered as a religious community.

"Within this very limited meaning, and bearing in mind biblical mentality, Judaism of the times after Our Lord also objectively shares the collective responsibility for deicide in as far as this Judaism constitutes the free and voluntary continuation of Judaism at that time.

"An example taken from the Church will help us to understand this fact. Each time that a Sovereign Pontiff and an ecumenical Council take a solemn deliberation in the plenitude of their authority, although they are not elected by the catholic community on a democratic system, yet by this decision they render co-responsible now and for all centuries to come, all 'catholicism' and the whole community of the faithful."

(*Palestra del Clero*, 1st February 1965)

Let us take the most celebrated of the numerous texts implying the collective responsibility of Israel, the Gospel of St. Matthew.

By Judas' treason, Jesus was delivered to the chief priests and they "took council against Jesus to put him to death." Finally:

"When they had bound him they led him away and delivered him to Pontius Pilate . . . and the governor asked him, saying: 'Art thou the King of the Jews?' And Jesus said unto him: Thou sayest. And when he was accused of the chief priests and elders he answered nothing. Then said Pilate unto him: 'Hearest thou not how many things they witness against thee?' And he answered to him never a word; insomuch that the governor marvelled greatly. Now at that feast the governor was wont to release unto the people a prisoner, whom they would. And they had then a notable prisoner, called Barabbas. Therefore, when they were gathered together, Pilate said unto them: Whom will ye that I release unto you? Barabbas, or Jesus which is called Christ? For he knew that for envy they had delivered him. When he was set down on the judgment seat, his wife sent unto him saying, Have thou nothing to do with that just man: for I have suffered many things this day in a dream because of him. But the chief priests and elders persuaded the multitude that they should ask Barabbas and destroy Jesus. The governor answered and said unto them, Whether of the twain will ye that I release unto you? They said, Barabbas. Pilate saith unto them, What shall I do then with Jesus which is called Christ? They all say unto him, Let him be crucified. And the governor said, Why, what evil hath he done? But they cried out the more, saying, Let him be crucified. When Pilate saw that he could prevail nothing but that rather a tumult was made, he took water and washed his hands before the multitude, saying, I am innocent of the blood of this just person: see ye to it. Then answered all the people and said, His blood be on us and on our children. Then released he Barabbas unto them and when he had scourged Jesus, he delivered him to be crucified."

(Matthew xxvii.)

This Gospel formally implies the collective responsibility of the Jewish people for the death of Jesus.

What attitude will the Church adopt on this point after the last Council, and how does one reconcile the above passage with the 1965 schema?

Will the Church admit to the thesis of Jules Isaac, which asserts that St. Matthew is a liar, that he falsified historical truth and completely invented this dramatic scene solely in order to reproach the Jews, St. Matthew, who was of their race?

Or will the Church, on the contrary, uphold and defend the historical truth of the Gospels?

The Council and the Holy Father have already taken their decision. They have vigorously re-asserted the truth of the Gospels.

"An inextricable vote," wrote Abbé Laurentin in *Le Figaro*, speaking about the Jewish question at the Council. "An incredible hornet's nest," as *Paris-Presse* described it in an article from which we have quoted at length. Cardinal Tappouni, Patriarch of the Catholic Churches of the Oriental Rite, told me at Rome at the time of the conciliar discussions: "We Fathers of the Oriental Church have clearly taken our position. We have declared once and for all that any discussion of the Jewish problem was inopportune. I have nothing to add or retract from this declaration for a word too many or too few on such a neuralgic problem could lead to disaster. The facts have proved us right, and no good will come out of it either for the Christians or the Jews."

Cardinal Tappouni was probably right but in fact the question has been raised and it can no longer be eluded. It has already caused quite a stir throughout the world, as Mgr. Carli remarks in his articles:

"The declaration on non-Christian religions . . . has unleashed an indignant Press campaign, it has provoked political and diplomatic complications and, unfortunately, in the East it has provided an excuse for some to abandon Catholicism in favour of Orthodoxy. The Fathers who support it are slandered with having sold themselves to international Jewry, whereas those who, for various reasons, consider the declaration inopportune or at least want to see it modified, are labelled anti-Zionists and practically held co-responsible for the Nazi camps."

Jules Isaac protests violently in his works against the principle of the collective responsibility of Israel, and Rabbi Kaplan echoes him.

But on the subject of collective responsibility, the Jews place themselves in a false position which renders them very vulnerable. *They furiously repulse any suggestion of collective responsibility when they themselves risk being found guilty of it but vehemently insist on it when it is to their advantage to do so.*

In chapter ten of this work we have quoted a typical article by Vladimir Jankélévitch, an important personality in Israel. In *Le Monde*, 3rd January 1965, speaking of Hitler's Jewish victims, he wrote:

"This crime without name is a crime that is truly infinite . . . of which one is compelled to say that only Germanic sadism could be guilty. . . . The methodical, scientific and administrative massacre of six million Jews is not a wrong *per se*, it is a crime for which a whole people is accountable."

Indeed, the German people was declared collectively responsible at Nuremberg for Hitler's anti-Jewish measures and every taxpayer in Federal Germany (except those in Eastern Germany under the Soviet régime) pays considerable sums every year to the State of Israel by way of indemnification for the wrongs undergone by international Judaism at the hands of Hitler.

But one cannot refuse the principle of collective responsibility when it is not to one's advantage and claim it when it is. One must choose one way or the other. If this principle is not admitted, and it would seem that the Council opted in favour of the negative, it is hard to see why Israel continues to exact a heavy tribute from the German people. Similarly, in this light the Nuremberg trial loses part of its justification.

An inextricable vote. An incredible hornet's nest.

There is a third point on which it is to be hoped that the Church will clarify her position following the Council vote, for it is susceptible of very different interpretations and has formidable consequences; the problem of anti-Semitism and persecution. It is a problem which has arisen in every country in the past three thousand years in which an appreciable number of Jews have resided.

This is what the schema adopted by the Council says:

"The Church condemns all persecutions of any men; she remembers her common heritage with the Jews and, acting not from any political motives, but rather from a spiritual and evangelical love, deplores all hatred, persecutions and other manifestations of anti-Semitism, whatever the period and whoever was responsible."

(*De Ecclesiae*, ibid., p. 7)

It is a text which looks short, simple and irrefutable, one on which agreement ought to be unanimous; the Church has always reproved persecution, and here the whole world will agree with her.

It is however bristling with difficulties and complex problems, and it is very much to be hoped that the Church will explain what will be her position henceforth.

Anti-Semitism and persecution are words liable to provoke emotional outbursts.

Let us begin with anti-Semitism. What exactly are manifestations of anti-Semitism? The ideas of anti-Semitism vary entirely according as to whether one examines them from the Jewish point of view or from the point of view of the non-Jews.

In Jewish eyes, every measure of defence and protection against the penetration of Jewish ideas and conceptions, against anti-Christian Jewish heresies, against Jewish control of the national economy, and in general every measure in defence of national Christian traditions, is a manifestation of anti-Semitism. Furthermore, many Jews consider that the very fact of the recognition of the existence of a Jewish question constitutes a declaration of anti-Semitism. "Their ideal", says Wickham Steed, in his remarkable work, *The Hapsburg Monarchy*, "seems to be the maintenance of Jewish international influence as a veritable *imperium in imperiis*. Dissimulation of their real objects has become to them a second nature, and they deplore and tenaciously combat every effort to place the Jewish question frankly on its merits before the world." (p. 179)

Let us take the concrete example concerning the Church. Jules Isaac, as we have abundantly shown at the beginning of this work, Jules Isaac accuses all the Fathers of the Church of anti-Semitism, St. John Chrysostom, St. Augustin, St. Agobard, the celebrated Pope St. Gregory the Great, etc. He treats them as perverters of the truth and torturers for their attitude towards Judaism. He accuses them of having unleashed the savagery of the beast and of being the real people responsible for German anti-Semitism and the gas chambers at Auschwitz. He finds them even worse than Hitler and Streicher and others, for their system resulted in the Jews being tortured slowly and being left to live and suffer interminably.

"Henceforward we perceive the radical difference which separates the Christian system of vilification from its modern Nazi imitator—blind and ignorant are they who ignore their thousand profound connections: the latter was only a stage, a brief stage preceding the massive extermination; the former on the contrary involved survival, but a shameful survival in contempt and disgrace; thus it was created to endure and to injure and slowly torture millions of innocent victims."

(J. Isaac: *Genèse de l'Antisémitisme*, pp. 168-72)

What will the attitude of the post-conciliar Church be on this point? What is the meaning of the phrase: "deplores all manifestations of anti-Semitism, whatever the period and whoever may have been responsible"?

Does the Church admit Jules Isaac's thesis and plead guilty?

Must Masses be said for the repose of the soul and pardon of the sins of St. John Chrysostom, St. Augustin, St. Gregory the Great and other great saints in the Christian liturgy, guilty of the crime of anti-Semitism?

Must their teaching be rectified and purified, according to the injunctions of Jules Isaac?

Must the Gospels be purged of many a passage which bears the taint of anti-Semitism?

"Can one," writes Mgr. Carli, "Can one legitimately make the Catholic Church, as such, assume such an enormous responsibility which would make of her the cruellest and vastest association of evil-doers that has ever existed on the face of the earth? The Jews today no longer want to be considered responsible for everything which was done to Jesus Christ by their ancestors, to whom even now they grant the benefit of good faith; but they demand that the Catholic Church of today should feel responsible and guilty for everything which, according to them, the Jews have suffered for the past two thousand years."

"I do not think that the Church, even out of charity or humility alone, can officially adopt such an interpretation of history. At least she ought not to accuse herself of such a transgression, which soils her image before her sons and the whole world, until after a minute and impartial investigation for which the few lines of the conciliar schema naturally cannot suffice (quite apart from their conclusive value).

"Nobody means to deny by this, and all the world is ready to regret, that there have arisen, to a greater or lesser degree, through ignorance and sometimes through bad faith, prejudiced anti-Jewish Christians; in the same way that certain Jewish rabbinical literature insulted Jesus and the Holy Virgin Mary, and inspired hatred and cursing against the Christians.

"But, rather than engaging in historical proceedings and demanding each other to admit to guilt, it would be much more useful for each to formulate exact doctrinal principles and to practise esteem and charity, and so to bring down mutual prejudices. In this sense one can subscribe to the words of the Chief Rabbi of Denmark: 'We will probably continue to remain a sign of mutual contradiction, but we will no longer devour each other.'

(cf. *Oikoumenikon*, 1st August, 1963, p. 270)

"But on condition that 'we deny none of our principles. For us Catholics, without denying or passing in silence over any of the points contained in Holy Scripture or in the divine, apostolic tradition.'

"Let us then work out a text which will be acceptable 'to all our Jewish friends', but which will above all be acceptable to all who love objective truth. . . .

"Were two thousand years of history so filled, as the Jewish thesis has it, with the moral faults of the Church towards the people of Israel, it cannot and ought not to change the terms of the question, as expressed on the lips of Jesus, St. Peter, St. Paul, etc. . . .

"The decision carried in the 1964 schema coincided with what the Jews propose and hope for. May I be permitted to doubt that it is acceptable according to objective truth."

(Mgr. Carli: *Palestro del Clero*, 1st May 1965)

What is the attitude of the Church towards persecution?—a term which the Jews always associate with the word anti-Semitism.

The Church reproves all forms of persecution from whatever side they come. Once again everybody will be in agreement, provided that the phrase "whatever the period and whoever may have been responsible" is clarified.

To hear and read Jewish authors, one would believe that only they are the victims of persecution in the world. In the modern world only anti-Jewish persecution arouses the democratic conscience. There are many victims of persecution in the history of the world, and they are not only Jewish.

In the review *Palestra del Clero*, 15th February 1965, Mgr. Carli wrote very justly:

"Certainly, no one ought to condemn hatred and persecution more than a Catholic, especially when their pretext is religious or racial motives. But it does seem peculiar, to some, to say the least, that in a conciliar document only those wrongs suffered by the Jews 'either in previous times or in our own days' are expressly condemned, as if others had not existed and do not, unfortunately, still exist today no less worthy of explicit condemnation. We refer to the massacre of the Armenians, and to the genocides and inumerable killings perpetrated under the banner of Marxist Communism", and Mgr. Carli added:

"With regard to the persecution of the Jews, certainly neither the Roman emperor Claudius, nor the German leader Hitler, to take only the first and the last of anti-Semitic persecutors in the Christian era, took their inspiration from religious principles."

Finally, since we are concerned with persecution, we must also mention those for which Jewish people are responsible, for they, who always set themselves up as innocent, crucified victims, are terrible persecutors when they have the upper hand. This subject is dealt with in chapter ten of this work, and we will not repeat again what we have said there.

In a work written in 1921 called *Le Problème Juif*, George Batault said:

"The attitude adopted by many Jews in attributing the secular phenomenon of anti-Semitism uniquely to the basest sentiments and to the crassest ignorance is absolutely untenable. It is perfectly infantile perpetually to seek to contrast the good Jewish sheep, steeped in pious meekness, with the bad non-Jewish wolf, thirsting for blood and howling with ferocious jealousy. The philosophy of history which consists in describing as a pogromist anyone who attempts to tackle the Jewish problem in a spirit which is not deliriously apologetic, this philosophy must be abandoned."
(G. Batault: *Le Problème Juif*, Paris 1921)

The following experience is a recent example of this state of mind. In October 1965 I went to Rome and delivered to more than two thousand Council Fathers, as well as a certain number of eminent personalities, a pamphlet entitled *Le Problème Juif face au Concile*, two-thirds of which were printed in Italian and the remainder in French. It contained a brief history of the role of Jules Isaac in the preparation of the conciliar schema on the Jewish question and a summary of the theses of his and other masters of contemporary Jewish thought on the question of the relations between Judaism and Christianity. It was neither abusive nor insulting, being simply an exposé of texts which I confined myself to presenting in a clear and coherent fashion. For I considered that it was essential for the Council Fathers to have a knowledge of these texts, since they formed the very basis on which the Fathers had been called to vote. A preliminary enquiry had rapidly convinced me that practically all the Council Fathers were completely unaware both of the existence of the texts and of the importance of the role of Jules Isaac.

In contrast with Jules Isaac, H. Fesquet of *Le Monde* and other laymen who exerted great influence at the Council, I did not issue any advice or directives, but simply put forward some information, adding: "The decision now rests with the Council Fathers and it is they who will carry the responsibility for it."

Several big papers in France, led by *Le Monde*, drew attention to my intervention and to the distribution of my pamphlets. All accused me, in rather disagreeable phraseology, of "anti-Semitism". In their issue of 17th October, speaking of "the incredible number of advances, visits, letters, tracts, pamphlets and pressures with which the secretariat for unity had been assailed (on the declaration on the Jews)", *Le Monde* said, "people will be amazed at so much passion, aberration, hatred and in a word, ignorance and stupidity".

Since my name was clearly mentioned a little further on in the article, this criticism was obviously directed at me, a criticism in which, naturally, passion, hatred, ignorance and stupidity played no part.

One of my relations sent my pamphlet to a priest whom I did not know, who is headmaster of a Catholic school and a renowned preacher, and received this letter in reply:

> "I enclose the distressing pamphlet by Mr. de Poncins, which shows so little pity towards Israel, so little charity and such a narrow interpretation of history. These eternal snippets from Joshua Jehouda are very irritating. Does Mr. de Poncins imagine that Mgr. de Provenchères and the Council Fathers are unaware that the Jews and the Moslems fiercely reject the Incarnation? Is that what it is all about?
>
> "When the Council's text appears in the Press, you will see. It is in a word the work of Cardinal Bea, a Jesuit and an exegete of eighty years who is greatly travelled and read and who undoubtedly has a great love of men and a great sense of justice. It is this motive, and not ignorance, which impelled him to sup-

port the schema, and upon which, under the guidance of the Holy Spirit, some two thousand Catholic bishops will vote."

Thus in the eyes of this worthy priest it is not Jules Isaac and the others who are provoking by attacking the great doctrines of Christianity; no, it is I who am provoking since I have actually quoted them and made them known. But there is no doubt that the disclosure of these deadly texts was exceedingly embarrassing to the success of the Jewish progressive manœuvre, and if they could have been published earlier they would have been even more effective.

The conclusion is very obvious: these "anti-Semites", who use a formidable weapon, the texts of Jewish authors themselves, must at all costs be silenced. This is what Abbé Laurentin said in scarcely veiled terms, when he wrote in Le Figaro on 15th October 1965:

"Is the 1965 text sufficient to tear out the roots of Christian anti-Semitism, which has expressed itself so vigorously these last months?"

In other words, one of the aims of the 1964 text was to impose silence on the "anti-Semites". However, though admirably prepared, the manœuvre did not succeed, or only very partially, for the 1965 text leaves the way open for restricted possibilities in this field.

On the other hand, no restriction whatever impedes Jewish writers or their allies.

With impunity Jules Isaac can write large works, recently republished, in which he describes the Evangelists as liars, the Fathers and the great saints of the Church as scurrilous pamphleteers, perverters of the truth and torturers, and in which he calls on the Church to recognise, abjure and make amends for her criminal wrongs towards the Jews. Bishops such as Mgr. de Provenchères publicly express their esteem, respect and affection for him. Mgr. Gerlier, the cardinal archbishop of Lyon, writes a laudatory preface in a book by Abbé Toulat called *Juifs mes Frères*, in which the role of Jules Isaac is exalted and glorified. Mgr. Liénart, the cardinal archbishop of Lille, patronises Jules Isaac's own Amitié judéo-chrétiennes. But because I simply quote Jules Isaac, Joshua Jehouda and others, I am described as a despicable anti-Semite—a typical example of passion, aberration, hatred, ignorance and stupidity, if one is to believe Le Monde.

Finally, the progressive clergy reserves its favours for the enemies of religion and pours sarcasm, scorn and hostility on those who defend their own tradition.

As far as common biblical relationship with the Jewish people is concerned, this indeed is indisputable, but we must beware of pushing the argument too far.

The New Testament marks a great turning-point in the history of religious thought and a profound break with the Old Testament. The split has only increased over the centuries.

The 1965 text says:

> "This sacred council remembers the bond by which the people of the New Testament is spiritually linked to the line of Abraham. The Church of Christ recognises that in God's plan of salvation, the beginnings of her own election and faith are to be found in the Patriarchs, Moses and the Prophets. . . . The Church cannot, therefore, forget that it was through that people, with whom God in his ineffable mercy saw fit to establish the Old Covenant, that she herself has received the revelation of the Old Testament. She takes her nourishment from the root of the cultivated olive-tree on to which the wild-olive branches of the Gentiles have been grafted (cf. Romans xi. 17-24). The Church believes that Christ, who is our Peace, has reconciled Jews and Gentiles through the cross and has made us both one in himself (cf. Ephesians ii. 14-16). . . .
>
> "Holy Scripture is witness that Jerusalem has not known the time of her visitation (cf. Luke xix. 44). The Jews have not, for the most part, accepted the Gospel; some indeed have opposed its diffusion (cf. Romans xi. 28). Even so, according to the Apostle Paul, the Jews still remain very dear to God, for the sake of their fathers, since he does not repent of the gifts he makes or the calls he issues (cf. Romans xi. 28-29). In company with the Prophets and the same Apostle, the Church looks forward to that day, known to God alone, when all peoples will call on the Lord with one voice and 'serve him with one shoulder'.
>
> (Soph. iii. 9; cf. Isaiah lxvi. 23; Psalms lxv. 4; Romans xi. 11-32)
>
> "Given this great spiritual heritage common to Christians and Jews, it is the wish of this sacred Council to foster and recommend a mutual knowledge and esteem, which will come from biblical and theological studies, and brotherly discussions."
>
> (*De Ecclesiae*, ibid., pp. 5-6)

In his article in *Palestra del Clero*, Mgr. Carli clearly explains Catholic doctrine on this point:

> "At a certain moment in history Israel broke the Covenant with God, not so much because it had transgressed the commandments of God, or in other words, because it had not fulfilled the con-

ditions of the Covenant (it had committed this sin so often and God had always forgiven it!) as because it had refused the fulfilment of the Covenant itself by refusing Jesus: 'for Christ is the fulfilment of the law' (Romans x, 4). Henceforth it was no longer a question of accidental terms of the Covenant, but of its actual substance. Automatically, Israel's 'election' was completely frustrated, it lost its purpose, and the privileges which were attached to it lost their sufficient reason. . . . Israel ended up by becoming institutionalised after a fashion into global, official and adamant opposition to Christ and his doctrine, despite the great 'sign' of the Resurrection of the Messiah.

"The mosaic religion which, by a disposition made known by God, was to issue into Christianity to find in it its own end and perfection, on the contrary constantly refused to adhere to Christ, thus 'rejecting' the cornerstone laid by God. It is not a question of the renunciation pure and simple of God's plan (which is already a very grave error), but of positive opposition; in this respect, the relationship between Christianity and Judaism is much worse than the relationship between Christianity and the other religions. For Israel alone had been chosen for and received a vocation, gifts and history, etc., very different from all other people on earth: in God's plan, Israel was entirely and completely 'relative' to Christ and Christianity. Having failed to achieve, through its own fault, such an important 'relativity', it had of itself put itself in a state of objective 'rejection'. This state will last as long as the Judaic religion throughout the world refuses to recognise and officially accept Jesus Christ.

"In my opinion, Holy Scripture justifies this interpretation and patristic tradition confirms it."

The rupture between the Old and the New Testament has continually increased as the Torah, or Law of Moses, made way for the growing influence of the Talmud as the source of inspiration of the Hebrew religion. The modern Jew studies not the Mosaic law but the Talmud; and between the Gospel and the Talmud there is an irreducible antagonism. We would but remind the reader that we have dealt with this question in chapter five of this work.

Will this antagonism endure until the end of time?

No, answers Catholic doctrine as formulated by St. Paul, for at the end of time, the whole Jewish people will be converted:

"At the end of time the mass of the Jews will save themselves; this assertion of St. Paul's is an essential part of Christian hope. . . . God's gifts are given absolutely, that is to say, once given they are never taken away; but for those who refuse them or do not use them at the appropriate time, they turn into articles of condemnation....

"This position was freely accepted by Israel, and as long as it persists the 'objective' state of accursedness remains with all its consequences. But one must categorically deny that any human authority whatever, whether private or public, may, under no matter what right or pretext, execute the punishment attached to the divine judgment: God alone may do it, in the manner and at the time he chooses."

(Mgr. Carli: *Palestra del Clero*, 15th February 1965)

But the masters of contemporary Judaism oppose this belief with haughty contempt and scorn. We have quoted particularly striking passages from Jehouda to illustrate this point. It is not the Jews who will convert to Christianity, which in their eyes is a bastard religion, a corrupted branch of Judaism—it is the Christians who must return to Israel. The following recent passage serves to confirm and strengthen this opinion:

"Let us be under no illusions: if they think they are going to exculpate us in order to win us more easily, they deceive themselves. We will not be changed. We must be accepted as we are —with our absolute and indivisible monotheism, with our fierce desire to survive as a distinct community, with our categoric refusal of every other 'truth'. We do not want to convert, we consider that we are adult men capable of choosing our own path ourselves. We want to be treated accordingly. But if your religion obliges you to proselytise, we do not object. Only, we warn you: you will be wasting your time. We will remain as we are, and no force on earth or in heaven will change us. For we are made from a substance as hard as the rock; we resisted God in our youth and men in our maturity. Thus we can wait. For this reason, the only attitude worthy of a Jew towards the ecumenical Council is one of polite impassiveness. Let us keep quiet and pursue our own work, waiting with serenity. For whatever the results may be, we must continue alone along our inconceivable route."

(Alexander Reiter, in an article on *Les Juifs et le Concile*, published by the weekly *Terre retrouvée* 15th June, 1964)

The conclusion may be drawn in a few words; it stems clearly from the numerous texts we have quoted from Jewish authors.

A religious agreement between Western Christians and Jews of Talmudic discipline will be very difficult to achieve, for, as Mgr. Carli says, speaking about the Jewish religion:

"It is not a question of the renunciation pure and simple of God's plan . . . but of positive opposition; in this respect the relationship between Christianity and Judaism is much worse than the relationship between Christianity and the other religions."

The generous intentions—or illusions—of the Council will always come up against a major obstacle, Jewish intransigence. The Jews demand everything but concede nothing; they refuse to assimilate, they refuse to convert; far from assimilating, they judaise, far from converting, they seek to impose their convictions on others.

"The Jewish problem presents an insoluble enigma more than two thousand years old, and today it is still one of the most formidable questions facing our times", wrote George Batault in *Le Problème juif*.

These prophetic words date from 1921. Notwithstanding so many dramatic events, so many disasters and world upheavals, they are still relevant today in 1967. Proof of it is the importance of the discussions on the Jewish question at the Second Vatican Council.

14

TRACTS AGAINST THE COUNCIL

THIS is the title of an article on page 154 of the special issue of 6th March 1966 of the *Osservatore Della Domenica* on "Vatican Council II". The book as a whole gives a very complete history of the Council, and this particular article, which we reproduce below, was written by Ugo Apollonio, and is devoted to pamphlets on the Jewish question which had been widely distributed among the Council Fathers during the Council; in the course of the article my name is clearly singled out, and I am violently taken to task. This is what the article says:

Vatican Council II has been the object, as indeed might be expected, of the greatest praise and of the severest criticism. One cannot be surprised then, at the anti-conciliar literature which burst out, and it is perhaps worthwhile calling it to mind again briefly, if only out of curiosity. Unfortunately there is not enough space to examine Communist dailies and periodicals which frequently twisted the intentions and discussions of the Council Fathers in every country, nor can we deal with the secular Press, which in Italy and elsewhere often presented the works of the Council from a one-sided point of view.

Thus we will limit our study to a certain section of books and pamphlets, of limited quantity and quality, whose common characteristics suggest a common source, at least in their inspiration:

1. They all come from latin countries (in particular, from France, Spain, Latin-America);
2. They reflect the ideas of certain ultraconservative Catholic circles;
3. They are all either anonymous or pseudonymous; in certain instances they are concealed behind signatures subsequently discovered to be either imaginary or false;
4. They have been translated into several languages (the Italian translation is usually rather poor);
5. Most were distributed through the post and sent direct to the Council Fathers.

As far as their contents are concerned, it must be added that many of these publications are entrenched behind a suspect preoccupation with orthodoxy, which they use as a pretext for ill-considered attacks on cardinals and bishops, whom they accuse of introducing heresies, seeking to subvert the Church, selling the Church for earthly rewards, and so on; on the other hand, others are distinctly anti-Semitic in tone and unjustly attack many representatives of the Church.

The first and most massive document—around which all the other lesser pamphlets which followed may be said to gravitate—was published in August 1962 under the pseudonym of Maurice Pinay. According to the introduction, this work should have contained "terrible revelations", whereas it contains, on the contrary, a jumble of gratuitous and illogical accusations against the Council Fathers, whom—as it says in the Appeal to the Reader—"are conspiring in order to destroy the most sacred traditions by carrying out audacious and noxious reforms on the lines of Calvin, Zwingli and other great heretics, by pretending to modernise the Church and bring it up to date, but with the secret intention of opening the doors to Communism, accelerating the ruin of the free world, and preparing for the future destruction of Christianity."

In a number of ronetyped leaflets, which arrived from America in 1964, one Hugh Mary Kellner attacks "the devastating results of secularism" and accuses the leaders of the Church of failing to "check the catastrophic decadence of Catholicism which has become apparent in recent decades". According to this man, many Council Fathers were "victims of a satanic seduction suggestive of the use of the apparently laudable word of Christ to weaken and destroy the Church".

However, the most important and bitter attacks were directed against "falsely converted Jews" and the "international Judaeo-Masonic B'nai B'rith organisation". A number of pamphlets and circular letters were sent to the Council Fathers at their private addresses, asserting that "the Jewish people alone is the deicide people" and that as a result, it must be "fought and exterminated", since "through Masonry, Communism and all the subversive organisations which it has created and directs, Judaism arrogantly and implacably continues to combat Christ".

Racism, fanaticism and the most obstinate opposition were displayed by certain anti-Jewish groups in numerous small publications urging ferocious persecution against the Jews, "fathers of deceit and calumny", quoting Church dogma or teaching in support or approval. As an example we quote from some which we have before us: *The Jews and the Council in the light of the Holy Scriptures and tradi-*

tion, anonymous—according to the pamphlet, the author is "Bernardus"; *The Jewish people is the deicide people* by Mauclair; *The Council and the attack of the central-European bloc* by Catholicus; *Judaeo-Masonic action in the Council* by an anonymous author who claims to be "a group of priests, some of whom belong to religious orders, and others to the secular clergy"; *The declaration in favour of the Jews favours a racism which infringes the legitimate right of defence of other peoples*, by one E. di Zaga; *The problem of the Jews at the Council* by L. de Poncins, etc. In all these pamphlets, just as in *Common Sense*, printed in New Jersey, and in yet others, the accusations are the same, and they spring from the same roots of misunderstanding, intolerance, scorn and hatred of the Jewish people.

The campaign, as we have remarked above, was not confined to Italy, but spread over the whole of the latin world. The principal people accused were clearly indicated. These are the "heretics": the German theologians, Oesterreicher and Baum, both of the Jewish race, whose task was to "judaise the Christians"; Fr. Klyber, who "brainwashed Catholics in favour of the Jews"; and Cardinal Bea, who "in presenting his proposed decree in favour of the Jews and in opposition to the Evangelists, concealed from the Council Fathers that he was repeating the theses which had been suggested to him by the Masonic order of the B'nai B'rith".

Cardinal Bea, who as we know created a study group in the heart of the Secretariat for Christian Unity, in obedience to the express wishes of Pope John, in order to examine from the solely theological and religious point of view the relations between the Church and the Jewish people, and who drafted the declaration on the Jewish problem—Cardinal Bea was attacked by all the anonymous authors of the various pamphlets with incredible vehemence and hostility. It is enough to remark that they attempted to prove his Jewish origin by maintaining that "in the past centuries the name of 'Beha' is found in several families in Germany and in Austria, a name which is the phonetic equivalent of the sephardic 'Beja', from the latinisation of which one arrives at the Jewish or crypto-Jewish Cardinal Bea" . . . .

In conclusion, it is sad to relate that even His Holiness Paul VI was not spared from the avalanche of venomous attacks unleashed against the Hierarchy. A little leaflet printed in November 1965 in California, U.S.A., and signed by the "Militant Servants of our Lady of Fatima", states among other things that the Pope committed a "detestable error, comparable to an apostasy, by pronouncing a speech before the atheist representatives of the United Nations", and that 4th October—the date the Pope visited U.N.O.—is to be regarded as a black day in the calendar which has only been eclipsed by the crucifixion of Jesus, since on that day the Pontiff handed over the Mystical Body of Christ to the United Nations, an organisation controlled by Jews, Freemasons and Communists. What then was to be done? We are told: each Council Father was to submit to the rite of exorcism to drive out the devil which became incarnate in their persons in the Council; all the Council decisions were to be regarded as annulled; and they were to renew all their priestly offices and pray God to enable them to resist every other assault of Lucifer and his agents. Only thus could the Pope and the Council Fathers purify themselves of the odious crime of apostasy.

Any comment would be superfluous.

Ugo Apollonio.

Let us note that there are two *Osservatores* at Rome, both of which are produced in the Vatican City in the same office.

The *Osservatore Romano* daily is the official Vatican newspaper.

The position of the *Osservatore della Domenica*, on the other hand, is much less clear. As its name indicates, it is a weekly, and its editors are distinctly progressive which perhaps in part explains the tone of the article in which I am implicated.

Nevertheless, and this is very important, it is a special number which makes a big book of 225 pages. It contains a complete history and résumé of the Council, and there is a preface by His Eminence, Cardinal Cicognani, Secretary of State for the Vatican, and by Monsignor Felici, Secretary General of the Council. It has all the characteristics of an official Vatican document.

Thus the accusations against the authors of pamphlets on the Jewish problem, and against me in particular, are of exceptional gravity.

Although as a general rule I avoid all personal polemics, I find I am obliged to put this matter straight, since I carry the entire responsibility for the material I publish. Otherwise Catholics throughout the world who read this article will receive the impression that I am a fanatical anti-Semite, boiling over with fury and hatred, plotting massacres and persecution, and showering the Council Fathers with a jumble of gratuitous, illogical and calumnious accusations.

Let us then examine the accusations brought against me one by one.

The first accusation is that "they (the authors of these pamphlets) are all either anonymous or pseudonymous; in certain instances they are concealed behind signatures subsequently discovered to be either imaginary or false".

As far as I am concerned, this accusation is completely false, for my pamphlet was signed by my name.

The second accusation is that "many of these pamphlets are entrenched behind a suspect preoccupation with orthodoxy, which they use as a pretext for ill-considered attacks on Cardinals and Bishops, whom they accuse of introducing heresies, seeking to subvert the Church, selling the Church for earthly rewards, and so on; on the other hand, others are distinctly anti-Semitic in tone and unjustly attack many representatives of the Church".

However, I did not make an ill-considered attack on Cardinals and Bishops. I did not accuse them unjustly of seeking to subvert the Church.

Relying on Jewish sources, I demonstrated that through ignorance of the Jewish question they had fallen into a trap most skilfully prepared by the leaders of great Jewish organisations in conjunction with a small minority of progressives.

Doubtless the Council Fathers are well acquainted with the biblical Judaism of the Old Testament, but what do they know of contemporary talmudic Judaism?

The third accusation is the common origin of these pamphlets. "The first and most massive document—around which all the other lesser pamphlets which followed may be said to gravitate—was published in August 1962 under the pseudonym of Maurice Pinay. According to the introduction, this work should have contained 'terrible revelations', whereas it contains, on the contrary, a jumble of gratuitous and illogical accusations against the Council Fathers."

The pamphlet which I circulated at the Council has nothing in common with Maurice Pinay's book, nor for that matter, with any of the other pamphlets published at Rome. As far as I am aware, I am the only person to have made known the role of Jules Isaac, spokesman of the great Jewish organisations, in the Vatican Council, and the only person to have circulated to the Council texts from the works of Jules Isaac, Joshua Jehouda and other doctors of Israel, texts which were fundamental to a comprehension of the issue on which the Council Fathers voted.

The fourth accusation is that of inciting to massacre and persecution against the deicide people. "However, the most important and bitter attacks were directed against 'falsely converted Jews' and the 'international judaeo-masonic B'nai B'rith organisation'. A number of pamphlets and circular letters were sent to the Council Fathers at their private addresses, asserting that 'the Jewish people alone is the deicide people', and that as a result, it must be 'fought and exterminated', since 'through Masonry, Communism and all the subversive organisations which it has created and directs, Judaism arrogantly and implacably continues to combat Christ'."

Nowhere have I ever written that the Jewish deicide people had to be fought and exterminated.

The article continues: "Racism, fanaticism and the most obstinate opposition were displayed by certain anti-Jewish groups in numerous small publications urging ferocious persecution against the Jews, 'fathers of deceit and calumny', quoting Church dogma or teaching in support or approval. As an example we quote from some of these violent publications which we have before us: *The Problem of the Jews at the Council* by L. de Poncins, etc. In all these pamphlets, just as in *Common Sense*, printed in New Jersey and in yet others, the accusations are the same and they spring from the same roots of misunderstanding, intolerance, scorn and hatred of the Jewish people."

Racism, fanaticism, ferocious persecution, intolerance, incomprehension, scorn and hatred towards the Jewish people! I have never written one single line which could be construed as a foundation for any of these accusations, but since I am virtually described as a "pogromist", I would ask the fair-minded reader to consider the degree of violence implicit in the methods and proposals for a solution to the Jewish problem which I drew up shortly before the outbreak of the last war, in a document which was sent to Heads of State and Jewish leaders all over the world, and which is reproduced here in full in Appendix I.

The fifth accusation is that "the campaign, as we have remarked above, was not confined to Italy, but spread over the whole of the latin world. . . . Cardinal Bea, in presenting his proposed decree in favour of the Jews and in opposition to the Evangelists, concealed from the Council Fathers that he was repeating the theses which had been suggested to him by the Masonic order of the B'nai B'rith. Cardinal Bea, who as we know created a study group in the heart of the Secretariat for Christian Unity, in obedience to the express wishes of Pope John, in order to examine from the solely theological and religious point of view the relations between the Church and the Jewish people, and who drafted the declaration on the Jewish problem—Cardinal Bea was attacked by all the anonymous authors of the various pamphlets with incredible vehemence and hostility. It is enough to remark that they attempted to prove his Jewish origin by maintaining that 'in the past centuries the name of "Beha" is found in several families in Germany and Austria, a name which is the phonetic equivalent of the sephardic "Beja", from the latinisation of which one arrives at the Jewish or crypto-Jewish Cardinal Bea'. . . ."

I did not attack Cardinal Bea with "incredible vehemence and hostility"; I only wrote the following few lines about him. Some time after (his visit to the Pope), Isaac "learned with joy that his suggestions had been considered by the Pope and handed on to Cardinal Bea for examination. The latter set up a special working party in the bosom of the Secretariat for Christian Unity, to study relations between the Church and Israel, which finally resulted in the Council Vote on 20th November 1964."

The sixth and final accusation is that "it is sad to relate that even His Holiness Paul VI was not spared from the avalanche of venomous attacks unleashed against the Hierarchy".

But the only mention that I made of Pope Paul VI was in the following lines: "(After the vote in November 1964) the Sovereign Pontiff, considering that a vote with such considerable bearings on politics and doctrine needed ripe reflection, refused to ratify it, and postponed the decision to the next and final session of the Council, which is to open on 14th September 1965. The final vote on the Jewish question took place on 14th October 1965 and was promulgated by the Pope on 28th October."

In a word, then, the accusations against me in the *Osservatore della Domenica* are completely false, and can only be accounted for by the ignorance or bad faith of the author of this article. All who struggle against the forces of subversion in the modern world encounter this procedure. Nesta Webster, who specialised in the study of revolutionary movements, relates her own experiences in her *Secret Societies and Subversive Movements* (preface, v):

"When I first began to write on revolution a well-known London publisher said to me, 'Remember that if you take an antirevolutionary line you will have the whole literary world against you.' This appears to me extraordinary. . . . If I was wrong either in my conclusions or facts I was prepared to be challenged. Should not years of laborious historical research meet either with recognition or with reasoned and scholarly refutation? But although my book received a great many generous and appreciative reviews in the Press, criticisms which were hostile took a form which I had never anticipated. Not a single honest attempt was made to refute either my *French Revolution* or *World Revolution* by the usual methods of controversy; statements founded on documentary evidence were met with flat contradiction unsupported by a shred of counter-evidence. In general the plan adopted was not to disprove, but to discredit by means of flagrant misquotations, by attributing to me views I had never expressed, or even by means of offensive personalities. It will surely be admitted that this method of attack is unparalleled in any other spheres of literary controversy.

"It is interesting to note that precisely the same line was adopted a hundred years ago with regard to Professor Robison and the Abbé Barruel, whose works on the secret causes of the French Revolution created an immense sensation in their day."

There is nothing new in these methods, but it is perhaps surprising to find a publication, which by all appearances is the spokesman of the Vatican, using similar methods when it is a question as serious as a conciliar vote which may alter the age-old doctrine of the Church, and the behaviour of millions of Catholics throughout the world.

However, now that the reader has been informed of all the necessary documents in the case, he may judge for himself.

15

HOW THE JEWS CHANGED CATHOLIC THINKING

THE article in the *Osservatore della Domenica* takes me to task for having brought calumnious and totally unjustified accusations against Cardinal Bea.

But a bomb exploded on 25th January 1966, for on that date an American review published documents of the highest interest on the role of Cardinal Bea and the world Jewish organisations in Vatican Council II.

In their issue of that date the magazine *Look*, which numbers 7,500,000 readers, published a leading article entitled "How the Jews changed Catholic Thinking"—written by their senior editor, Joseph Roddy—which gave many details of the secret negotiations held in New York and Rome by Cardinal Bea with the leaders of the great world Jewish organisations, such as the B'nai B'rith, the American Jewish Committee, and others.

The author begins the article by recalling the responsibility of the Catholic Church, for, as he says, her doctrinal teaching is the principal cause of anti-Semitism in the modern world, and it is worth noting that on this point he faithfully follows Jules Isaac's thesis.

Space prevents us from reproducing more than the following important passages, which we have selected from the article:

> "The best hope that the Church of Rome will not again seem an accomplice to genocide is the fourth chapter of its *Declaration on the Relation of the Church to Non-Christian Religions*, which Pope Paul VI declared Church law near the end of Vatican Council II. At no place in his address from the Chair of Peter did the Pope talk of Jules Isaac. But perhaps the Archbishop of Aix, Charles de Provenchères, had made Isaac's role perfectly clear some few years earlier. 'It is a sign of the times', the Archbishop said, 'that a layman, and a Jewish layman at that, has become the originator of a Council decree.'"

Roddy then mentions the work of Jules Isaac and the book which he published on the question of the relations between Jews and Christians. To return to the article:

"Isaac's book was noticed. In 1949, Pope Pius XII received its author briefly. But eleven years went by before Isaac saw real hope. In Rome, in mid-June 1960, the French Embassy pressed Isaac on to the Holy See. Isaac wanted to see John XXIII. Isaac went to Augustin Bea, the one German Jesuit in the College of Cardinals. 'In him I found powerful support', Isaac said. The next day the support was even stronger. John XXIII . . . reached for Jules Isaac's hand, then sat beside him. 'I asked if I might take away some sparks of hope', Isaac recalled. John said he had a right to more than hope. After Isaac left, John made it clear to the administrators in the Vatican's Curia that a firm condemnation of Catholic anti-Semitism was to come from the Council he had called. To John, the German Cardinal seemed the right legislative whip for the job.

"By then, there was a fair amount of talk passing between the Vatican Council offices and Jewish groups, and both the American Jewish Committee and the Anti-Defamation League of B'nai B'rith were heard loud and clear in Rome. Rabbi Abraham J. Heschel of New York's Jewish Theological Seminary, who first knew of Bea in Berlin thirty years ago, met with the Cardinal in Rome. Bea had already read the American Jewish Committee's *The Image of the Jews in Catholic Teaching*. It was followed by another A.J.C. paper, the twenty-three page study, *Anti-Jewish Elements in Catholic Liturgy*. Speaking for the A.J.C. Heschel said he hoped the Vatican Council would purge Catholic teaching of all suggestions that the Jews were a cursed race. And in doing that, Heschel felt, the Council should in no way exhort Jews to become Christians. About the same time, Israel's Dr. Nahum Goldmann, head of the World Conference of Jewish Organisations, whose members ranged in creed from the most orthodox to liberal, pressed its aspirations on the Pope. B'nai B'rith wanted the Catholics to delete all language from the Church services that could even seem anti-Semitic. Not then, nor in any time to come, would that be a simple thing to do.

"The Catholic liturgy, where it was drawn from writings of the early Church Fathers, could easily be edited. But not the Gospels. Even if Matthew, Mark, Luke and John were better at evangelism than history, their writings were divinely inspired, according to Catholic dogma, and about as easy to alter as the centre of the sun. That difficulty put both Catholics with the very best intentions and Jews with the deepest understanding of Catholicism in a theological fix. It also brought out the conservative opposition in the Church and, to some extent, Arab anxieties in the Middle East. The conservative charge against the Jews was that they were deicides, guilty of killing God in the human-divine person of Christ. . . . Clearly, then, Catholic Scripture would be at issue if the Council spoke about deicides and Jews. Wise and long-mitred heads around the Curia warned that the bishops in Council should not touch this issue with ten-foot staffs. But still there was John XXIII, who said they must.

"If the inviolability of Holy Writ was most of the problem in Rome, the rest was the Arab-Israeli war. . . . In Rome the word from the Middle East and the conservatives was that a Jewish declaration would be inopportune. From the West, where 225,500 more Jews live in New York than in Israel, the word was that dropping the declaration would be a calamity. . . .

"Still, for the bishops, there was quite a bit of supplementary reading on Jews. Some agency close enough to the Vatican to have the addresses in Rome of the Council's 2,200 visiting Cardinals and Bishops, supplied each with a 900 page book, *Il Complotto contro la Chiesa (The Plot Against the Church)*. In it, among reams of scurrility, was a kind of fetching shred of truth. Its claim that the Church was being infiltrated by Jews would intrigue anti-Semites. For, in fact, ordained Jews around Rome working on the Jewish declaration included Father Baum, as well as Mgr. John Oesterreicher, on Bea's staff at the Secretariat. Bea, himself, according to the Cairo daily, *Al Gomhuria*, was a Jew named Behar.

"Neither Baum nor Oesterreicher was with Bea in the late afternoon on 31st March 1963, when a limousine was waiting for him outside the Hotel Plaza in New York. The ride ended about six blocks away, outside the offices of the American Jewish Committee. There a latter-day Sanhedrin was waiting to greet the head of the Secretariat for Christian Unity. The gathering was kept secret from the Press. Bea wanted neither the Holy See nor the Arab League to know he was there to take questions the Jews wanted to hear answered. 'I am not authorised to speak officially,' he told them. 'I can, therefore, speak only of what, in my opinion, could be effected, indeed, should be effected, by the Council.' Then he spelled out the problem. 'In round terms,' he said, 'the Jews are accused of being guilty of deicide, and on them is supposed to lie a curse.' He countered both charges. Because even in the accounts of the Evangelists, only the leaders of the Jews then in Jerusalem and a very small group of followers shouted for the death sentence on Jesus, all those absent and the generations of Jews unborn were not implicated in deicide in any way, Bea said. As to the curse, it could not condemn the crucifiers anyway, the Cardinal reasoned, because Christ's dying words were a prayer for their pardon.

"The rabbis in the room wanted to know then if the declaration would specify deicide, the curse and the rejection of the Jewish people by God as errors in Christian teaching. Implicit in their question was the most touchy problem of the New Testament.

"Bea's answer was oblique. 'Actually,' he went on, 'it is wrong to seek the chief cause of anti-Semitism in purely religious sources —in the Gospel accounts, for example. These religious causes, in so far as they are adduced (often they are not), are often merely an excuse and a veil to cover over other more operative reasons for enmity'. . . .

"Not long after that, the Rolf Hochhuth play *The Deputy* opened to depict Pius XII as the Vicar of Christ who fell silent while Hitler went to the Final Solution. Montini, the Archbishop of Milan, wrote an attack on the play in the *Tablet* of London, and a defence of the Pope, whose secretary he had been. A few months later, Pope John XXIII was dead, and Montini became Pope Paul VI.

"At the second session of the Council, in autumn 1963, the Jewish declaration came to the bishops as chapter four of the larger declaration *On Ecumenism* . . . but the session ended without the vote on the Jews or religious liberty, and on a distinctly sour note, despite the Pope's announced visit to the Holy Land. 'Something had happened behind the scenes', the voice of the National Catholic Welfare Conference wrote. '(It is) one of the mysteries of the second session.'

"Two very concerned Jewish gentlemen who had to reflect hard on such mysteries were 59-year-old Joseph Lichten of B'nai B'rith's Anti-Defamation League in New York, and Zachariah Shuster, 63, of the American Jewish Committee. The strongest possible Jewish declaration was their common cause."

The article in *Look* then gives a detailed report of the frantic efforts made in Rome by the representatives of the great Jewish organisations, and we learn that apparently the New York *Times*, whose owners and directors are Jewish, was the best informed paper on the progress of the negotiations. "To find out how the Council was going, many U.S. bishops in Rome depended on what they read in the New York *Times*. And so did the A.J.C. and the B'nai B'rith. That paper was the place to make points."

Then, "Mgr. George Higgins, of the National Catholic Welfare Conference in Washington, D.C., helped arrange a papal audience for U.N. Ambassador, Arthur J. Goldberg, who was a Supreme Court Justice at the time. Rabbi Heschel briefed Goldberg before the Justice and the Pope discussed the declaration . . . and Cardinal Cushing arranged an audience with the Pope for Heschel. With the A.J.C's Shuster beside him, Heschel talked hard about deicide and guilt, and asked the Pontiff to press for a declaration in which Catholics would be forbidden to proselytise Jews. Paul, somewhat affronted, would in no way agree . . . and the audience did not end as cordially as it began. . . .

"The Rabbi's audience with Paul in the Vatican, like Bea's meeting with the A.J.C. in New York, was granted on the condition that it would be kept secret. It was undercover summit conferences of that sort that led conservatives to claim that American Jews were the new powers behind the Church.

"But on the floor of the Council, things looked even worse to the conservatives. There, it seemed to them as if Catholic bishops were working for the Jews. At issue was the weakened text. . . . The Arab bishops argued that a declaration favouring Jews would expose Catholics to persecution as long as Arabs fought Israelis. Their allies in this holy war were conservative Italians, Spaniards and South Americans. They saw the structure of the faith being shaken by theological liberals who thought Church teaching could change.

"When the declaration reappeared at the third session's end, it was in a wholly new document called *The Declaration of the Relation of the Church to Non-Christian Religions*. In that setting, the bishops approved it with a 1,770 to 185 vote. There was considerable joy among Jews in the United States because their declaration had finally come out.

"In fact it had not.

"There were troubles to face. In Segni, near Rome, Bishop Luigi Carli wrote in the February 1965 issue of his diocesan magazine that the Jews of Christ's time and their descendants down to the present were collectively guilty of Christ's death. A few weeks later, on Passion Sunday, at an outdoor Mass in Rome, Pope Paul talked of the Crucifixion and the Jews' heavy part in it. Rome's chief rabbi, Elio Toaff, said in saddened reply that in 'even the most qualified Catholic personalities, the imminence of Easter causes prejudices to re-emerge'.

"On 25th April 1965, the New York *Times* correspondent in Rome, Robert C. Doty . . . said the Jewish declaration was in trouble . . . and that the Pope had turned it over to four consultants to clear it of its contradictions to Scripture and make it less objectionable to Arabs. It was about as refuted as a *Times* story ever gets. When Cardinal Bea arrived in New York three days later, he had his priest-secretary deny Doty's story by saying that his Secretariat for Christian Unity still had full control of the Jewish declaration. Then came an apologia for Paul's sermon. 'Keep in mind that the Pope was speaking to ordinary and simple faithful people—not before a learned body', the priest said. As to the anti-Semitic Bishop of Segni, the Cardinal's man said that Carli's views were definitely not those of the Secretariat. Moriss B. Abram of the A.J.C. was at the airport to greet Bea and found his secretary's views on that reassuring.

"In Rome a few days later, some fraction of the Secretariat met to vote on the bishop's suggested *modi*. On 15th May, the Secretariat closed its meeting, and the bishops went their separate ways . . . all with lips sealed.

"In fact, the study was finished, the damage was done, and there existed what many regard as a substantially new declaration on the Jews.

"At Vatican II's fourth and last session, there was no help in sight. And things were happening very fast. The text came out weakened, as the *Times* said it would. Then the Pope took off for the U.N., where his *jamais plus la guerre* speech was a triumph. After that, he greeted the president of the A.J.C. in an East Side Church. That looked good for the cause. . . . But the opposition, not content with a weakened declaration, wanted the total victory of no declaration at all. For that, the Arab's last words were 'respectfully submitted' in a twenty-eight-page memorandum calling on the bishops to save the faith from 'Communism and atheism and the Jewish-Communist alliance'.

"In Rome, the bishops' vote was set for 14th October and to Lichten and Shuster, the prospects of anything better looked almost hopeless. There were telephone calls to be made to the A.J.C. and the B'nai B'rith in New York, but these were not much help at either end. . . . Lichten sent telegrams to about twenty-five bishops he thought could still help retrieve the strong text, but Higgins quietly told him to give up. Abbé René Laurentin, a Council staff man (and correspondent of *Le Figaro*) wrote to all the bishops with a last-minute appeal to conscience.

"Finally, the vote took place, and exactly 250 bishops voted against the declaration, while 1,763 supported it. Through much of the U.S. and Europe, the Press minutes later made the complex simple with headlines reading VATICAN PARDONS JEWS, JEWS

NOT GUILTY or JEWS EXONERATED IN ROME. Glowing statements came from spokesmen of the A.J.C. and B'nai B'rith, but each had a note of disappointment that the strong declaration had been diluted. Bea's friend Heschel was the harshest and called the Council's failure to deal with deicide 'an act of paying homage to Satan'.

"A view popular in the U.S. was that some kind of forgiveness had been granted the Jews. The notion was both started and sustained by the Press, but there was no basis for it in the declaration. . . . And one of the hypotheses that B'nai B'rith and the A.J.C. must ponder is that much Arab resistance and some theological intransigence were creatures of Jewish lobbying. . . . There are Catholics close to what went on in Rome who think that Jewish energy did harm. . . . There were many bishops at the Council who felt Jewish pressure in Rome and resented it. They thought Bea's enemies were proved right when the Council secrets turned up in American papers. 'He wants to turn the Church over to the Jews,' the hatemongers said of the old cardinal, and some dogmatics in the Council thought the charge about right.

"Father Felix Morlion at the Pro Deo University, who heads the study group working closely with the A.J.C. thought the promulgated text the best. . . . Morlion knew just what the Jews did to get the declaration and why the Catholics had settled for its compromise. *'We could have beaten the dogmatics'*, he insisted. *They could indeed, but the cost would have been a split in the Church.*"

(Look, 25th January 1966, pp. 19-23)

This article is of the utmost interest for it gives us numerous details of Cardinal Bea's secret negotiations with the leaders of the great American Jewish organisations, and in particular with the B'nai B'rith.

The author of the article is obviously in close contact with these leaders and it must almost certainly have been they who supplied him with his documentation. Cardinal Bea has all his sympathy and is depicted as making incessant efforts for the triumph of the Jewish cause at Rome.

Far from being the product of "anti-Semitic" opponents, it is written and produced by parties eminently favourable to the Jewish cause, and thus cannot be dismissed as a work motivated by hatred or bad faith.

It was read by 7,500,000 people at least, and yet, as far as I know, the publication of this extraordinary document produced no reaction at Rome or anywhere else. In the whole Catholic Church no one has risen to express astonishment or ask for an explanation.

In these circumstances we would be glad to read at least a reasoned reply from the Vatican, failing which we are obliged to conclude that Cardinal Bea came to a secret understanding with the leaders of the great American Jewish organisations, and in particular with the B'nai B'rith, to work for the triumph of the Jewish cause, despite the opposition of the conservatives in the Curia and elsewhere.

However that may be, the spectacle of a cardinal in one of the highest posts of the Catholic Hierarchy offering excuses to American Jews because the Pope had read from and commented on the Gospel account of the Passion in Holy Week, is something which had never yet been seen in the whole two thousand years of the history of Christianity.

This claim of the Jews to have the Gospels censored has spread since the new attitude adopted by the Council. On 1st January 1966, *La Terre Retrouvée*, a Zionist publication from Paris, published an article about a six volume Sacred History by Hachette. The following is a typical passage from the article in question:

> "What we take exception to in these very beautiful colour printed volumes, is their conformity. . . .
>
> "Their pictures are a servile and pious amplification of the text. And the text, as far as the Old Testament is concerned, is resumed in conformity with the official doctrine of the Church on the role of Christ, as is shown, for example, by the title of the fourth volume in the series—*From David to the Messiah*. It is taken for granted that the Messiah has come, that David's line leads to him, and that the Messiah is Jesus. Doubtless one can argue this problem of the Messiah with Israel in theology, or in all sorts of other fields. *But boys and girls should not be served with a truth which is only a Gospel truth and which the whole teaching of Israel denies.*
>
> "Of course, we do not claim that only ecumenical Sacred History may be taught. That would be impossible. Nor do we claim that Christian teaching should censor itself, except—and we believe that in this matter, since the Council, it has a positive obligation —when it is a question of replacing the doctrine of contempt of the Jews with the doctrine of esteem . . . the idea of one sewing hatred in the souls of the boys and girls for whom these books were written is a frightful thing to contemplate."
>
> (Paul Giniewski: *La Terre Retrouvée*)

Thus, according to *La Terre Retrouvée*, spreading the knowledge of the Gospels is to propagate throughout the world a frightful seed of hatred!

APPENDIX I

APPEAL TO HEADS OF STATE

WE give below the text of an appeal personally addressed by the author almost exactly one year before the Second World War broke out to the heads of State all over the world, suggesting the creation of an international commission as the first step to be taken towards a peaceful solution of the Jewish problem:

The experience of forty centuries of history bears witness over a longer period than any other known example to the fact that there is such a thing as the Jewish problem.

For forty centuries the essential features of the problem have scarcely changed, whether in the political, religious or economic fields.

At first sight, it would appear that it is insoluble and that all that one can do is to let events take their course, accepting crisis after crisis, persecution after persecution and a permanent element of disorder as an inherent part of the very constitution of the white races. In this case there would be no problem to solve. It would simply be a question of recording Jews and non-Jews pursuing with all their power and with the aid of as many allies as possible the enslavement and destruction of their adversary.

Today events seem to be moving towards this dangerous state of affairs.

The stakes are as high as the danger is immense. Conquered, the West would lose its historic personality and be obliged to renounce its mission.

Conquered, the Jews would emerge from the struggle crushed as they had never been before. But what a price the West would have to pay for its victory.

We write this with the full courage of our convictions—as we always have—but we do not think that a catastrophe is inevitable, nor that the problem can only be solved by an Apocalyptic conflagration in which atrocious violence and persecution is unleashed. If the problem with which we are concerned has till now appeared insoluble, it seems to us that this is largely due to the fact that it has never been studied in a spirit of rigorous and scientific impartiality. And doubtless this is because, blinded by passion, *neither side have really wanted to study it, because, for various reasons, neither side have really wanted to solve it.*

Violence, curses and complaints are none of them valid arguments bringing a solution to the problem.

We must approach the problem as scholars using scholarly arguments in order to attempt to elucidate a difficult question to some purpose.

We consider that Jews and non-Jews, anti-Semites and philo-Semites in good faith alike, who are convinced that they have something essential to defend and maintain, both have something essential to gain from an attentive and comprehensive study of the question that divides them.

Without being under any illusion as to the magnitude and difficulty of the task before us, but in an endeavour to achieve at least some useful results, we have taken the initiative in suggesting the foundation of an INTERNATIONAL INSTITUTE TO STUDY THE JEWISH QUESTION.

The Institute would be strongly organised and established in some neutral and symbolical town such as Geneva or the Hague. Competent and representative personalities, Jewish and non-Jewish, hostile and favourable to Judaism, but all of indisputably high moral and intellectual standing, would collaborate in it.

A certain number of precise and well-defined questions, drawn up by the Institute's Council of Direction, composed of Jews and non-Jews, would be set before the Institute's two departments for the criticism and defence of Judaism and its influence, who would share them out among the competent sections. The results obtained on either side would be brought together and discussed in interdepartmental sessions. The conclusions adopted in common agreement would be communicated to the governments of the Western nations and brought to the knowledge of public opinion in all countries. In case of disagreement, a strictly objective summary of the arguments produced by both sides would be published in order to pave the way for future studies.

The very fact that common agreement could be reached on studying the Jewish problem, which is so delicate and so complex, in a spirit of rigorous scientific impartiality, would constitute a great step forward in itself likely to diminish passions which today have become so dangerously exasperated.

We have no doubt that all the States, all the Governments and all the great Jewish organisations of the whole world, whatever attitude they may adopt with regard to the Jewish question, will give our idea consideration and support its immediate realisation.

We appeal to all people of good will to seek out the truth, remembering Dostoievsky's words that "whoever sincerely seeks the truth is already, by that fact, armed with a terrible force" and that finally, if men "enter into the path of truth, they will find it".

It is in this firm conviction that we launch our appeal with indestructible confidence.

Something must be done!

Apart from high Authorities to whom it is destined, the present Appeal will be sent to a great number of personalities in all countries of every shade of opinion. We would be obliged if those who are interested would write and offer us their reflexions, suggestions and criticism. And we will be especially grateful to those who make a material contribution towards a special fund which wiil be set up to help us diffuse our idea and achieve our object.

LEON DE PONCINS
GEORGE BATAULT

The World War, which broke out shortly afterwards, put an end to our endeavours.

APPENDIX II

SIX MILLION INNOCENT VICTIMS

SIX million dead, such is the fearful figure with which the organisations of Jewry ceaselessly confront the world; it is the unanswered argument of which they availed themselves at the Council in order to obtain a revision of the Catholic Liturgy.

This figure of six million, to which the Jewish organisations testified, was neither verified nor checked in any way whatsoever, and it served as the foundation for the prosecution at the time of the Nuremberg Trial, and was widely disseminated by the Press of the whole world.

Today many facts and documents have come to light which were not known at that time and it is no longer possible to give credence to this figure.

A French Socialist of the left, who was himself deported to Buchenwald, Mr. Paul Rassinier, has made a prolonged and extremely detailed study of this question, which he published in four large volumes, summarised in this chapter.

Rassinier reached the conclusion that the number of Jews who died after deportation is approximately 1,200,000, and this figure, he tells us, has finally been accepted as valid by the Centre Mondial de Documentation Juive Contemporaine. Likewise he notes that Paul Hilberg, in his study of the same problem, reached a total of 896,292 victims.

So many exaggerations and impostures have completely distorted the facts that we deem it only fair to make known to the reader, who is concerned for historical truth, what were the real ingredients of an incontestibly tragic drama, but one which, reduced to its proper proportions must be seen in the entire context of the Second World War, which indeed numbered many millions of innocent victims on all sides.

The notes which follow are taken from the two most recent works of Rassinier: *Le Véritable Procès Eichmann ou les Vainqueurs Incorrigibles* and *Le Drame des Juifs européens*. The author must bear the responsibility for what he has written. For our part it would seem that these books represent a testimony of great value, for they

APPENDIX II SIX MILLION INNOCENT VICTIMS

bring to light important facts and documents which lay open to question everything that has been written on this aspect of the war.

The following is a résumé of Rassinier's thesis:

It was during the course of the trial of major German war criminals at Nuremberg, 1945-46, that the number of Jews alleged to have been the victims of German concentration camps and gas chambers was first put forward.

In his speech of indictment on 21st November 1945, Mr. Justice Jackson declared that of 9,500,000 Jews who had been living in Germany-occupied Europe, 4,500,000 had disappeared.

This figure was not retained by the court, but was nevertheless soon transformed by the Press to ten millions, and then reduced to an average of six million, where it scored a resounding success, and was definitely accepted by the whole world.

It had been approximately established by specialists in Jewish demography by two methods:

Either, as was done by the World Jewish Congress, by comparing the data of, respectively, the pre-war and post-war figures of the Jewish population of the various European occupied countries, resulting in a loss of six million. Unfortunately these statistics do not take into account important emmigration movements by the Jewish population of Europe between 1933-45, particularly towards Palestine and the United States, which meant that they were established on completely false foundations;

Or by means of the oral or written declarations of "witnesses" which for the most part have proved, after serious investigation, to be full of contradictions, exaggerations and falsehoods, and which cannot therefore any longer be taken into consideration.

Indeed, some of these "witnesses", such as Pastor Martin Niemöller, who had been a fervent adherent of National Socialism, have felt a need to clear themselves and outbid everyone else, so as to appear more sincere.

"Pastor Niemöller claimed in a lecture which he delivered on the 3rd July 1946, and which was published under the title of *Der Weg ins Freie* by Franz M. Helbach at Stuttgart that '238,756 persons were incinerated at Dachau'."

However, "On 16th March 1962, Mgr. Neuhäussler, the auxiliary Bishop of Munich, made a speech at Dachau itself before the representatives of fifteen nations who had come there to celebrate the liberation of the camp, which was reported next day in *Le Figaro* in these words:

" 'This afternoon, in intense cold and despite the aggravation of snow, the pilgrims have gathered together in the camp at Dachau

where 30,000 men were exterminated of the 200,000 persons from thirty-eight nations who were interned there from 1939-45.' "
(Paul Rassinier: *Le Drame des Juifs européens*, p. 12)

The testimony of men such as Rudolph Hess, the SS officers Hoelbrigel, Hoettl, Wisceliceny, and others ... who were amongst the accused at Nuremberg, and who were faced with the prospect either of being condemned to death or with the hope of obtaining a reprieve, is highly suspect. Having been frequently subjected to ill-treatment or threats during their detention, they seem to have said or written what was desired of them.

Others, who had survived the German concentration camps, perhaps felt guilty for reprehensible acts which they had committed and for which they might now be required to answer before a court; such was the case of the Czech Communist doctor, Blaha, who had belonged to the self-direction committee of the camp at Dachau, or Professor Balachowsky of the Institut Pasteur of Paris, who was deported to Buchenwald, and who had a predilection for dabbling in crime. Those most directly affected fell back, to exculpate themselves, on the necessity of obeying orders under pain of disappearing. It is not surprising that under these conditions there should be something a little "forced" about their declarations. Other survivors only witnessed what happened at second-hand, such as Dr. Kautsky; they based their declarations not upon what they themselves "saw" but upon what they "heard", always from "reliable" sources, who by some chance are almost always dead and thus not in a position to confirm or invalidate their statements.

Scant testimony indeed upon which to establish with absolute certainty the number of victims in the camps. And yet this figure of six million dead has been given world-wide publicity and accepted as an article of faith without being checked or verified in any way whatsoever. It owes its success to the abundant growth of concentration-camp literature, which is cosmopolitan and mainly Jewish, full of both imposture and falsehood.

We give below a list of some of the most typical titles of works of this kind, headed by *Axis Rule in Occupied Europe*, by Professor Rafael Lemkin, a Polish Jew, who fled to England and was the first to accuse National Socialist Germany of the crime of genocide. Numerous writers subsequently took up this thesis:

Chaines et Lumières by Abbé Jean-Paul Renard.
The Destruction of the European Jews by Paul Hilberg.
Le Bréviaire de la Haine by Léon Poliakov.
Le 3ème Reich et les Juifs by L. Poliakov and Wulf.
Documentation sur les gaz by H. Krausnik.

APPENDIX II SIX MILLION INNOCENT VICTIMS

Mémoires de Rudolf Hess, published in part under the title of *Le Commandant d'Auschwitz parle.* . . .
Le Vicaire by Rudolf Hochhuth.

But the palm, Rassinier tells us, is undoubtedly awarded to the unbelievable work of the Jewish Hungarian Doctor, Miklos Nyizli: *Médecin à Auschwitz*.

By its falsification of facts, the evident contradictions and shameless lies, this book seems to show that Dr. Nyizli is speaking of places which it is transparent he has never visited, not to mention that it is a document of extremely doubtful authenticity, as Rassinier has shown. (*Le Drame des Juifs européens*, p. 52).

If one is to believe the distinguished "Doctor of Auschwitz", 25,000 victims were exterminated each day for four and a half years. This amounts to 1,642 days which, at 25,000 a day, produces a total of forty-one million victims, in other words, two and a half times the total pre-war Jewish population of the world.

When Rassinier attempted to discover the identity of this strange "witness", he was told that "he had died some time before the publication of the book".

Today, when numerous documents still unknown at the time of the Nuremberg Trial have been exhumed and made public, it would seem to be difficult to continue to maintain the figure of six million Jewish victims, as do both Jules Isaac, in his two books *Jésus et Israel* and *Genèse de l'Antisémitisme* and Vladimir Jankélévitch, Professor of the School of Arts and Humane Sciences, at Paris, in the article in *Le Monde* from which we have quoted an extract above, and it is becoming increasingly recognised that this figure has been considerably exaggerated, and that it does not in any way correspond to reality.[1]

During the trial of Eichmann at Jerusalem the figure of six million was not mentioned in court:

"The prosecution at the Jerusalem trial was considerably weakened by its central motif, the six million European Jews[2] exterminated in the great mass of the gas-chambers.

"It was an argument that easily won conviction the day after the war ended, amidst the general state of spiritual and material chaos. Today many documents have been published which were

---

[1] However, the world Press continues to publish these figures. The weekly *Paris-Match*, in its special issue of 20th March 1965, on the capture of Berlin, wrote that "in the death camps fifteen million deportees were assassinated".

[2] This figure was only mentioned by the Press and by witnesses; the charge drawn up by Mr. Gideon Haussner simply said "some" millions.

not available at the time of the Nuremberg trials, and which tend to prove that if the Jewish nationals were odiously wronged and persecuted by the Hitler régime, there could not possibly have been six million victims." (P. Rassinier, ibid., p. 125)

Indeed, contrary to the estimates put forward at Nuremberg by Mr. Justice Jackson and at Jerusalem during the Eichmann trial by Professor Shalom Baron, the total Jewish population of Europe was far from being as high as 9,600,000, as the former claimed, or 9,800,000, as maintained by the latter.

Between 1933 and 1945 large numbers of Jews from Central Europe emigrated to other countries in order to avoid first the interference and later the persecution of the Germans. Recent statistics confirm this. In his book *Le Drame des Juifs européens*, Rassinier deals with this point in the light of extremely precise information. We recommend the reader who is interested to consult the work himself.

This is the gist of what he says:

Taking into account the constant flow of emigration, Mr. Arthur Ruppin, the most authoritative of the Jewish statisticians, estimates the population at that time at 5,710,000; the Centre de Documentation Juive of Paris and Doctor Korherr put it as respectively 5,294,000 and 5,500,000, and the latter would appear to be the closest to reality. Thus, omitting this calculation, the statistics of survivors established in 1945 are found to be completely false and the margin of error in relation to them represents about 40 per cent of the real figure. The number of survivors, therefore, was not 1,651,000 as was claimed at that time, but something in the order of 4,200,000 or more, which reduces the figure of the missing to between one and one and a half million, and represents a large percentage of the victims.

Another source of error in the calculation of the number of victims stems from the fact that as the Russian troops advanced, deportees were brought back from Poland to the western camps of Buchenwald, Dora, Dachau, and others (J. Rassinier: *Le Véritable Procès Eichmann*, pp. 94-95). These men, who had been registered upon their arrival at Auschwitz or elsewhere, were not to be found when these camps were liberated, and were put down as missing or exterminated in the gas-chambers if they were Jews. In reality they were alive and kicking in the German camps further west, but the timing of their arrival had rendered their subsequent registration impossible and no real record of it had been kept.

There is a further point to consider. The toll of mortality in camps reserved for Jews was undoubtedly higher than in the others. But after minute investigation one must perforce admit that, in general, if the responsibility for the high mortality of the camps rested with the SS men who were in charge of them, it rested even more with the detainees who were in charge of the administration of these camps.

According to Rassinier, the number of missing evaluated above is corroborated today by the statistical studies of the Centre Mondial de Documentation Juive Contemporaine, which gives a figure of 1,485,292 Jewish victims. As we have noted, Paul Hilberg accounts for 896,292 victims.

But of one fact, he tells us, and it is the most explosive to emerge from his books, there is now no doubt at all. Very serious investigations carried out on the sites themselves have revealed with irrefutable proof that contrary to the declarations of the above-named "witnesses", whether it is a question of Buchenwald, Dora, Mathausen, Bergen-Belsen or Dachau, not one of the camps throughout the whole of German territory was fitted with gas-chambers. This fact has been recognised and attested by the Institute of Contemporary History at Munich, a model of hostility to National Socialist Germany.

At Dachau the construction of a gas-chamber had in fact been begun but it was only completed at the end of the war by SS men who had taken the place of the deportees.

Nevertheless Doctor Blaha has given up copious details of the exterminations which apparently took place in this camp, Fr. Jean-Paul Renard wrote in his book *Chaines et Lumières* that he "had seen thousands upon thousands of people" in the gas-chambers at Buchenwald ... which were non-existent, and numerous "witnesses" again declared at the Eichmann trial at Jerusalem that they had seen deportees at Bergen-Belsen setting out for the gas-chambers.

As far as the Polish camps occupied by the Germans are concerned, the sole document attesting the existence and utilisation of gas-chambers at Chemno, Belzec, Maidanek, Sobidor and Treblinka comes from a man named Kurt Gerstein. Drawn up in French by this ex-*Waffen* SS man—we will never know why since the man in question "committed suicide" in his cell after composing this peculiar confession—the document was considered of such doubtful authenticity from the moment it appeared that, produced at Nuremberg on the 30th January 1946, it was not admitted by the Court, and not included in the charge against the accused. This did not prevent the Press from upholding it as authentic, and it continues to circulate in three different versions—two in French and one in German—which moreover do not agree with each other. The latter version featured in the Eichmann trial at Jerusalem in 1961. Bad faith, as we see, dies hard.

It is probable that there was a gas-chamber in existence at Belzec. At Auschwitz, on the other hand, it seems to have been established that there was one in existence and functioning; a great deal of evidence exists, but it is so often divergent and contradictory that it is difficult to disentangle the truth. If any such chambers were in operation at Auschwitz, it can only have been from the 20th February 1943, when they were completed, until the 17th November 1944—in other words, for seventeen to eighteen months, from which a certain number of months must be deducted since, according to the report of Dr. Rezso Kasztner, president of the Committee for the Salvation of the Jews of Budapest from 1942 to 1945, these chambers were out of operation from the autumn of 1943 to May 1944.

It would be difficult to form any idea of the number of victims who are said to have passed through these chambers, since no exact and credible assessments appear to have been made, and the accounts given by the various witnesses are more akin to the realm of extravagance than reality. So many "witnesses" have "committed suicide" —or been forced to do so—and so many others have died who perhaps never even existed, that it is impossible to lend faith to their statements; for what strikes one more forcibly than anything else upon attempting to discover precise evidence and the original documents is the way in which both of these sources, whose sole factor in common is their "good faith", have "disappeared".

Rassinier's study clearly shows that if Hitler's Germany was racialist and did not, as such, consider the Jews as nationals, that she did not, in the beginning at least, wish to exterminate the Jews, but to place them outside the national community—which is precisely what the State of Israel did when she drove back into Jordan 900,000 Arabs who had been living in Palestine.

"Germany under Hitler was a racialist State. Now, as we know, (the theory of) the racialist State postulates the expulsion of minority races outside the frontiers of the national community. The State of Israel is another example of this assumption.

"According to Article 4 of the twenty-five point programme of the National Socialist Party published in Munich on the 24th February 1920, 'Only a patriot can be a citizen. Only a person who has German blood in his veins, irrespective of his religion, can be a patriot. A Jew cannot be a patriot. . . .'

"Article 5 concluded: 'A person who is not a citizen can only live in Germany as a guest and is subject to the legislation for aliens.'

"When National Socialism came to power on the 30th February

1933, the German Jews automatically became subject to the Statute of Aliens, which in every country of the world excludes foreigners from positions of influence in the State or the Economy. Such is the juridical foundation of the racial laws in Hitler's Germany....

"The only difference between Germany under Hitler and other States, is that in the latter one is a foreigner by virtue of one's nationality, whereas under National Socialism a foreigner was classified by virtue of his race. But in Israel Arabs no longer teach, or work in the Treasury, or administer a kibbutz, or become Ministers of State. What is happening in Israel does not justify what has happened in Germany, I agree—doubtless because one wrong does not right another—but I am not attempting to justify, I am offering an explanation, and to do so I am taking a mechanism to pieces: if I quote Israel, it is only to show at the same time that the evil of racialism in the sense in which National Socialism understood the word is much greater than is generally believed, since the champions of anti-racialism have today become its protagonists and, contrary to popular opinion, Hitler's Germany is not, so to speak, its only example."

(P. Rassinier, *Le Véritable Procès Eichmann*, pp. 100-101)

The promulgation of the racial laws after the Congress of Nuremberg in September 1935 led the German Government into negotiations seeking to transfer the Jews to Palestine on the basis of the Balfour Declaration. When this failed, the government asked other countries to take charge of them. They refused.

"Since there was no Jewish State with which to draw up a bilateral agreement or international treaty on the model of Geneva or the Hague, and since, despite reiterated offers from the National Socialist Government, not a single country had agreed either to permit them to immigrate or to take them under their wing, they lived in Germany until the declaration of war enjoying the status of stateless foreigners, which was no guarantee to the safety of their persons, since, as such people all over the world are, they were at the mercy of those in power." (P. Rassinier, ibid., p. 20)

It was only in November 1938, after the assassination of von Rath, the Councillor of the German Embassy in Paris, by Grynspan, who was Jewish—a crime which provoked violent anti-Jewish reaction in Germany—that the leaders of the Third Reich proposed the introduction of an over-all solution to the Jewish problem and re-launched the idea of transfering them to Palestine. The project, which had dragged on since 1933, broke down because Germany could not negotiate their departure on the basis of 3,000,000 marks, as demanded by Britain, without some agreement for compensation. Moreover Germany was unable to negotiate the emigration of the Jews on a massive scale with other countries, since they refused to establish import-export agreements in compensation which would have made emigration possible. France likewise, at the end of 1940, did not agree to their transfer to Madagascar:

"After the defeat of France and the failure to conclude peace with England, the German leaders conceived the idea that the Jews could be gathered together and then transferred to a French colonial territory, for example, Madagascar. In a report on the 21st August 1942, the Secretary of State for the Ministry of Foreign Affairs of the Third Reich, Luther, decided that it would be possible to negotiate with France in this direction and described conversations which had taken place between July and December 1940, and which were brought to a halt following the interview with Montoire on 13th December 1940 by Pierre-Etienne Flandin, Laval's successor. During the whole of 1941 the Germans hoped that they would be able to reopen these negotiations and bring them to a happy conclusion." (P. Rassinier, ibid., p. 108)

It was only after successive rebuffs, and for several other reasons, as we shall see, that Germany's attitude in relation to the Jews hardened.

First of all, there was the letter sent by Chaim Weizmann, President of the Jewish Agency, to Chamberlain, Prime Minister of Great Britain, in which he informed him that "we Jews are on the side of Great Britain and will fight for democracy". It was published in the *Jewish Chronicle* of the 8th September 1939 and constituted a veritable declaration of war by World Jewry against Germany.

Earlier Leon Blum had urged the democracies to destroy the racist ideology in an article which was published in *Paris-Soir* on the 23rd March 1939:

"The re-organisation, the reconciliation and the co-operation of all the States in the world that are attached to liberty and peace, and the stimulation and exaltation of the democratic system, and at the same time the systematic destruction of the racist ideology, that is the essential task incumbent on the great movements of public opinion, without which the governments would be impotent."

The Jewish writer Emil Ludwig, a naturalised Swiss of German origin, who was decorated with the Légion d'Honneur by the French

Government in April 1939, launched an appeal with a great deal of to-do about the same time "for a new Holy Alliance to be concluded between the three great democracies of the world", and scarcely disguised the invitation to war:

". . . the influence of the United States in this alliance will be the decisive factor. Because this new alliance is first and foremost designed as a threat and a deterrent, the chief role falls to America. . . ."   (E. Ludwig: *A New Holy Alliance*, p. 94)

"All countries may join the new Holy Alliance . . . among the Great Powers the Soviet Union will be the first. . . . (p. 101). The national philosophy will decide whether or not a state is to be admitted into the alliance . . . the alliance is directed against Germany, Italy and similar states which might adopt such principles at any moment . . . it issues its challenge in even more forceful language than that of the dictators. (p. 104)
for
". . . the political aims of this century are: socialism as the national expedient, and the United States of Europe as the international policy. Is it possible to reach both goals without war? . . ." (p. 120)

It seems hardly likely, and Ludwig makes no attempt to disguise the fact, since he concludes his appeal with the words:

"Religions, philosophies, ideals have always been formulated and guarded by solitary thinkers. But they have always been defended by armed men, at the peril of their lives."
(E. Ludwig, ibid., p. 123)

To return to the position of the Jews in Germany.

"In September 1939, from the very moment hostilities began, the authorities representing the World Jewish Congress, as if to reproach England and France with having delayed so long, recalled that 'the Jews of the entire world had declared economic and financial war on Germany as early as 1933' and that they had 'resolved to carry this war of destruction through to the end', and at the same time they authorised Hitler to place all those to hand in concentration camps, which is the way countries all over the world treat enemy aliens in time of war. As events developed the European Jews found themselves in the same boat as their brethren in Germany, and when there was no longer any hope of their emigrating outside Europe—and the last chance vanished with the failure of the Madagascar plan at the end of 1940—it was decided to regroup them and to put them to work in one immense ghetto which, after the successful invasion of Russia, was situated towards the end of 1941 in the so-called Eastern territories near the former frontier between Russia and Poland: at Auschwitz, Chelmno, Belzec, Maidaneck, Treblinka, etc. . . . There they were to wait until the end of the war for the re-opening of international discussions which would decide their fate. This decision was finally reached at the famous interministerial Berlin-Wannsee conference which was held on the 20th January 1942, and the transfer had commenced in March."

(P. Rassinier, *Le Véritable Procès Eichmann*, p. 20)

Then came the declaration of war against Russia, the massive bombardment of Dresden, Leipzig and Hamburg, and lastly the publication of a book by an American Jew, Theodor N. Kaufman, called *Germany must perish*:

"In his book, Kaufman flatly states that Germans, solely because they are Germans, do not deserve to live . . . and that after the war 25,000 doctors will be mobilised and each will be given 25 German men or women to sterilise every day, so that in three months there would not be a single German alive in Europe capable of reproduction and in sixty years the German race would be totally eliminated from the continent. He said, moreover, that the German Jews shared his view.

"Hitler ordered this book to be broadcast over all German radio stations, and one can imagine the effect it produced on the German public."

(P. Rassinier, pp. 108-109)

Finally let us deal with the Morgenthau plan.

This scheme, which had been drawn up in the United States by Henry Morgenthau, one of Roosevelt's advisers, and Harry Dexter White (both men were Jewish, the latter of Eastern European origin), provided for the complete destruction of German industry and the definite transformation of Germany into an agricultural country.

It was approved at the Quebec Conference of 1943, and as soon as the war was ended the Allies put it into operation and began dismantling the factories in the Ruhr. It was quickly realised that it was completely senseless and abandoned. Meanwhile Harry Dexter White had been discovered to be a Soviet agent. He died of a heart attack the day before he was due to be arrested.

But with reference to Germany; in the face of the Morgenthau plan, the Kaufman plan, the declaration by Chaim Weizmann and the World Jewish Congress of war to the bitter end, the declaration

APPENDIX II SIX MILLION INNOCENT VICTIMS

of Casablanca confirming the decision to accept only an unconditional surrender, the campaign of terror-bombing of the civilian population of German towns (135,000 died at Dresden), the Germans were now convinced that the Allies had decided on their extermination, and in these conditions one is not surprised to find that the Jews collected in the camps served as hostages and that terrible reprisals fell upon them.

It was in these circumstances that there commenced the massive and brutal deportation of Jews towards the Polish camps, particularly Auschwitz.

To bring this chapter to a conclusion, we wish to quote the evidence of a Jewish witness, the importance of which will not escape the reader. In the issue of 15th December 1960 of *La Terre Retrouvée*, Doctor Kubovy, director of the Centre Mondial de Documentation Juive Contemporaine at Tel-Aviv, recognised that no order for extermination exists from Hitler, Himmler, Heydrich or Goering (Rassinier: *Le Drame des Juifs Européens*, pp. 31, 39). It would seem then that the exterminations by gas were the work of regional authorities and a few sadistic Germans.

According to Rassinier, the exaggeration in the calculation of the number of victims is inspired by a purely material problem:

". . . It is simply a question of justifying by a proportionate number of corpses the enormous subsidies which Germany has been paying annually since the end of the war to the State of Israel by way of reparation for injuries which moreover she cannot be held to have caused her either morally or legally, since there was no State of Israel at the time the incriminating deeds took place; thus it is a purely and contemptibly material problem.

"Perhaps I may be allowed to recall here that the State of Israel was only founded in May 1948 and that the Jewish victims in Germany were nationals of many States with the exception of Israel, in order to underline the dimensions of a fraud which defies description in any language; on the one hand Germany pays to Israel sums which are calculated on roughly six million dead, and on the other, as at least four-fifths of these six million were decidedly alive at the end of the war, she is paying substantial sums by way of reparation to the victims of Hitler's Germany to those who are still alive in countries all over the world other than Israel and to the rightful claimants of those who have since deceased, which means that for the former (the six million, i.e.), or in other words, for the vast majority, she is paying twice."

(P. Rassinier: *Le Drame des Juifs Européens*, pp. 31 and 39)

With this we conclude our examination of Rassinier's arguments. Not having made a personal study of this question, we are limited to an examination of this author's conclusions, for which he must bear the full responsibility, but it would seem that the facts and documents which he adds to the dossier of war crimes merit full and impartial investigation. The question of six million Jewish victims who died in Hitler's camps can no longer be considered an article of faith.

BIBLIOGRAPHY
of works quoted

* indicates foreign works available in the British Museum.

BATAULT, G. *Le Problème Juif*, 1921. *Israel contre les Nations*, 1939*.
BENAMOZEGH, E. *Israel et l'Humanité*, 1961*.
BONSIRVEN, Rev., S.J. *Le Judaisme Palestinien au temps de Jésus-Christ*, 1934.
COHEN, K. *Nomades*, 1928.
DE ECCLESIAE. *Declaration on the Relation of the Church to Non-Christian Religions*, Trans. by T. Atthill, C.T.S., 1966.
DHORME, E. *Revue de l'Histoire des Religions*.
DIMONT, MAX I. *Jews, God and History*, 1964.
DISRAELI, B. *Coningsby*, 1849.
DOENITZ, Admiral. *Ten Years and Twenty Days*, 1959.
FAURE, E. *L'âme juive*, in *La Question Juive vue par vingt-six éminentes personalités*, 1934.
FEJTO, F. *Dieu et son Juif*, 1960*. *Les Juifs et l'Antisémitisme dans les Pays communistes*, 1960.
FLEG, E. *Israel et Moi*, 1936*.
GRAETZ, *History of the Jews*.
ISAAC, J. *Jésus et Israel*, original edition 1946; 1959. *Genèse de l'Antisémitisme*, original edition 1948; 1956*.
JEHOUDA, J. *L'Antisémitisme, Miroir du Monde*, 1958*.
LANE, A. BLISS. *I Saw Poland Betrayed*, 1948.
LAPOUGE, VACHER DE. *Les Selections sociales*, cours professé à l'Universite de Montpellier, 1888-9.
LAZARE, BERNARD. *Anti-Semitism*, 1903, New York.
LENIN. *The Proletarian Revolution and Kautsky the Renegade*, 1920.
LEWISOHN, L. *Israel*, 1926.
LOEB, I. *La Littérature des Pauvres dans La Bible*.
LOVSKY, F. *Antisémitisme et Mystère d'Israel*, 1955.
LUDWIG, E. *A New Holy Alliance*, 1938.
MADAULE, J. *Les Juifs et le Monde Actuel*, 1963*.
MASSOUTIÉ, L. *Judaisme et Hitlerisme*, 1935*. *Judaisme et Marxisme*, 1939*.
MEMMI, A. *Portrait of a Jew*, 1963.
NEUMANN, alias Neuberg. *L'Insurrection armée*.
NOSSIG, A. *Integrales Judentum*, 1922.
PASMANIK, Dr. D. *Qu'est-ce que le Judaisme?* 1930.
PÉGUY, C. *Notre Jeunesse dans Oeuvres en Prose*, 1909-14.

PONCINS, LÉON DE. *Le Plan Communiste d'Insurrection Armée*, 1939*.
L'Enigme Communiste, 1942.
RABI. *Anatomie du Judaisme français*, 1962*.
RASSINIER, P. *Le Mensonge d'Ulysse*, 1955*. *Ulysse trahi par les Siens*, 1961*. *Le Véritable Procès Eichmann*, 1962*. *Le Drame des Juifs Européens*, 1964*.
RENAN, J. E. *The Antichrist*, 1899 (tr. by W. G. Hutchinson).
ROSENBERG, A. *A History of Bolshevism*, 1934.
ROUDINESCO, Dr. A. *Le Malheur d'Israel*, 1956.
SALLUSTE (pseud.) *Les Origines Secrètes du Bolchevisme*, 1930.
SAROLEA, C. *Impressions of Soviet Russia*, 1924.
SARTRE, J. P. *Portrait of the Anti-Semite*, 1948.
SERANT, P. *Les Vaincus de la Liberation*, 1964.
SOMBART, W. *The Jews and Modern Capitalism*, 1913.
SPIRE, A. *Quelques Juifs et demi-juifs*, 1928*.
STEED, H. W. *The Hapsburg Monarchy*, 1913.
THORWALD, J. *Wlassow contre Staline*, 1953.
TROTSKY, LEV. *The Defence of Terrorism*, 1921.
VALLAT, X. Article in *Aspects de la France*, 21st January 1965.
WEBSTER, N. H. *Secret Societies and Subversive Movements*, 1964.
WEBSTER, N. H. *World Revolution*, 1921.
WEBSTER, N. H. *French Revolution*, 1919.

INDEX

Aaron, 145
Abel, 57
Abraham, 55, 155
Abram, M. B., 172
Abranavel, J., 118
Adam, 57
Adler, 109
Albigensians, the, 90
Algazi, L., 12
Al Gomhuria, 169
Alliance Israelite Universelle, 140
Aman, 74
America, 141
American Jewish Committee, 135, 140, 141, 167-73
American Reform Judaism, 34
Amitiés judéo-chrétiennes, 12, 29, 30, 71, 154
Amos, 56
Antichrist, 27
Anti-Defamation League of the B'nai B'rith, 168, 170
Anti-Semitism, 11, 20-22, 34-37, 60, 62, 67, 71, 82-88, 110, 119, 120, 130, 134, 136, 137, 140, 141, 148-50, 153, 154, 160, 162, 168, 170, 173
Apollonio, U., 159
Appio, 86
Apro, A., 108
Artaxerxes, 74
Aspects de la France, 49
Assuerus, 74
Atheism, 36, 49, 119, 125, 172
Auschwitz, 11, 18, 22, 28, 32, 150, 181, 182, 184, 188, 189
Azef, 109

Balachowsky, Prof., 180
Balfour Declaration, 70, 185
Barabbas, 17, 146, 147

Baron, Prof. S., 182
Barruel, Abbé, 166
Bartolocci, 117
Batault, G., 48, 78-80, 88, 90, 112, 152, 158
Baum, Father, 161, 169
Bea, Cardinal, meets Jules Isaac, 12; commissioned by Pope to study his suggestions, 13; in favour of the schema on the Jews, 133; attacks upon by anti-Semitic tracts, 137-41, 161, 164, 165; an exegete, his love of men and justice, 153; his relations with B'nai B'rith, AJC, and other world Jewish organisations, from the article in *Look* magazine, 167-74
Belzec, 183, 184, 188
Benamozegh, E., 32, 37, 38, 88, 121, 122, 130
Benda, J., 98
Bergen-Belsen, 183
Beria, 98
Berman, J., 108
Bernadotte, Count, 110
"Bernardus", 161
Berzine, 107
Birobidjan, 75
Blaha, Dr., 180, 183
Bloch, M., 62
Blum, L., 95, 129, 186
B'nai B'rith, 10, 31, 34, 35, 130, 140, 160, 161, 164, 167, 168, 170, 172-4
Boerne, L., 62, 117
Bolshevism, 104, 106, 107
Bonsirven, Rev. S. J., 47
Borodin, 106
Boudnitchenko, Colonel, 98

INDEX

Buber-Neuman, M., 100
Buchenwald, 97, 180, 182, 183
Buddhism, 138
Buxtorf, 117
Bykadorov, Captain, 99

Cabbalism, the Cabbala, 36, 77, 115, 118, 121
Caiaphas, 17, 39
Cain, 21, 57
Calvin, 36, 118, 160
Carli, Mgr., 133-5, 142, 144, 145, 147, 150-2, 155, 157, 171, 172
Casablanca, the declaration of, 189
Catholicus, 161
Catholicism, the attack on the traditional form of, 11, 33, 35, 37, 49, 50, 69, 76, 150
Celsus, 116
Centre Mondial de Documentation Juive Contemporaine, 178, 183, 189
Centre de Documentation Juive de Paris, 182
Chamberlain, 186
Chaplin, C., 80
Chemno, 183
Chiang Kai-shek, 106
Chizuk Emuna, 117
Churchill, 144
Cicero, 86
Cicognani, Cardinal, 162
Claudius, Emperor, 152
Clement III, 92
Clement VIII, 92
Coetus internationalis patrum, 134
Cohen, Kadmi-, 92-95, 129
Collective responsibility, the principle of, 97, 144-6, 148, 167
Committee for the Salvation of the Jews of Budapest, 184
Commission Théologique de L'Oeuvre Evangelique suisse, 73
Common Sense, 161, 164
Communism, 36, 68, 119, 124, 128, 152, 159, 160, 162, 164, 172

Conference of European Rabbis in Great Britain, 1960, 50
Congar, Father, 9
Contempt, "the teaching of contempt", 12, 14, 21, 24, 27, 150, 174
Conversion, to Christianity, 31, 37, 39, 54, 55, 58, 59-62, 73, 76, 90, 114, 115, 157, 171; to monotheism, Judaism, 35, 38, 78, 79, 114, 115, 120-2
Corriere della Sera, 139
Constantine, Emperor, 113, 114
Council of Trent, 25
Cushing, Cardinal, 171

Dachau, 179, 180, 182, 183
Daniel, 56
Daniel, Father, 49
Daniélou, Father, 12
Darmesteter, 80, 111, 116, 120, 129
Declaration of Moscow, 1943, 51
De Ecclesiae, The Declaration on the Relation of the Church to non-Christian Religions, 9, 10, 13, 33, 130, 133-7; the text of the final form of, 140, 143, 144, 149, 155, 165, 167, 171
Deicide, the deicide charge, 15, 21, 23, 134, 135, 139, 142-5, 163, 164, 169, 170
Delo, 100
Demann, Father, 12
Deutero-Isaiah, 56, 79
Deuteronomy, 91
Deutsch, H., 40-42
Dhorme, E., 92
Dimont, M. I., 10, 53, 73, 77, 90, 91, 130
Disraeli, B., 93, 117
Djerdjinsky, 106
Doenitz, Grand Admiral, 51, 106
Dora, 182, 183
Dostoievsky, 177
Dresden, the destruction of, 188, 189
Dreyfus affair, 70, 88

Ecumenism, 31, 33, 157, 170
Edict of Nantes, 62

INDEX

Ehrenburg, I., 106
Eichmann, A., 51, 181-3
Einstein, 77, 80
Eisendrath, Rabbi M., 34
Eisenmenger, J. A., 86
Eisner, K., 104
Eitani, R., 49
Elias, 78
Engels, 103-105
Esraism, 54
Esther, 74
Exodus, 56
Ezekiel, 54, 56, 78, 145

Farkas, M., 109
Farkas, W., 109
Faure, E., 68, 69, 76-78, 81, 83-85, 130
Fejtö, F., 56, 57, 67, 68, 75, 108, 114, 115
Felici, Mgr., 162
Feltin, Cardinal, 34
Fenyes, 109
Fesquet, H., 9, 133, 136, 153
Le Figaro, 51, 133, 134, 137, 141, 147, 154, 172, 179
Fineberg, 109
Flandin, P. E., 186
Fleg, E., 12, 130
France-Soir, 134
Frederick, Emperor, 116
Freemasonry, 160, 162, 164
French Revolution, 35, 36, 65, 71, 116, 117, 119, 166
Freud, 77, 80
Freudenberg, Pastor, 12
Friends, The, of Jules Isaac, 29

Galen, alias General Blücher, 106
Gaulle, General de, 126
Gemara, 55, 59
Geouffre de la Pradelle, Maitre Raymond de, 51
Gerlier, Cardinal, 34, 154
Gero, 108
Gerstein, K., 183
Gnostics, 86
Goering, Field-Marshal, 101, 189
Goldberg, A. J., 171

Goldmann, N., 10, 47, 71, 72, 168
Graetz, 61, 62, 119
Grebnjakov, V., alias Dora, 101
Grynspan, 110, 185
Guershouni, 109

Hagada, 55
Halaka, 55
Hamburg, the destruction of, 188
Hanan, 17
Hatvany, Baron, 41
Haussner, G., 181
Hegira, the, 38
Heine, H., 62, 102, 117, 129
Heschel, Rabbi A. J., 168, 171, 173
Hess, R., 180, 181
Heydrich, 189
Higgins, Mgr. G., 171, 172
Hilberg, P., 178, 180, 183
Himmler, 189
Hitler, A., 19, 32, 48, 70, 87, 88, 92, 95, 97, 100, 101, 144, 148, 150, 152, 170, 182, 184, 185, 187, 189, 190
Hochhuth, R., 170, 181
Hoelbrigel, 180
Hoettl, 180
Holmogor, 101
Holtzmann, 109
Homer, 77
Honorius III, 91
Hosea, 56

Impropria, suppression of the prayer of, 33
Inquisition, the, 62, 72, 90, 91
Institute of Contemporary History, Munich, 183
International Institute to Study the Jewish Question, suggestion of the foundation of, 176
Isaac, Jules, 10; the gist of his thesis, 11, 12; organises Judaeo-Christian dialogues and had private audiences with Pius XII and John XXIII, 12; the result, 13; his revised version of the Gospels, 14-19, of the Church Fathers, 20-22, and of the Doctors of the Church, 22-

28; his demands of the Council, 29; supported in Catholic circles, 29, 30; his visit to Rome, 31-33; H. Deutsch intervenes on behalf of with Paul VI, 40, 41; 82, 86, 111, 112, 114, 116, 130, 140, 144, 148-50, 152-4, 163, 165, 167; the author's thesis of influence of on declaration on Judaism in Vatican Council II confirmed in *Look* article, 167, 168; 181
Isaiah, 54, 56, 78, 155
Islam, 90, 138
Israel, the State of, 48-51, 148, 184, 185, 189

Jackson, Justice, 179, 182
Jacob, P., 34
Jankélévitch, V., 96, 148, 181
Janson, 107
Jehouda, J., 30-32, 34-38, 47, 71, 73, 82, 85, 115, 117-20, 129, 140, 154, 157, 163
Jehovah, Jahve, Jahweh, 20, 56, 57, 89, 112
Jeremiah, 54, 56, 78
Jesus, 14-18, 21, 26, 39, 40, 55, 58, 77, 115, 117, 122, 125, 134, 143, 145-7, 150, 151, 156, 162, 170, 174
Jewish Chronicle, 186
John XXIII, 12, 30, 136, 161, 164, 168-70
Joshua, 56
Jullie, Cardinal, 12
Juvenal, 86

Kaplan, Grand Rabbi J., 12, 135, 142, 148
Kasztner, Dr. R., 184
Katyn Forest Murder, 101
Katz, L., 10, 34
Kaufman, Dr. T. N., 188
Kautsky, Dr., 180
Kautsky, K., 102
Kellner, H. M., 160
Kennedy, President J. F., 110
Keri, 109

Kibbutz mapam, 49
Kiziewicz, General, 108
Klauzner, J., 39, 115
Klyber, Father, 161
Koestler, 73
Korherr, Dr., 182
Krasnov, General, 99
Krasnov, Colonel S., 99
Krausnik, H., 180
Kubovy, Dr., 189
Kuhn, Bela, 104, 106, 107, 109

Lagrange, Father, 112
Lane, A. Bliss, 108
Lapine, Captain, 99
Laptchinski, Lieut., 99
Lassalle, F., 102, 117
Lateran Council, the Fourth, 91
Lattés, S., 12
Laurentin, Abbé, R., 134, 135, 147, 154, 172
Laval, 186
Lazare, B., 54, 55, 57, 58, 80, 83, 84, 93, 102, 117, 129
Lazareff, P., 134
Lefebvre, Mgr., 133
Leipzig, the destruction of, 188
Lemkin, Prof. R., 180
Lenin, 75, 105
Leo XIII, 97, 136
Leroy-Beaulieu, A., 63
Lewisohn, L., 65, 66, 129
Lichten, J., 170, 172
Liebnecht, 102, 104
Liénart, Cardinal, 12, 34, 154
Lieven, M., 104
Litvinoff, M., alias Wallach, etc., 109
Loeb, I., 79, 80
Look, article "How the Jews changed Catholic Thinking", 167-73
Lopinot, Father C., 12
Losovsky, 107
Louis XIV, 116
Lovsky, Prof. F., 12, 50, 60, 74, 92, 121
Ludwig, E., 129, 186
Lukacs, G., 108

INDEX

Lunel, 29
Luther, 36, 76, 86, 118
Luther, Secretary of State for the Third Reich, 186
Luxembourg, Rosa, 102, 104

Madaule, J., 12, 47-50, 71, 76
Madagascar, 186, 187
Maidanek, 183, 188
Maimonides, Moses, 80
Malachi, 38
Malychkine, General, 99
Mao Tse-tung, 106
Manicheans, 86
Marrou, H., 12
Martin, J., 12
Martin V, 91
Marx, K., 37, 68, 76, 77, 81, 102-105, 117
Marxism, 67, 75, 87, 100, 102, 103, 116, 152
Massoutié, L., 61-63, 86
Mathausen, 183
Mauclair, 161
Maxentius, 113
Maximos IV, Patriarch, 141
Meandrov, General, 99
Memmi, A., 32, 37, 123-8, 130
Mendelssohn, M., 69
Il Messagero de Roma, 143
Messiah, messianism, 30, 31, 37, 39, 55, 58, 71, 102, 113, 115, 120-2, 143, 146, 156, 174
Micah, 56
Mihajlov, 100, 101
Militant Servants of Our Lady of Fatima, 161
Minc, 108
Mishna, 53-55, 59
Le Monde, 9, 34, 40, 51, 71, 72, 96, 100, 101, 133, 135, 137, 139, 143, 148, 153, 154, 181
Monotheism, 30-32, 34, 35, 37, 56, 77, 89, 119, 120, 157
Montaigne, 80
Montini, Archbishop of Milan, 170
Montoire, 186
Morgenthau Plan, 188

Morlion, Father, F., 173
Moses, Mosaic Law, 53-56, 77, 91, 92, 134, 145, 155, 156
Mouret, 29
Moyne, Lord, 110

Nantet, J., 12
National Catholic Welfare Conference, 170, 171
Nebuchadnezzar, 93
Neue Rheinische Zeitung, 103
Neuhäussler, Mgr., 179
Neumann, alias Neuberg, 104, 105, 107
Nicholas, I, 136
Niemöller, Pastor, M., 179
Nietzsche, 37
Nieuwenhuys, D., 104
Nizzachon, 117
Nossig, Rabbi A., 64, 65, 76, 129
Nuremberg trial, 139, 144, 148, 178-83
Nyizli, Dr. M., 181

Oesterreicher, Father, 161, 169
Official Report of the Portuguese Government to the Committee of Non-Intervention, 107
Oikoumenikon, 151
Origen, 59, 116
Osservatore della Domenica, 162, 167
Osservatore Romano, 143, 159, 162, 165
Oswald, L., 110
Ottaviani, Cardinal, 12

Palanque, Father, 29, 30
Palestra del Clero, 134, 142, 144, 146, 151, 152, 155, 157
Pange, J. de, 12
Paris-Match, 181
Paris-Presse, 41, 137, 147
Paris-Soir, 95, 186
Parny, 117
Patriarch of Antioch, 136
Pasmanik, D., 46, 47, 70, 77
Paul IV, 92
Paul VI, 40, 41, 133, 135, 137, 138, 161, 165, 167, 170-2, 174

INDEX

Pauker, A., 108
Péguy, C., 93
Pentateuch, 53
Peter, G., 109
Petlioura, H., 110
Pfefferkorn, J., 36, 118, 119
Pharaohs, The, 93
Pharisees, The, 53-55, 59, 113, 117
Philostrates, 89
Pico de Mirandola, 36, 118
Pilate, Pontius, 15-18, 84, 146
Pinay, M., 160, 163, 168
Piperno, Dr. S., 143
Pius XII, 12, 168, 170
Plehve, 109
Pogany, 109
Poliakov, L., 180
Poncins, Leon de, 104, 106, 134, 136, 153, 161, 164
Pravda, 104
Primao, R., (or Primakoff), 107
Protestantism, 62, 76, 86, 139
Proust, M., 80
Provenchères, Mgr. de, 29, 30, 153, 154, 167
Psalms, 155

Quebec Conference, 188

Rabi, 32, 33, 37, 39, 47, 50, 71, 102, 115, 121, 130
Radkiewicz, 108
Rakosi, 108
Rassinier, P., 97, 100, 101, 178, 180-6, 188-90
Rath, von, 110, 185
Rathenau, W., 129
Reformation, The, 35, 36, 76, 80, 116-19
Reinach, S., 80
Reiter, A., 157
Renaissance, The, 35, 36, 80, 116-19
Renan, E., 85
Renard, Abbé, J.-P., 180, 183
Reuchlin, J., 36, 118
Revai, 108
Revue des Deux Mondes, 101
Richard the Lion-Hearted, 80
Robison, Prof., 166
Roddy, J., 167

Roosevelt, 188
Rosenberg, A., 102
Rosenbergs, The, 69
Rothschilds, 41
Roudinesco, Dr. A., 46, 55, 56, 59, 60, 66, 69, 70, 83, 87, 88, 91, 122
Routenberg, 109
Rubinstein, J., 110
Rudenko, General, 101
Ruppin, A., 182

Sadducees, 53
St. Agobard, 11, 25, 27, 28, 33, 149
St. Ambrose, 11, 22, 27, 33
St. Thomas Aquinas, 92
St Augustine, 11, 21-25, 28, 33, 59, 130, 149, 150
St. Avit, 60, 74
St. John Chrysostom, 11, 22, 23, 25, 28, 33, 130, 149, 150
St. Clement of Alexandria, 59
St. Cyril of Jerusalem, 22
St. Ephrem, 22
St. Epiphany, 22
St. Francis of Assisi, 80
Pope St. Gregory the Great, 11, 25, 28, 33, 130, 149, 150
St. Gregory of Nyssa, 22
St. Hilary of Poitiers, 22
St. Joan of Arc, 128
St. Jerome, 22, 59
St. John, 14, 16, 17, 33, 140, 143, 145, 168
St. Luke, 14-16, 40, 155, 168
St. Mark, 14, 16, 40, 168
St. Matthew, 14-17, 19, 29, 33, 40, 113, 140, 145-7, 168
St. Paul, 20, 25, 68, 77, 78, 81, 151, 155, 156
St. Peter, 139, 151
Pope St. Pius V, 92
Salluste, 76
Sarolea, C., 103, 104, 107
Sartre, J. P., 67
Satan, 23, 27, 28, 162, 173
Scarioli, N., 100
Scemama, A., 71, 72
Schourski, 29

INDEX

Schuster, Z., 141, 171, 172
Schwartzbart, 110
Schweitzer, M., 109
Secretariat for Christian Unity, 161, 164, 169, 172
Seelisberg, the Ten Points of, 12
Seneca, 86
Sepher Toledot Jeschu, 28
Scrant, P., 97, 98
Sergius, Grand Duke, 109
Sérot, Colonel, 110
Shapiro, M., 49
Sigaud, Mgr. de Proenca, 133
Silberberg, 109
Simon the Magician, 139
Slansky, 69, 108
Sobidor, 183
Socialism, 104
Soekarno, President, 138
Sombart, W., 61, 62, 77
Spanish Revolution, 107
Specht, alias Olszewski, 108
Spinoza, 31, 77, 80
Spire, A., 71, 111, 116, 120, 130
Spychalski, 108
Stalin, 68, 103
Statute of London, 1945, 51
Steed, H. W., 45, 46, 53, 64, 65, 73, 149
Steinberg, A., 50
Stolypine, 109
Streicher, 23, 28, 32, 150
Stürgkh, Count, 109
Szamuelly, 104
Synagogue, the, 26-28, 53, 66, 77, 86, 91, 114, 120

The Tablet, 10, 170
Tacitus, 86, 112
The Talmud, 36, 39, 53, 54-56, 58, 59, 90, 102, 115, 117-20, 156, 157, 163
Tappouni, Cardinal, 147
Tcherkassy, General Prince B., 99
Terre de Provence, 29
La Terre retrouvée, 157, 174, 189
Times, the New York, 170-2
Tisserand, Cardinal, 12
Tiza, Count, 109

Toaff, E., Chief Rabbi of Rome, 143, 171
Togliatti, 124
Toldoth Jesho, 117
Tolstoi, Count Ivan, 100
Tollier, V., 25
Torah, 53, 54, 56, 58
Torquemada, 63
Toulat, Abbé, 154
Toussenel, 87
Treblinka, 183, 188
Trotsky, L., 104, 105
Troukhine, General, 99
Union of Jewish Congregations in America, 34
United States of Europe, 187
U.N.O., 162, 172
Uritski, M., 107

Vacher de Lapouge, 83
Vallat, X., 49
Vas, 108
Vichy, the Government of, 48, 49
Vieillard, Abbé, 12
Vita, 100
Voltaire, 87, 116, 117

Wagenseil, 117
Wallach, M. G. M., alias Buchmann, Finkelstein, Harrison and Litvinoff, 109
Webster, N. H., 165, 166
Weigel, Rev. S. J., 141
Weizmann, Chaim, 186, 188
White, H. D., 188
Wildenbruch, von Pieffer-, 41
Wilke, F., 41
Wisceliceny, 180
Wlassow, General, 98-100
Wolf, 117
World Jewish Congress, 10, 31, 34, 35, 130, 140, 168, 179, 187, 188
World Zionist Organisation, 47, 71, 72

Yourowski, J., 106

Zaga, E. di, 134, 136, 161
Zionism, 67, 69-72, 141, 142
Zoroaster, 86
Zwingli, 118, 160